Reporting Talk

Reported speech, whereby we quote the words of others, is used in many different types of interaction. In this revealing study, a team of leading experts explores how reported speech is designed, the actions it is used to perform and how it fits into the environments in which it is used. Using the most recent techniques of conversation analysis, the authors show how speech is reported in a wide range of contexts – including ordinary conversation, story-telling, news interviews, courtroom trials and medium–sitter interactions. Providing detailed analyses of reported speech in naturally occurring talk, the authors examine existing linguistic and sociological studies, and offer some pioneering insights into the phenomenon. Bringing together work from the most recent investigations in conversation analysis, this book will be invaluable to all those interested in the study of interaction, in particular how we report the speech of others, and the different forms this can take.

ELIZABETH HOLT is Senior Lecturer in English at Huddersfield University. She has contributed to the journals *Research on Language and Social Interaction, Text, Social Problems* and *Language in Society.*

REBECCA CLIFT is Lecturer in Linguistics at the University of Essex. She has contributed to the journals *Language, Language in Society, Journal of Sociolinguistics* and *Lingua.*

Studies in Interactional Sociolinguistics

EDITORS
Paul Drew, Marjorie Harness Goodwin, John J. Gumperz, Deborah Schiffrin

Reporting Talk

Reported Speech in Interaction

Edited by
ELIZABETH HOLT AND

REBECCA CLIFT

CAMBRIDGE
UNIVERSITY PRESS

CAMBRIDGE UNIVERSITY PRESS
Cambridge, New York, Melbourne, Madrid, Cape Town, Singapore, São Paulo

CAMBRIDGE UNIVERSITY PRESS
The Edinburgh Building, Cambridge CB2 2RU, UK

Published in the United States of America by Cambridge University Press, New York

www.cambridge.org
Information on this title: www.cambridge.org/9780521824835

First published 2007

Printed in the United Kingdom at the University Press, Cambridge

A catalogue record for this publication is available from the British Library

ISBN-13 978-0-521-82483-5 hardback
ISBN-10 0-521-82483-4 hardback

Contents

Contributors

PROFESSOR STEVEN CLAYMAN
Department of Sociology, University of California, Los Angeles, USA

DR REBECCA CLIFT
Department of Language and Linguistics, University of Essex, Colchester, UK

DR ELIZABETH COUPER-KUHLEN
Institut fur Anglistik & Amerikanistik, University of Potsdam, Germany

DR RENATA GALATOLO
Department of Communication Disciplines, University of Bologna, Italy

PROFESSOR CHARLES GOODWIN
Applied Linguistics, University of California, Los Angeles, USA

DR MARKKU HAAKANA
Department of Finnish Language, University of Helsinki, Finland

DR ELIZABETH HOLT
School of Music and Humanities, University of Huddersfield, UK

JOANNE KERBY
Formerly School of Human and Life Sciences, Roehampton University, London

DR JOHN RAE
School of Human and Life Sciences, Roehampton University, London

DR ROBIN WOOFFITT
Department of Sociology, University of York, UK

Acknowledgements

We are deeply indebted to Paul Drew for encouragement at all stages of the production of this volume and for helpful comments on the final draft. Makoto Hayashi also provided generous intellectual support with his wide-ranging knowledge of work on reported speech. We also thank Andrew Winnard, Helen Barton, Jayne Aldhouse and all those at Cambridge University Press for their careful shepherding of the manuscript through the presses.

Transcription conventions

The method of transcription used within this volume was developed by Gail Jefferson (but see the Appendix to Chapter 6 for some additional notations used within that chapter.) The system attempts to capture some of the features of the interaction relevant to its organisation, including turns, overlapping talk, pauses, and intonational features such as emphasis and marked rises and falls in intonation.

This summary of transcription notations relies heavily on Atkinson and Heritage (1984) and ten Have and Psathas (1995).

Simultaneous turns

Where turns are begun simultaneously they are marked by a single left-hand bracket at the start of the turns:

```
[    Tom:     [I used to smoke a lot when I was young
[    Bob:     [I used to smoke Camels
```

Overlapping turns

When turns do not start simultaneously, the point where the new turn begins is marked by a left-hand bracket within the first turn and at the start of the new turn:

```
[    Tom:     I used to smoke [a lot
[    Bob:                     [He thinks he's real tough
```

Where overlapping talk stops, it is marked by right-hand brackets:

]   Tom: I used to smoke [a lot] more than this
]   Bob: [I see]

Contiguous turns

When turns are latched (i.e. there is no interval between the end of
one turn and the beginning of a next) equals signs are used at the
end of the first turn and the beginning of the second:

=   Tom: I used to smoke a lot=
=   Bob: =He thinks he's real tough

    Equals signs are also used where a transcriber has put on to a
new line elements of a turn that form part of the continuous flow of
speech often due to intervening overlapping talk:

=   Tom: I used to smoke [a lot more than this=
       Bob: [You used to smoke
=   Tom: =but I never inhaled the smoke

When overlapping turns end simultaneously and a subsequent turn
is begun without an interval, the overlapping turns are followed by
right-hand brackets and equal signs. The new turn is marked by a
left-hand bracket at the beginning:

]=   Tom: I used to smoke [a lot]=
]=   Bob: [I see]=
=   Ann: =So did I

Intervals within and between turns

Intervals in talk are timed to the tenth of a second and marked by
numbers in parentheses either within a turn at talk:

(0.0)   Lil: When I was (0.6) oh nine or ten

or between turns:

       Hal: Step right up
(0.0)   (1.3)
       Hal: I said step right up

An interval of less than, or around, one tenth of a second is marked by a period within parentheses:

(.)   Dee: Umm (.) my mother will be right in

Characteristics of speech delivery

Punctuation is used to convey characteristics of speech delivery rather than grammatical units.

Sound stretch

A colon indicates a stretched sound:

:   Ron: What ha:ppened to you

        Longer stretches of sound are indicated by multiple colons:

::   Mae: I ju::ss can't come
:::   Tim: I'm so::: sorry re:::ally I am

Cut-off

A single hyphen indicates that the prior word or sound is cut off (i.e. abruptly terminated):

-       C: Th' U:sac- uh:, sprint car dr- dirt track...

Intonation

A full stop indicates a fall in tone usually at the end of a unit:

.   Jenny: They're a lovely family now aren't they.

        A comma indicates a continuing intonation:

,   Tony: That really makes me ma:d,

        A question mark indicates a rise in intonation:

?   V: A do:g? enna cat is different.
        P: Yih ever take'er out again?

Marked rises or falls in intonation are marked by upward- or downward-pointing arrows immediately before the shift:

↑↓   L: <u>AND</u> uh ↑<u>we</u> <u>were</u> looking rou-nd the ↓sta:lls 'n <u>p</u>oking about...

Less marked rises or falls in intonation along with some stretching can be marked by underlining immediately preceding a colon for a fall:

<u>a</u>:   L: we (.) really didn't have a lot'v ch<u>a</u>:nge...

and underlining of a colon for a rise:

a<u>:</u>   P: I'm (h) eyeing your cho<u>:</u>p up m<u>i:</u>nd.

   An exclamation mark indicates an animated tone:

!   C: An that! so what he sez.

Emphasis

Underscoring indicates emphasis:

<u>Still</u>   L: ...he said <u>oh</u>: hh<u>e</u>llo Lesley (.) ↑<u>still</u> trying to buy
                       Something <u>f</u>' nothing,

Croaky voice

An asterisk indicates croaky voice in the immediately following talk:

*   D: Wul mayb- maybe *uh- uh good thing...

Volume

Increased volume is marked by the use of upper case letters:

PUT   D: ↑PUT THE F<u>I</u>:RE ON

   Decreases in volume are marked with a degree symbol at the start and end of the quiet talk:

° °   J: . . .I'll go ahea:d, and, .hh pay for it when it comes
            and °he'll never kno:w°,

Aspiration

A series of 'h's preceded by a dot indicates an in-breath:

.hhh   L: .hhhhhh Santa Claus.

Out-breath is indicated by a series of 'h's without a preceding dot.

hh   J: I'm not sure hh- who it belongs to

Laughter and smile voice

Laughter is indicated by an attempt to convey the sound using 'h's
and vowels, while laughter particles within words are indicated by
an 'h' or 'h's in parenthesis:

eh   D: ↑UH you fin:nished with that ch↑o::p p↓et eehh he he
                °he [he he he°
(h)   P: [I'm (h) eyeing your cho:p up [mi:nd.
        D: [hah hah hah hah .hhh
                it's cool. . .

Smile voice is indicated by pound or dollar signs immediately
before and at the end of the affected talk:

$/£   P: . . .und you might $knock a few blocks out of
                position$

Speed of delivery

Talk which is noticeably quicker than surrounding talk is marked
by 'more than' and 'less than' symbols either side of the fast talk:

> <   P: >In fact d'yuh think they will< enjo:y co:mpany.

Indecipherable sounds

Where a transcriber is unable to make out a sound or a series of
sounds, spaces within parenthesis are used to convey the approxi-
mate extent of the missing talk:

```
         D:      huh hee it'd [bust
( )      P:                   [( )
```

Where the transcriber is able to guess at the words or sounds used, these are included within parentheses:

```
(in)     J:      ↑Santa Claus brou:ght it. (in his sle::d).
```

Where the transcriber is unsure of who made a sound, empty parenthesis may be used instead of a name or initial:

```
( )      ( ):     ( )
```

Verbal descriptions

Double parenthesis is used to enclose a description of the talk or some other phenomenon present during the interaction that the transcriber does not want to convey by attempting to represent the sound. For example, in the following extract an 'f' in double parenthesis marks falsetto intonation:

```
(( ))    J:      ((f)) ↑Da:ddy Mommy:
         Bob:    ((sniffle)) He thinks he's tough
```

Presentation conventions

Horizontal arrows to the left of the transcription indicate a turn that the author wants to call the reader's attention to. The significance of the turn will be explained in the text.

```
→        Vera:→    Well I said tuh Jean how abou:t it...
```

Horizontal ellipses
These indicate that parts of the same turn are omitted:

```
...      D:      ...as I say yu- yuh go down steep...
```

Vertical ellipses
These indicate that intervening turns have been omitted:

```
 .       Mum:      ↑oh: dea:r. Thursday.
 .                      .
 .                ((20 lines omitted))
                        .
         Mum:      Oh: they make you pay f'r putting it on again too:.
```

Numbering of lines or turns

This is done for convenience of reference. Intervals within talk are also numbered.

44	Les:	Yes well we s<u>e</u>nt the money str<u>a</u>ight aw<u>a</u>:y
45		(0.4)
46	Les:	.p

1

Introduction

Rebecca Clift and Elizabeth Holt

(I)n real life people talk most of all about what others talk about – they transmit, recall, weigh and pass judgement on other people's words, opinions, assertions, information; people are upset by others' words, or agree with them, contest them, refer to them and so forth.

(Bakhtin, 1981: 338)

1.1 Introduction

This volume is an investigation of reported speech in naturally occurring spoken interaction. We recurrently use talk to report talk, whether we are reporting the compliment someone gave us or conveying how we made a complaint or told a joke. In the following extract, for example, the speaker uses reported speech as part of a story relating how she was the victim of a nasty put-down (arrowed):[1]

(1) [Holt: C85: 4: 2–3] (Lesley has been looking around the stalls at a church fair)

```
1   Lesley:   AND uh  ↑we were looking rou-nd the
2             ↓sta:lls 'n poking about 'n he came
3             up t'me 'n he said Oh: hhello Lesley, (.)
4        →    ↑still trying to buy something f'nothing,
5        →    .tch! .hh [hahhhhhhh!
6   Joyce:              [.hhoohhhh!
```

Lesley's animation of the man's words is the culmination of her reporting of a series of actions. It is this phenomenon – the reproduction of prior talk in a current interaction – that the studies

---

[1] For a key to transcription symbols, see pages xi–xvii.

in this volume are concerned with. Together they bear witness to the use of reported speech and its variant forms across the range of interactional contexts from ordinary conversation to so-called institutional talk such as political interviews and debates. While engaging with material as diverse as story-telling, witness testimony in court, interaction between spiritual mediums and their sitters and video data of an aphasic man, the chapters have a central focus: the design and placement of reported speech – and thought – in sequences of interaction. Aspects of design include its lexical and prosodic construction; issues of placement relate to how turns in reported speech are built to follow particular others, and the responses that they in turn generate. In the extract above, for example, Lesley introduces reported speech as the climax of the story she has been telling; story climaxes, as we shall see, are one of the recurrent interactional sites for reported speech. The design and sequential placement of reported speech thus display systematicities which are only available by close analytic attention to several instances of the same phenomenon; the chapters in this volume are characterised by a commitment to such analytic attention.

A more detailed survey of the contents follows in due course, but first we sketch the background to existing work on reported speech and the main theoretical issues to have emerged from it. As we shall see, the relatively recent advent of interactionally grounded studies of reported speech has promised to illuminate many of the theoretical issues formerly regarded as intractable. The rationale for adopting the rigorously empirical approach of conversation analysis is duly set out here, followed by some of the earlier findings from conversation analytic work on reported speech; it is in this work that the current contributions have their origins.

1.2 Background and main themes

Work on reported speech in recent years has emerged from a variety of disciplines, most prominently literary theory, philosophy, linguistics and sociology.[2] The proposal of the Bakhtin/Volosinov circle

---

[2] For a comprehensive bibliography of work on reported speech, see Güldemann et al. (2002).

that much of what we say is permeated with the voices of others has proven highly influential beyond the domain of literary theory; much subsequent empirical work has pursued Bakhtin's notion of 'polyphony' and his claim that any utterance contains 'the half-concealed or completely concealed words of others' (1981: 92). Within philosophy, reported speech has been of interest in its reflexive capacity (D. Davidson, 1968–9, 1984; Quine, 1960) and in this respect converges with work on metapragmatics within linguistics (see, for example, the collection in Lucy, 1993), which has its origins in Jakobson's concern with reported speech as 'a speech within speech, a message within a message...' (1971: 130). It is the work in linguistics that has produced the most diverse range of perspectives. Across this diversity it is nonetheless possible to identify three central concerns in the literature: that with **forms** of reported speech; with its **authenticity**, and with **what it does**. While all three, as we shall see, continue to be the focus of ongoing research, it is evident that the concern with forms of reported speech generally predated work on its authenticity, and it is only in relatively recent years that research has focused on what reported speech does in interaction. This latter focus marks the increasing influence on linguistic research of work in sociology, and it is at the intersection of these two domains that much conversation analytic work on reported speech has emerged and where the current study has its starting point. To chart the route to this point, we now briefly sketch the three main preoccupations of previous work in reported speech.

1.2.1 Forms of reported speech

Of structural linguistic studies, a major focus has been the distinction between so-called direct reported speech (DRS) and so-called indirect reported speech (IRS). Jespersen proposed that:

When one wishes to report what someone else says or has said (thinks or has thought) – or what one has said or thought oneself on some previous occasion – two ways are open to one. Either one gives, or purports to give, the exact words of the speaker (or writer): *direct speech*. Or else one adapts the words according to the circumstances in which they are now quoted: *indirect speech* (oratio obliqua).   (1924: 290)

On Jespersen's account, extract (1) – cited above – shows an instantiation of the former; the extract below, in which a speaker
is summarising or conveying the gist of a previous thought or
locution, is an example of the latter:

```
(2)  [Rahman: II:4]  (Simplified)
1      Jenny:   An' I:van had said to me in the mo:rn ing
2         →      would I run 'im through to Saltburn .hh
```

Jenny here conveys what Ivan purportedly said without claiming
fidelity to his original utterance, the presence of the pronoun 'I'
clearly indicating that Jenny is speaking from her perspective.
Besides this proposed distinction in the linguistics literature between DRS and IRS, more recent work has focused on what has
come to be known as either 'free indirect' or 'quasi-direct' speech
(Coulmas, 1986; Banfield, 1973, 1982; for a survey, see McHale,
1978), an amalgam of direct and indirect reported speech:

```
(3) [NB: II: 2: 10]
1      Nancy:   ... I only had o:ne (0.3) .hhhhhh (0.4)
2                dero:gatory rema:rk? if: you c'd call it
3                tha:t a:nd ah,h (0.6) u-it ca:me from a
4         →      gi:rl (0.2) and she said she fe:lt thet
5         →      I: would of gott'n more out'v the cla:ss
6         →      if I hed not been en eVOIder, h w'tever
7         →      sh'meant by tha:t, .hhhhh u-but that
8         →      ah:::, (0.5) I will c'ntinue t'remember
9         →      th'class en gro:w from it. Er sump'n (.)
```

The majority of Nancy's report here is indirect: the pronouns are
from the point of view of the current speaker, not the original
speaker. However, 'en eVOIder' (line 6) appears to be directly
reported. Elements of the last part of the reported speech – 'will
c'ntinue t'remember th'class en gro: w from it' (lines 8–9) – appear
also to be directly reported.

Much linguistic research has been grounded in this proposed
three-way distinction between direct, indirect and quasi-direct
speech. Thus Li (1986) provides a detailed characterisation of the
differences between direct and indirect reported speech in lexico-
syntactic and prosodic terms; Banfield (1973), Partee (1973),

Mayes (1990) and Longacre (1985) have also compared direct and indirect reported speech with respect to their distinctive structural characteristics. Of more functionally oriented research, Coulmas claims that, while IRS is related from the current speaker's point of view (see also Leech and Short, 1981), DRS:

> is not the reporter's speech, but remains the reported speaker's speech whose role is played by the reporter.   (1986: 2)

And according to Li (1986), DRS is used to convey both the form and content of the reported utterance, including gestures and facial expressions. In IRS, however, the speaker has the option of communicating a comment on the utterance as it is uttered. Thus, if the utterance is reported in an angry voice, in direct form the anger will be heard as the reported speaker's, and in indirect form it will be heard as the current speaker's comment on the utterance.

The concern with different forms of reported speech has led to lively interest in its introductory components, sometimes called 'quotatives' (Mathis and Yule, 1994), most commonly in English – as in extract (1) – a pronoun and a *verbum dicendi* such as 'say'. Such quotatives may be present in what is identifiably both DRS and IRS, although in English one common characteristic of indirect reports is that the quotative is followed by the complementiser 'that' (Li, 1986).[3] However, while variants of *pronoun + say* may be considered the paradigmatic introductory component of reported speech, research has identified a number of alternatives. So Tannen's (1989) survey of quotatives includes 'tell', 'go' and 'like'. The apparently increasing use of *be + like* as an introductory component has been the focus of recent attention by Blyth et al. (1990), Romaine and Lange (1991), Ferrara and Bell (1995), Tagliamonte and Hudson (1999), Macaulay (2001) and Cukor-Avila (2002). The claim by Romaine and Lange that 'like' blurs the boundary between DRS, IRS and reported thought, claiming less commitment to the original than 'say' does, touches on the second of the three main concerns in the linguistics literature in this domain: the authenticity of reported speech.

---

[3] See Haakana (this volume) for Finnish as a contrast case.

1.2.2 The authenticity of reported speech

Research into reported speech began with the assumption (derived
from the lay assumption (see Mayes, 1990: 330–31)) that direct
speech is more accurate than indirect speech. Thus, Bally (1914)
viewed DRS as 'a phonographic reproduction of the thoughts and
words' of the original speaker (quoted in Clark and Gerrig, 1990:
795). But more recent work has shown how DRS is, in fact, rarely
an accurate rendition of a former locution. Volosinov (1971) was
the first to criticise the assumption that reported speech is an
authentic rendition of the original, proposing that the meaning of
the original utterance is inevitably altered in the reporting context
(see Dubois (1989) on what she calls 'pseudoquotation', and Sternberg (1982) on claims regarding the reframing of reported speech).
This claim has been supported by psycholinguistic research. Thus
Lehrer (1989) shows that, in experiments to test the memory of
prose, subjects tend to remember the meaning of utterances rather
than the form, and that verbatim recall is unusual. Mayes (1990:
331) investigated the authenticity of the reported speech in her
corpus and claimed that at least 50 per cent were inventions by
the current speaker. Included in her collection, along with 'plausible
quotes' and 'improbable quotes' (for example, a speaker reporting
an utterance made twenty years earlier), were 'highly improbable
quotes' (such as a 'Greek chorus' where a quote is attributed to
more than one person) and 'impossible quotes' (including hypothetical quotations). Thus it would seem that the term 'reported
speech' is somewhat of a misnomer;[4] as we shall see, one of the
concerns of this volume will be to engage with the reasons for this.

1.2.3 What does reported speech do?

While early linguistic studies of reported speech were overwhelmingly concerned with structural questions for which the use of constructed exemplars or literary texts was perceived to be adequate,
the past twenty years have seen an increasing number of empirical
studies of reported speech. In part this is due to a convergence of

---

[4] Tannen (1989) goes so far as to adopt the term 'constructed dialogue' for
these reasons.

structural and comparative linguistic concerns: many languages grammaticalise quotative constructions (see, for example, Cohen et al. (2002) on a range of East African languages, and the collection in Aikhenvald and Dixon (2003), and there has been keen interest amongst typologists in this grammatical encoding of reported speech (see the collections in Lucy (1993) and Güldemann and von Roncador (2002)). This move away from literary and textual materials towards naturalistic speech data in a variety of languages has also engendered an increasing interest in functional and pragmatic aspects of reported speech. So comparative linguistic studies, grounded in the ethnographic tradition, have investigated aspects of reported speech in the languages of North America (see, e.g. Collins, 1987; Moore, 1993; Urban, 1993), Austronesia (see, e.g. Besnier, 1993; Parmentier, 1993; McGregor, 1994), South and Central America (see, e.g. Adelaar, 1990; Basso, 1986; Shoaps, 2004) and Africa (see, e.g. Aaron, 1992; Clements, 1975).

Of linguistic studies concerned with the generic properties of reported speech, many have remarked on the dramaturgical quality of DRS in particular (see Li, 1986; Tannen, 1989; Wierzbicka, 1974). It has been proposed that reported speech is used in stories not only to replay an interaction but also to enable the speaker to simultaneously convey his or her attitude towards the reported utterance. Labov (1972) distinguishes between 'external evaluation', where the point of a story is explicitly explained, and 'internal evaluation' where it is conveyed through the story itself. DRS is, he argues, a means of internally evaluating the story and is therefore more effective because it allows the recipient to draw his or her own conclusions about the characters and events recounted. Mayes (1990) notes how reported speech is often used at the climax of stories and proposes this as an effective way of conveying the point of a narrative.[5]

Much research in recent years, aiming to pursue the interactional motivations for the use of reported speech, has shown the influence of the sociologist Erving Goffman's observations on social interaction. Goffman noted that:

---

[5] The association between reported speech and the climax or punchline of stories is not restricted to English (see, for example, Polanyi, 1982; Li, 1986; Larson, 1987).

In daily life the individual ordinarily speaks for himself, speaks, as it were, in his 'own' character. However, when one examines speech, especially the informal variety, this traditional view proves inadequate...When a speaker employs conventional brackets to warn us that what he is saying is meant to be taken in jest, or as mere repeating of words by someone else, then it is clear that he means to stand in a relation of reduced personal responsibility for what he is saying. He splits himself off from the content of the words by expressing that their speaker is not he himself or not he himself in a serious way.   (1974/1986: 512)

In observing that reported speech is an intrinsic feature of the way we interact, Goffman echoes Bakhtin; but Goffman subsequently proposed that reported speech is a natural upshot of a more general phenomenon in interaction: shifts of 'footing', defined as 'the alignment of an individual to a particular utterance...' (1981: 227). Goffman is concerned to break down the roles of speaker and hearer into their constituent parts. The speaker subsumes the roles of 'animator' – 'the sounding box', the 'author' – 'the agent who scripts the lines' and the 'principal' – 'the party to whose position the words attest' (1981: 226). All three roles may be played by a speaker at the same time, but often they are not. For instance, the vice-president reading out the speech on behalf of the president is only the animator. The author may be the president in conjunction with a scriptwriter. The principal is the president, as well as the represented political party she represents. In reporting the speech of another person the speaker is the animator but not the author or principal. Thus, our ability to use reported speech stems from the fact that we can adopt different roles within the 'production format', and it is one of the many ways in which we constantly change footing as we interact (see Levinson (1988) for an elaboration of Goffman's proposal).

The 'reduced personal responsibility' that Goffman claims for reported speech therefore appears to account for much of the licence that speakers seem to take in using it; thus, Goffman (1981) notes how curses and taboo utterances may be used with greater freedom than if speakers are speaking 'in their own voice'.

Goffman's work has proven foundational in the investigation of reported speech in interaction because it recognises that as much is to be learned from examining the context of reported speech – and the switch from non-reported to reported speech – as examining (as many structural studies had) just the reported speech itself. While Goffman is not in his own work concerned with the analysis of actual instances of interaction (for a critique, see Schegloff, 1988), it provides a framework for researchers concerned with investigating reported speech in its most basic environment of occurrence: ordinary conversation. Before examining some of the products of this research, we provide a brief sketch of some of the basic tenets of conversation analysis.

1.3 Conversation Analysis: a brief sketch

Conversation analysis (CA) – the adopted name for what is perhaps more accurately termed the study of talk-in-interaction – takes as a basic tenet the fact that social interaction is not haphazard but orderly, and that the methodical, organised nature of our social life can be studied by close attention to naturally occurring materials (for more detailed explication of the methods of CA, see Atkinson and Heritage, 1984; Heritage, 1984a, Chapter 8; and Psathas, 1995). The transcription of these audio- or video-recorded materials according to the system devised by Gail Jefferson (see 'Transcription conventions' on pages xi–xvii) involves registering features of the production and articulation of talk – and its absence – which capture the temporal unfurling of turns-at-talk. So features such as overlapping talk, in-breaths, the infiltration of laughter into talk, aspects of pace and prosody – all elusive to memory or intuition – are captured in the transcript and so accessible for their possible interactional import. These transcriptions then make the data available for repeated inspection and analysis. This has two important consequences: it allows for methodological transparency, such that the presence of the data makes any analysis accountable to it, and disputable because of it; and it also enables the collection of multiple examples of the same phenomenon, which reveals the systematicities underlying the apparent disorder and fragmentation of interaction. It is in establishing these systematicities that interpretation becomes analysis. And, because the analysis focuses on patterns observable in the data, analysts are able to avoid speculating about participants' intentions and understandings, or external constraints and influences that might impact on their conduct. Schegloff and Sacks note of their pioneering work in this field:

We have proceeded under the assumption (an assumption borne out by our research) that in so far as the materials we worked with exhibited orderliness, they did so not only to us, indeed not in the first place for us, but for the co-participants who had produced them. If the materials (records of natural conversation) were orderly, they were so because they had been methodically produced by members of the society for one another, and it was a feature of the conversations we treated as data that they were produced so as to allow the display by the co-participants to each other of their orderliness, and to allow the participants to display to each other their analysis, appreciation and use of that orderliness. Accordingly, our analysis has sought to explicate the ways in which the materials are produced by members in orderly ways that exhibit their orderliness and have their orderliness appreciated and used, and have that appreciation displayed and treated as the basis for subsequent action.   (1973: 290)

Turns are, in the first instance, built to contribute to the sequence of actions in which they occur; thus to analyse them in isolation is to ignore the way they are built to display analysis of, and participation in, the actions embodied by prior turns. Every turn-at-talk therefore displays the participant's definition of the situation; it displays an understanding of the activity sequence to which it contributes, and of what is an appropriate contribution to that sequence. This has an important methodological upshot: the analyst can use the sequential nature of turns at talk as a resource for accessing the participants' analysis of the nature of the actions engaged in.[6] From this perspective we can see how Goffman's observations on footing and the relationship between reported and non-reported speech have been an important influence on conversation analytic research into reported speech. It is to this work – the foundation for the current volume – that we now turn.

1.4 CA studies of reported speech

In some respects, detailed analysis of reported speech in context has highlighted differences between claims by linguists and sociolinguists and conversation analytic ones, while in others CA research has supported and extended previous findings. We begin by considering some of the discrepancies illuminated by existing CA work.

---

[6] For a more detailed consideration of CA method and its contribution to linguistics, see Clift (2005).

In section 2 we identified three main concerns in the linguistics literature regarding reported speech. The first of these was an overwhelming concern with a proposed distinction between direct and indirect forms of reported speech; different structural and functional features were attributed to each form. What CA is able to investigate, grounded as it is in participants' own orientations, is whether this purported distinction is an interactionally salient one. And indeed it would seem that it is not: recent empirical work has demonstrated that in practice these distinctions are often less clear-cut than authors have suggested, and functions attributed to one form are demonstrated by other forms. For example, above we saw that Li (1986) claims that prosodic features may be used to distinguish between direct and indirect forms. Given that DRS is thought to be a replaying of a former utterance conveying both form and content, while in indirect speech the current speaker can comment on the reported utterance, it seems reasonable to assume (as many authors have) that they will recurrently have different prosodic contours. So this would suggest that DRS may be accompanied by dramatic shifts in prosody or voice quality to distinguish it from the current speaker's unfooted utterances, highlighting that these are not the speaker's own words, and conveying the way in which the utterance was 'originally' said. In indirect speech, on the other hand, it is claimed that prosody or voice quality may be used to convey the current speaker's attitude towards the reported utterance. However, in a study of reported speech in German, Günthner notes that prosody and voice quality played a crucial role in staging dialogues in her data. She claims that:

simple dichotomies of direct versus indirect speech unduly reduce the complexities of reporting past dialogue: direct speech may also incorporate and contextualise the reporter's interpretation and evaluation of the reported dialogue.   (1997b: 250)

Indirect as well as direct speech, she finds, is used to present both *what* was said and *how* it was said. Günthner concludes that alternating between different forms of reported speech may contribute to a range of activities, such as distinguishing between different speakers, or to help differentiate background information from the climax of the story. However, these functions cannot be straightforwardly attributed to the different forms; rather 'we seem to be dealing with a complex web of factors in the dynamic interrelationship of reported and reporting discourse' (1997b: 268; see also Klewitz and Couper-Kuhlen (1999) for an account of the prosodic features marking out reported speech sequences). Thus, analysis of reported speech in interaction has revealed that distinctions between DRS and IRS are not always clear-cut. For example, a speaker may begin reporting an utterance with what appears to be DRS, but then switch to IRS (Holt, 1996). Indeed as Bolden (2004) shows, the boundaries of reported speech and other non-reported talk may not be clear-cut at all; in her study of conversational Russian, she shows how what she calls 'fading out' (2004: 1106) may be deployed to a number of inter-actional ends; in particular, potential problems of alignment and evidentiality.

In spite of the fact that CA research has shown that a clear-cut distinction between IRS and DRS is not always warrantable, and that uses or actions attributed to one form may also be demon-strated by the other, research focusing on DRS in interaction has substantiated and extended linguistic and sociolinguistic claims. For example, the fact that DRS purports to be a replaying of a prior locution has proved to be central to many aspects of the use made of the device in interaction. According to Holt (1996: 229), DRS gives the recipient 'access' to the reported utterance, enabling the recipient 'to assess it for himself or herself'. Wooffitt (1992), in an analysis of accounts of the paranormal, finds that speakers use DRS to make their claims more robust. Direct speech has long been seen as a way of not simply recalling a locution but also giving evidence about its form and content. Holt demonstrates that DRS can be used in interaction to give evidence of a former locu-tion: the reported speaker appears to be 'allowed to speak for himself or herself' (1996: 230). However, shifts in prosody or voice quality, as well as other components in the sequence such as story prefaces, can implicitly convey the speakers' evaluation. Thus, recipients are able to be the first to explicitly evaluate the reported incident, with tellers sometimes concurrently joining in with the evaluation (Holt, 2000).

This characteristic of letting the recipient interpret the reported speech for himself or herself (or at least to appear to do so) may help to explain its recurrent association with certain types of activity sequences. Golato's studies of reported speech in German focus on the use of a particular quotative ('und ich so/ und er so' – 'and I'm like/and he's like') to report embodied actions (2000) and on self-quotation to report past decisions (2002). Both Drew (1998a) and Holt (2000) examine complaints with respect to reported speech, and propose that in complaints the recipient can be given 'access' to a reprehensible comment, enabling him or her to offer a negative assessment of it and thus support the teller's own evaluation. Both find that reported speech is recurrently associated with recounting the climax of a story involving a complaint.

Conversation analytic research has revealed other environments with which reported speech is recurrently associated. Reported speech is often associated with laughter and can occur in making a joke or telling an amusing story (Holt, 2000, this volume). Goodwin (1990), in a study of African-American children, finds that reported speech is used to report contentious comments by a third party to the child targeted by those comments. The reduction of responsibility for a reported utterance partially accounts for the association between reported speech and gossip. Being able to delegate responsibility for 'forbidden expressions' (Bergman 1993: 113) gives gossips more freedom to transgress normal rules and 'enjoy playing with taboo modes of expression and turns of phrase that offend good taste' (1993: 117). In a study of racial discourse on a college campus, Buttny (1997) found that speakers would use reported speech in order to evaluate themselves and others, but overwhelmingly to criticise others (see also Buttny and Williams, 2000).

Existing CA work has thus already done much to illuminate one of the central concerns in the linguistics literature – that of the existence or otherwise of distinct forms of reported speech. It has also, as we have seen, ranged substantially beyond past work, to hitherto uninvestigated contexts. In this respect the current volume consolidates and enhances existing conversation analytically informed work by grounding the accounts in sequential analysis. As we shall see, it engages with two of the central concerns of previous literature – the authenticity of reported speech and what reported speech does in interaction.

1.5 This volume

The reported speech in this volume is shown in its diverse manifest-
ations in a range of contexts. The conversation analytic focus of the
chapters that follow reveal the extent to which it is the collaborative achievement of all the participants. The chapters by Charles
Goodwin and Elizabeth Holt underline the intellectual debt owed
by today's work in reported speech to Bakhtin/Volosinov and
Goffman while also exploring the limitations of the frameworks
developed by them. Goodwin examines both the telling of a story in
conversation and the activities of an aphasic man able to speak only
three words ('yes', 'no' and 'and'). Video data of these two types of
interaction reveal the importance of analysing footing and reported
speech within embodied, multi-party processes of interaction. Holt,
using telephone data, similarly shows how reported speech is the
product of collaboration by both participants. By focusing on what
she calls 'enactments', where participants shift footing to enact a
character, she throws light not only on the joking scenarios that they
construct but also on the more specific characteristics of this type
of reported speech, such as the lack of any distinct introductory
component.

The chapters by Elizabeth Couper-Kuhlen and Rebecca Clift
both focus on hitherto little-studied forms of reported speech –
those produced in non-narrative contexts. Couper-Kuhlen, examining both reported speech and reported thought, discusses two
framing environments for these: assessments and accounts. She
goes on to claim that such non-narrative uses of reported speech
consist maximally of one turn-constructional unit (TCU). Clift, in
Chapter 5, produces additional evidence to endorse this claim, and
furthermore examines a recurrent context for such non-narrative
uses of reported speech: competition over rights to assess. She also
investigates the means by which reported speech is necessarily *not* a
reproduction of what was – or might have been – originally said.

The chapters by Markku Haakana and John Rae and Joanne
Kerby return reported speech and thought to what is perhaps its
most common environment: story-telling. Haakana, examining
Finnish data, focuses on reported thought in complaint stories
as examples of what is *not* said, and proceeds to examine the
framing of the reported utterance through the various introductory

components in Finnish. Rae and Kerby, examining a corpus of stories told by young offenders of their encounters – often with the police – reveal how speakers design contexts for reported speech. In addition, they explore how responsive actions are represented in reported speech.

Rae and Kerby's chapter is one of four which examine reported speech in institutional contexts. Renata Galatolo focuses on the reported speech deployed during a notorious Italian murder trial, and discusses the moral and evidential work it performs in such legal contexts. Steven E. Clayman, in work which once more reveals a debt to Goffman, investigates how broadcast journalists present themselves as speaking on behalf of the public, showing the strategic importance of such a practice in the increasingly adversarial domain of journalistic interviews. In the final chapter, Robin Wooffitt examines how reported speech is used by mediums to support their claims to have established contact with the dead.

By grounding their investigations in the analysis of sequences of action, the articles in this volume can thus be seen to return to many of the issues that have preoccupied students of reported speech over the years. In doing so, they have aimed to anchor what have hitherto been analytic preoccupations in the orientations of the participants themselves. And, in taking participants' orientations as the starting point, they have ranged far beyond the traditional domains of inquiry, illuminating further the diversity and richness of reported speech.

2

Interactive Footing

Charles Goodwin

2.1 Introduction

In 1929, V. N. Volosinov (1973) argued that the linguistics of his time was seriously flawed because it took as its primary object of study language structures that were isolated from both context and the social life of their speakers. He proposed that this situation could be remedied by focusing on reported speech, utterances in which the current speaker in some way quotes or reports the talk of another. Noting that 'what is expressed in the forms employed for reporting speech is an *active relation* of one message to another', Volosinov (1973: 116, italics in original) proposed that reported speech constituted a crucial site for recovering the intrinsic dialogic organisation of language. The cogency and power of this argument is well demonstrated by the large body of significant research on both reported speech and the dialogic organisation of language and culture that has flourished since the 1970s in a number of different fields.

In reported speech the voices of separate actors are found in a particular place, a complex strip of talk produced by a single speaker, albeit one quoting the talk of another. While recognising both the originality and the importance of Volosinov's insights, I will argue here that the precise way in which he conceptualised reported speech actually served to hide, and render invisible to analysis, crucial aspects of the very dialogic organisation of language that he sought to probe. These include: 1) dialogue as multiparty sequences of talk in which the voices of different participants are not only heard but actually shape each other; 2) the visible actions of hearers and thus the multi-party interactive organisation of utterances (which would seem central to Volosinov's (1973) interest in a word as shared territory); and 3) utterances which lack the syntactic and other complexity required to incorporate reported speech.

To investigate such issues I will look first at one of the most powerful and influential models for analysis of the different kinds of 'speakers' that can co-exist within a strip of reported speech: Goffman's deconstruction of the speaker in Footing (1981) (see also Goffman, 1974/1986). In presenting this model Goffman also offered an important framework for the study of participation, and indeed participation seems absolutely central to the dialogic organisation of human language (C. Goodwin, 1981, 1986a; M. H. Goodwin, 1990, 1997, 2000; Goodwin and Goodwin, in press, 1987; Heath, 1986; Rae, 2001). There are, however, serious problems with Goffman's approach to participation. What he provides is a typology of participants rather than analysis of how utterances are built through the participation of structurally different kinds of actors within ongoing courses of action. To probe how such issues are consequential for the investigation of actual talk I will first use Goffman's model of the speaker to describe the different entities visible within a strip of reported speech in a story. This model provides important analytic tools. However, its limitations become visible when analysis is expanded to include the actions of silent (though consequential) participants, such as the party whose talk is being quoted. To further examine the dialogic organisation of both utterances and the speaker I will then look at the impoverished talk of a man with aphasia so severe that he lacks the syntax to construct the rich, laminated utterances required by the frameworks of both Goffman and Volosinov. It will be argued that a quite different notion of both participation and the dialogic organisation of language is necessary to explicate the way in which this man functions as a powerful speaker by incorporating the complex talk of others within his own limited utterances. Such phenomena shed light on the constitution of the speaker and the hearer – the two participant categories that are most central to human language – and to the dialogic processes that provide organisation for the construction of talk through their interaction with each other within this framework.

```
                              (4.0)
 1  Ann:    Well- ((throat clear))           (0.4)
 2          We coulda used a liddle, marijuna.
 3          tih get through the weekend.
 4  Beth:   What h [appened.
 5  Ann:          [Karen has this new hou:se.
 6          En it's got all this like (0.2) ssilvery::g-go:ld
 7          wwa:llpaper,
 8          *hh (h) en D(h)o(h)n sa(h)ys,
 9          y'know this's th'firs'time we've seen this house.
10          =Fifty five thousn dollars in Cherry Hill.=Right?
11              (0.4)
12  Beth:   Uh hu:h?
─────────────────────────────────────────────────────────
13  Ann:    Do(h)n said (0.3)
14          dih-did they ma:ke you take this [wa(h)llpa(h)p(h)er?
15  Beth:                                    [hh!
16  Ann:    =er(h)di [dju    pi(h)ck  [i(h)t ou(h)t.
─────────────────────────────────────────────────────────
17  Beth:            [Ahh huh  huh [huh huh=
```

Figure 2.1. Extract (1)

2.2 Complex speakers

The deconstruction of the speaker offered by Goffman in Footing demonstrates the genuine power of an analytic framework that focuses on the dialogic interplay of separate voices within reported speech. Figure 2.1 is a story in which a teller quotes something that her husband said. The story is about one of the prototypical scenes of middle-class society. Friends have got a new house. As guests visiting the house for the first time, the speaker and her husband, Don, were in the position of admiring and appreciating their hosts' new possessions. However, while looking at the wallpaper in the house Don asked the hosts if they were able to pick it out, or were forced to accept it (lines 13–16).[1]

Who is speaking in lines 14 and 16? The voice that is heard is Ann's, the current story-teller. However, she is reporting something that her husband, Don, said, and moreover presenting what he did

[1] This same story was analysed from a different perspective, without reference to Footing, in Goodwin (1984). I am indebted to Gail Jefferson for transcribing this talk.

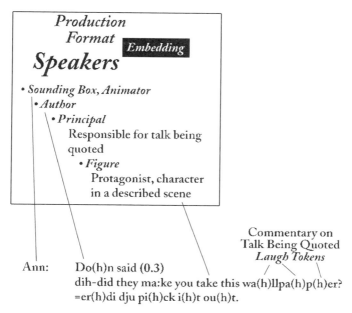

Figure 2.2. Production Format

as a terrible faux pas, an insult to their hosts in the narrated scene. She is both reporting the talk of another and also taking up a particular stance toward what was done through that talk. In a very real sense Ann (the current story-teller) and Don (the principal character in her story) are both 'speakers' of what is said in lines 14 and 16, though in quite different ways. The analytic framework offered by Goffman in Footing for what he called the Production Format of an utterance provides powerful tools for deconstructing the 'speaker' into a complex lamination of structurally different kinds of entities (see Figure 2.2).

In terms of the categories offered by Goffman, Ann is the *Animator*, the party whose voice is actually being used to produce this strip of speech. However, the *Author* of this talk, the party who constructed the phrase said, is someone else, the speaker's husband, Don. In a very real sense he is being held accountable as not only the *Author* of that talk, but also its *Principal*, a party who is socially responsible for having performed the action done by the original utterance of that talk. Goffman frequently noted that the talk of speakers in everyday conversation could encompass an entire theatre. And indeed here Ann is putting Don on stage as a character in the story she is telling, or in Goffman's terms *animating* him as a *Figure*.

Moreoever there is a complex laminated and temporal interdigitation among these different kinds of entities within the space of Ann's utterance. Thus it would be impossible to mark this as a quotation by putting quotation marks before and after what Don said. In addition to the report of this talk, the utterance also contains a series of laugh tokens, which are not to be heard as part of what Don said, but instead as the current speaker's, Ann's, commentaries on what Don did through that talk. Through her laugh tokens Ann both displays her own stance towards Don's utterance, formulating his talk as something to be laughed at, and, through the power of laugh tokens to act as invitations for others to join in the laughter (Jefferson, 1979), invites others to join in such treatment. Ann thus animates Don as a figure in her talk while simultaneously providing her own commentary on what he said by placing her own laugh tokens throughout the strip of speech being quoted.

In brief, in Footing Goffman provides a powerful model for systematically analysing the complex theatre of different kinds of entities that can co-exist within a single strip of reported speech. The analytic framework he develops sheds important light on the cognitive complexity of speakers in conversation, who are creating a richly inhabited and textured world through their talk. In addition to producing a meaningful linguistic sentence, Ann, within the scope of a single utterance, creates a socially consequential image of another speaker. His talk is thoroughly interpenetrated with another kind of talk that displays her stance toward, and formulation of both what he said (e.g. as a laughable of some type), and the kind of person that would say such a thing. Goffman's deconstruction of the speaker provides us with genuine analytic insights, and tools for applying those insights to an important range of talk.

2.3 Recovering the social and cognitive life of hearers

Goffman's speaker, a laminated structure encompassing quite different kinds of entities who co-exist within the scope of a single utterance, is endowed with considerable cognitive complexity. However, no comparable semiotic life animates Goffman's hearers. In a separate section of the article they are described as cognitively simple points on an analytic grid listing possible types of participation in the speech situation (e.g. Addressee vs Overhearer, etc.).

However, Ann's talk is actually lodged within a participation framework that has a range of structural features that carry it well beyond either a typology of participants, or dialogic text instantiated within the talk of a single speaker. Don, the principal character in Ann's story, the party whose faux pas is being reported, is not just a figure animated through the talk of the story, but an actual person who is present at the telling. Indeed he is seated right next to the story-teller. Elsewhere Goffman defined a social situation, such as the gathering where this story was told, as 'an environment of mutual monitoring possibilities' (Goffman, 1972: 63). Central to the organisation of the participants' monitoring of each other is the way in which those present 'jointly ratify one another as authorized co-sustainers of a single, albeit moving focus of visual and cognitive attention' (Goffman, 1972: 64). Within the field created by Ann's story it is appropriate and relevant for the others present to look at Don, the author of the terrible faux pas, when it is at last revealed. That place for scrutiny of the co-present offender being animated within the talk is defined by the sequential organization of the story, that is at its climax. As principal character in the story Don is faced with the task of arranging his body for the scrutiny it will receive when that moment arrives. When a videotape of the telling is examined it can be seen that, as Ann quotes what he said during lines 14 and 16, Don's face and upper body perform visual versions of her laughter. Indeed, on looking at the video, it appears that two separate bodies are performing the same laugh. For example, there is quite precise synchrony between escalation in Ann's vocal laughter and Don's visual displays. Thus, just as laugh tokens first appear in 'wa(h)llpa(h)p(h)er' in line 14, Don's face starts to form a smile/visual laugh. As Ann's laughter becomes more intense in line 16 Don's face matches her escalation with more elaborate head movements, wider opening of his mouth, etc.

The participation framework relevant to the organisation of Ann's story, and most crucially the quoted speech within it, thus extends far beyond structure in her talk to encompass the embodied actions of others who are present. Don is faced with the task of

systematically organising the displays being made by his body with
reference to the phenomenal field being constituted through the
unfolding structure of Ann's story. Moreover, the precision with
which he coordinates his actions with structure in Ann's talk suggests that he is not waiting to hear what she has actually said before
he begins to act, but instead projecting what she is about to say.
Structure in her talk provides resources for such projection. The
phrase 'Do(h)n said' marks that a quotation will be produced next
(the story clearly concerns what Don said to their hosts). Over
'Do(h)n said' in line 13, Don, who had been looking to his side
attending to something else, moves his head back to the focus of
Ann's story, and sits next to her in a posture that places his head in a
position where it is available for story-relevant scrutiny by others
(see 3 in Figure 2.3). However, he places his hand over his mouth,
the region of his face that will break into a smile a moment later
when Ann actually reports what he said. Thus, over line 13, he
positions himself like an actor moving to the wings just before his
projected entrance on stage.

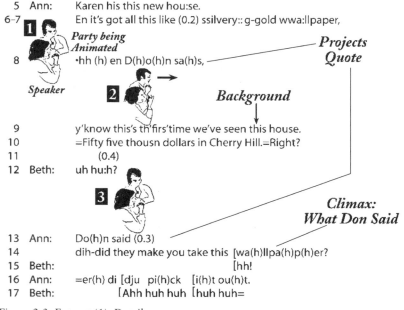

```
 5  Ann:    Karen his this new hou:se.
6-7         En it's got all this like (0.2) ssilvery:: g-gold wwa:llpaper,
            1   Party being                                   Projects
                Animated                                      Quote
 8          ·hh (h) en D(h)o(h)n sa(h)s, ─────────────
                Speaker
            2                          Background
 9          y'know this's th'firs'time we've seen this house.
10          =Fifty five thousn dollars in Cherry Hill.=Right?
11              (0.4)
12  Beth:   uh hu:h?
            3                                              Climax:
                                                        What Don Said
13  Ann:    Do(h)n said (0.3)
14          dih-did they make you take this [wa(h)llpa(h)p(h)er?
15  Beth:                                   [hh!
16  Ann:    =er(h) di [dju  pi(h)ck   [i(h)t ou(h)t.
17  Beth:             [Ahh huh huh  [huh huh=
```

Figure 2.3. Extract (1), Detail

The way in which Don moves to a preparatory position just before he becomes the story-relevant focus of attention in line 14 strongly suggests that he is using the emerging structure of Ann's talk to make projections about what he should do next within the multi-party interactive field invoked by the story.[2] Ann's story provides materials that permit more systematic investigation of this possibility. In line 8, with 'en D(h)o(h)n sa(h)s', Ann also projects that she is just about to quote the terrible thing that Don said to their hosts. Over this talk Don moves into a preparatory position (see Figure 2.4 on page 29) that is almost identical to the one he assumes several moments later over line 13. However, right after this, in lines 9–11, Ann abandons movement into the projected quotation and provides her hearers with additional background information about the house being assessed (its price and location). In essence, lines 9–11 constitute a parenthesis as additional background information is embedded within the climax segment begun in line 8.

The effect of this is that in line 9 Don has the rug pulled out from under his feet; the event that he had moved into position to be ready for – the quotation of his faux pas – is suddenly withdrawn. If Don is in fact organising his body with reference to projections about upcoming events in the story, then he is now positioned inappropriately (i.e. he has arranged his body for the scrutiny of others as his talk is quoted, but the speaker has suddenly shifted to further description of the house itself). As soon as the parenthesis is entered, Don abandons his preparatory position, and indeed visible orientation to the telling itself, by turning his gaze to his left and looking at how the person seated next to him is ladling soup from the pot in the centre of the table to his bowl (2 in Figure 2.3).

Don thus immediately adapts to the changes in Ann's talk so as to maintain the appropriateness of his participation for the structure of the talk currently in progress. Through such changes in his visible participation Don demonstrates his understanding of how the talk in progress is consequential for his own actions. As part of this process he visibly differentiates alternative kinds of units within Ann's story in terms of the participation frameworks each invokes.

---

[2] For more detailed analysis of how Don's embodied actions are organised with reference to interactive field invoked by Ann's telling, see Goodwin (1984).

The sequence as a whole provides strong evidence for the possibility that hearers are: first, visibly co-participating in the organisation of the talk in progress; second, engaged in detailed analysis of the unfolding structure of that talk; and third, using that analysis to make projections relevant to their own participation in it.

2.4 An alternative view of participation

Goffman's decomposition of the speaker provided us a model of an entity with complex internal structure, a multi-faceted player using language to perform interesting, laminated actions within a rich cognitive environment. However, no other participant category is decomposed in an equivalent fashion. Instead the complexity of participation status emerges through the accumulation of categories for types of recipients. Each of these categories, in marked contrast to the decomposition of the speaker, is treated as structurally simple and undifferentiated. Moreover, the complex ties between linguistic structure and forms of participation so prominent in Goffman's analysis of the speaker are entirely absent from his typology of possible recipients. Indeed, if one conceptualises the production of language as essentially a speaker's activity, this might seem entirely natural.

The model offered in Footing constitutes the point of departure for one very important approach to the study of participation. The categories for types of participants offered by Goffman were considerably expanded by Levinson (1988). Hanks (1990) then opposed open-ended category proliferation by noting how a range of different types of speakers and hearers could be logically accounted for as the outcome of more simple and general underlying practices, such as systematic embedding of one participation framework within another (as happens, for example, in quotation and other forms of reported speech).

Don's actions suggest an alternative framework for the study of participation, one that does not follow Footing by focusing on the construction of typologies categorising in a static fashion structurally different types of participants. Instead participation can be analysed as a temporally unfolding process through which separate parties demonstrate to each other their ongoing understanding of the events they are engaged in by building actions that contribute to the further progression of these very same events. Thus Don participates in the interactively sustained, multi-party interactive field that constitutes Ann's telling by organising his body with reference to how he is positioned within that field, while modifying his embodied displays as the emerging structure of Ann's talk makes relevant different kinds of participation alignments.

Shifting analysis – from the elaboration of typologies for participants, to study of the activities that parties must perform in order to participate appropriately in the events of the moment by building relevant action – has a number of important consequences. First, such a framework recovers the cognitive life of the hearer by focusing investigation on the analysis he or she must perform in order to co-construct action through differentiated participation in the talk of the moment. Second, a crucial component of the analysis hearers are engaged in focuses on distinguishing alternative units with the stream of speech in terms of the different possibilities for participation that each makes relevant. The actions of hearers thus shed important light on a key theoretical issue in the analysis of language structure; specifically the question of how participants parse the stream of speech into relevant units. Indeed, that task becomes visible here as a practical problem for participants, a constitutive feature of the forms of social organisation they build through talk, rather than simply a theoretical issue for analysts or transcribers. Third, important properties of this unit structure are provided by the sequential organisation of talk, including what different kinds of units count as forms of multi-party, multi-modal interaction. Fourth, this process also has a temporal dimension as, first, different kinds of units (with different participation possibilities) unfold through time and, second, hearers make projections about upcoming units in order to accomplish relevant simultaneous action.

2.5 Logocentrism

This view of participation has a number of consequences for how stories, reported speech and talk in interaction more generally are conceptualised. Most analysis of both reported speech and stories focuses exclusively on talk. However, the data examined here reveal that a story in face-to-face interaction is a multi-modal, multi-party field of activity. In addition to phenomena in the stream of speech, other kinds of signs displayed through, for example, the visible organisation of the body are also relevant.

Differences between kinds of sign systems, and their potential for being captured in writing, privilege one participant, the speaker, while obscuring all others. Because of the division of labour between speaker and hearer(s), speaker(s) produce most talk. Hearers' concurrent talk, though frequently informative about a recipient's analysis of what is being said and his or her stance toward it (Jefferson, 1973, 1983, 1984a), typically lacks the semantic and syntactic complexity of the speaker's talk. Characteristically, recipient actions, such as continuers (Schegloff, 1982) and assessments (Goodwin, 1986b), take the form of brief one- or two-syllable phrases. Indeed, if hearers were to provide substantive talk within another speaker's turn, extended overlap would occur. It might be argued that the actions of hearers can be recovered by focusing on later turns where former hearers who have now become speakers can display analysis of the talk they heard earlier. However, there is no reason whatsoever to treat such subsequent action as equivalent to their concurrent analysis and co-participation in the utterance while it was in progress (Goodwin and Goodwin, 1987). There are crucial differences between a hearer and a subsequent speaker. For example, though Don participated in the laughter while Ann reported what he said, in subsequent talk he tried to counter and minimise her interpretation of his talk, e.g. 'But I said it so innocuously y'know'. He responds to what Ann quotes him as saying in entirely different ways during her talk than he does later as a subsequent speaker.

The upshot of all of this is that focusing analysis exclusively on talk treats the speaker as the primary – indeed, on occasion, the sole – actor relevant to the construction of an utterance such as a story, while obscuring, or rendering completely invisible, the simultaneous actions of the hearer. Thus Don appears only as a cited figure in the transcript of Ann's story in Figure 2.1, not as a present actor. If data for study of the story consisted only of the talk transcribed there, none of his actions that were investigated above would be accessible to investigation. These include not only phenomena centred on the visible body, such as participation displays, but also his moment-by-moment analysis of the unfolding structure of the talk in progress.

Some argue that the genuine analytic problems raised by this situation can be avoided by using data such as phone calls where the participants' only access to each other is through talk. While this may be true for such limited cases, it seems clear that the primordial site for talk-in-interaction, and human interaction in general, is not one that is restricted to sound, but instead a situation in which participants are building relevant action together through talk while attending to each other as fully embodied actors, and frequently to relevant structure in their environment, the larger activities they are engaged in, etc. (Goodwin, 2000a, 2003a).

There are powerful reasons for such logocentrism. For thousands of years human beings have been grappling with the issues raised by the task of capturing significant structure in the stream of speech in writing. Writing systems, and the insights and methodological tools they have provided for the analysis of linguistic and phonetic structure, the creation of precise records that can endure in time and be transported from place to place, etc. are major accomplishments that provide a crucial infrastructure for much of research into language structure, verbal genres and more recently talk-in-interaction. However, despite efforts in kinesics, gesture studies, Labanotation, etc., there are no systems comparable to writing for the rapid and precise annotation of the other embodied modalities that contribute the organisation of face-to-face interaction. The problems posed are not simply methodological but, more importantly, require discovery of the crucial distinctions that participants attend to for the organisation of action through embodied interaction. Moreover, such perceptual bias toward what is being said, with other modalities receding into a more amorphous ground, seems to reflect in part the way participants themselves focus their explicit attention on the talk in progress. Thus, if asked what happened in an encounter, participants typically report what was said, not the work of constructing the embodied frameworks of mutual orientation that made interactive talk possible in the first place (Goodwin, 1981; Kendon, 1990).

Contemporary video and computer technology makes it possible to repeatedly examine the bodies as well as the talk of participants in interaction, and thus to move analytically beyond logocentricism. And indeed some evidence suggests that neither talk, nor language itself, are self-contained systems, but instead function within a larger ecology of sign systems (Goodwin, 2000a).

2.6 Mutual reflexivity

Within interaction participants treat their co-participants as reflexive actors. They expect each other to take into account for the organisation of subsequent action the projective frameworks provided by both talk and visible embodied displays. Don's actions provide one example of how hearers demonstrate ongoing analysis of emerging talk by building actions that make visible appropriate participation in it. Data beyond that included in this chapter demonstrate that speakers take the actions of hearers into account in ways that have strong consequences for the future trajectory of stories and other units of talk (C. Goodwin, 1981, 2002; M. H. Goodwin, 1980). A story is constructed, not by the speaker alone, but instead through the coordinated actions of different kinds of participants. Moment by moment each party must take into account: 1) the emerging structure of the activities in progress; 2) what precisely other parties are doing; and 3) the implications that this has for the trajectory of future action. Major resources for this process include the signs present in the structure of the talk and the displays being made by the bodies of the participants.

It is precisely this organisation of mutual reflexivity that is missing from Goffman's models of Footing and participation.

In Footing, instead of collaborating together to build talk, speakers and hearers inhabit separate worlds, with quite different frameworks being used for the analysis of each. One reason for this would seem to lie in the way in which speakers and hearers are described in quite separate sections of Footing. Such a rhetorical arrangement makes it difficult (perhaps impossible) to build a model in which utterances are constructed through processes of interaction in which different kinds of participants are building action in concert with each other. In Footing, building utterances is exclusively the work of speakers, who are thus endowed with all relevant cognitive structure.

It is most ironic that one of Goffman's most influential legacies is a powerful analytic framework that focuses on the talk of the speaker in isolation from the simultaneous actions of the hearer.

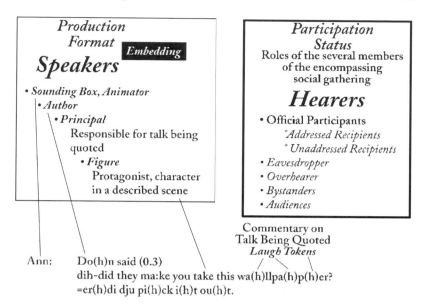

Figure 2.4. Participation Status

Goffman introduced into the study of human interaction terms such as 'mutual monitoring'. His whole career was devoted to intensive studies of processes of human interaction, and in work such as that on strategic interaction and mutual monitoring he showed deep concern for the ways in which participants were analysing each other to manipulate meaning and action. Why then in Footing did he develop an analytic framework that treats the talk of the speaker as an isolated, self-contained system?

Candy Goodwin and I were studying with Goffman while he was working on Footing. One day he urged us to read Volosinov (1973), which had only been recently published in English. Though I have no other evidence[3] whatsoever, I suspect that Goffman's thinking in Footing was influenced in part by his reading of Volosinov. His decomposition of the speaker, noted above, provides powerful tools for working with some of Volosinov's insights about reported speech. Most crucially, both Footing and Volosinov share a vision of how dialogic interaction can be embedded within the

---

[3] Volosinov is not listed in the references to Footing and is cited only once in Goffman's *Forms of Talk* (1981).

talk of a single speaker that has deeply shaped how subsequent scholars conceptualised both reported speech and participation status. Sapir (1968) notes that a word with its associated concept 'is not only a key; it may also be a fetter.' The genuine insights of both Volosinov and Goffman created a key through which important phenomena could be investigated in novel and important ways, while simultaneously constraining such study in hidden but powerful ways.

2.7 Volosinov's conception of dialogue

Marxism and the Philosophy of Language was published in the Soviet Union in 1929. Its author, V. N. Volosinov, was a member of the circle of scholars who clustered around Mikhail Bakhtin. Indeed it has been strongly argued that Bakhtin, not Volosinov, was the work's author. I take no position on that issue. Regardless of who might be named as author, the volume and its arguments are deeply tied to the analytic frameworks associated with Bakhtin, and indeed might be considered one of the canonical Bakhtinian texts. Here I wish to raise questions about the precise way in which Volosinov formulated the dialogic nature of language, essentially arguing that both the participation of the hearer and multi-party talk are rendered invisible in his conception of reported speech. However, in doing this I want to emphasise my deep appreciation for, and agreement with, the insights and perspectives so brilliantly enunciated in this book. My disagreement is not an attack on Volosinov, but a dialogue with him, and an attempt to expand the perspectives he offers by looking seriously at how he formulated crucial analytic phenomena. Moreover, I recognise only too well how subsequent scholars have used the work of Bakhtin and Volosinov to probe the interrelationship between language, ideology, stance, social positioning, voice and culture to develop powerful, original and important new ways of thinking about, and acting within, the lived social world.

When, at Goffman's urging, I first read Volosinov (1973) in the early 1970s, I was amazed that the book could have been written in the 1920s. It made arguments about the social and interactive organisation of language that prefigured my own interest in the participation of the hearer in the construction of utterances, but which I had not seen anywhere else. For example:

word is a two-sided act. It is determined equally by *whose* word it is and for *whom* it is meant. As word, it is precisely *the product of the reciprocal relationship between speaker and listener, addresser and addressee*. Each and every word expresses the 'one' in relation to the 'other'. I give myself verbal shape from another's point of view ... A word is territory shared by both addresser and addressee, by the speaker and his interlocutor ... constituting, as it were, the border zone between [the speaker] and his addressee.   (Volosinov, 1973: italics in original)

All of this – for example, proposing that the speaker shaped himself or herself from the point of view of the addressee – reson-ated directly with what I was finding in my own video analysis of utterance construction at that time, e.g. speaker's reconstruct-ing their emerging utterances, and displays of knowledge and cer-tainty, as gaze was moved from one type of addressee to another (C. Goodwin, 1979, 1981, 1987).

Moreover, in a critique that remained relevant to the formal linguistics of the late twentieth century (though originally directed against what Volosinov termed the Abstract Objectivism of Saus-sure), and which seemed to anticipate fields such as conversation analysis, Volosinov (1973: 117) argued that the primary locus for language was not the isolated monologic utterance or sentence, but instead 'the interaction of at least two utterances – in a word dialogue.'

However, in a series of subtle but most crucial moves, Volosinov lodged the problems posed by the study of dialogue, not in se-quences of multi-party talk, i.e. what one would consider to be the most natural, straightforward notion of dialogue, but instead within the consciousness of the individual speaker: 'How...is another speaker's speech received? What is the mode of existence of another's utterance in the actual, inner-speech consciousness of the recipient? How is it manipulated there?' (Volosinov, 1973: 117).

How can the interplay between the utterances of separate indi-viduals be analysed within the mind, and talk, of a single speaker? Volosinov's answer to this problem was original and important. He argued that reported speech, in which the current speaker incorpor-ates the talk of another into the current utterance, provides a place where the reception and transformation of another's talk can be systematically investigated. Ann's report of what Don said in lines 13–16 of Figure 2.1 provides a typical example, and indeed, as is demonstrated by Goffman's decomposition of the speaker in *Footing*, and much work by a host of other scholars, what Volosinov draws our attention to here is a rich and important phenomenon. Note, however, that dialogue is now transformed into something that can best be investigated within the talk and consciousness of a single speaker, albeit one quoting the talk of another.

Indeed Volosinov argues explicitly that what he is proposing as the key to the dialogical organisation of language, the process of 'words reacting on words' found in reported speech,

is distinctly and fundamentally different from dialogue. In dialogue, the lines of the individual participants are grammatically disconnected; they are not integrated into one unified context. Indeed, how could they be? *There are no syntactic forms with which to build a unity of dialogue.* (Volosinov, 1973: 116, italics in original)

Volosinov thus comes to the rather paradoxical conclusion that dialogue, multi-party sequences of talk, does not provide appropriate data for study of the dialogic organisation of language, 'the *active relation* of one message to another' (1973: 116, italics in original). The evidence he offers to support this, lack of syntactic ties linking the contributions of separate speakers, is simply not true as work such as that of Sacks (1992a: 144–147), on collaborative utterances and tying techniques (1992a: 716–721), clearly demonstrates.[4]

However, by making this argument Volosinov was able to define dialogue so that syntactically complex texts, rather than talk-in-interaction, constitute the primary site for the dialogic organisation of language and culture. And, indeed, within the larger politics of research fields competing to occupy the most relevant site for the analysis of human language, cognition and social action (and by offering his work as a critique of, and alternative to, Saussure Volosinov was explicitly engaging in such politics), defining *the*

---

[4] Note in this connection the significant body on research on reported speech, and the diverse grammatical practices of different languages, which have crucial differences in their sequential placement, which takes talk-in-interaction and research in conversation analysis as its point of departure (e.g. Hayashi, 1997; Holt, 1996; the introduction to this volume).

perspicuous site for research in this fashion, i.e. as reported speech, could be most useful to a literary critic such as Bakhtin. This position has strong implications for methodology and data as well. Since all relevant phenomena are located in the kinds of language structure that writing captures, it is not necessary for the analyst to look beyond the printed text, for example to investigate the bodies of either the speaker or active (though silent) participants such as hearers, or multi-party action. A radical argument about the importance of both the hearer and dialogue is thus subtly domesticated so that it fits comfortably within the boundaries of the traditional textual artefacts that thus continue to define where language will be analysed.

Volosinov and Footing thus share a number of key assumptions. In both, syntactically complex language in which the current speaker reports in some fashion the talk of another is used to build very interesting analysis of how single utterances constitute a site where the voices of multiple speakers dynamically interact with each other. However, by virtue of the way in which the multiple voices that constitute the dialogue being analysed are embedded in a single utterance, there is no need to investigate actual multi-party sequences of talk or phenomena outside the stream of speech. Parties other than the speaker are thus excluded from analysis. The crucial mutual reflexivity of speakers and hearers is lost. It becomes impossible to investigate how utterances are built through processes of interaction that include the participants' ongoing analysis of each other. In essence the world being analysed is lodged within a single speaker's speech.

2.8 Multi-party speakers and participation

While the insights of both Volosinov and Footing lead to very interesting analysis of a rich and important class of utterances, serious problems arise if models such as this are used for the general analysis of the dialogic organisation of language and culture, of stance and footing, and of the practices used by speakers to incorporate another's talk into a current utterance. For example, both Volosinov and Footing require, as a point of departure for the kinds of analysis they propose, utterances that have rich syntax, e.g. clauses in which the talk of another that is being reported is embedded within a larger utterance by the current speaker. The necessity of rich syntax not only excludes important activities – such as many greetings which, at least in English, are frequently done with one to two word utterances (e.g. 'Hi') – but also certain kinds of speakers. Because of a severe stroke Chil, whose actions we will now investigate, was able to say only three words: 'Yes', 'No' and 'And'. It is impossible for him to produce the syntax that Goffman's Production Format and Volosinov's reported speech seem to require (i.e. he can't produce a sentence such as 'John said X'). Someone such as Chil appears to fall beyond the pale of what counts as the competent speaker required for their analysis.

Chil in fact acts as a powerful speaker in interaction, and moreover one who is able to include the talk of others in his utterances. Describing how he does this requires a model of the speaker that moves beyond the individual. The sequence in Figure 2.5 provides an example. Chil's son Chuck and daughter-in-law Candy are talking with him about the amount of snow the winter has brought to the New York area where Chil lives. After Candy notes that not much has fallen 'this year' (which Chil strongly agrees with in talk omitted from the transcript), in line 11 she proposes that such a situation contrasts markedly[5] with the amount that fell 'last year'. Initially, with his '°yeah-' Chil seems to agree (in the interaction during the omitted talk Chil was strongly agreeing with what Candy was saying, and thus might have grounds to expect and act as though that process would continue here). However, he ends his agreement with a cut-off (thus visibly interrupting and correcting his initial agreement) and moves to strong, vivid disagreement in line 13. Candy immediately turns to him and changes her 'last year' to 'the year before last'. Before she finishes, Chil (line 15) affirms the correctness of her revised version.

Despite his severely impoverished language Chil is able to make a move in the conversation that is both intricate and precise: unlike what Candy initially proposed in line 10, it was not 'last year' but 'the year before last' when there was a lot of snow. Chil says this by getting someone else to produce just the words that he needs. The

---

[5] This contrast is signalled strongly by both the contrastive 'But', which begins line 11, and the displays of heightened affect and stance that follow.

The participants have been discussing snow in the area where Chil lives

1   Candy: You haven't had **that** much this year have you.

... ((8 lines omitted))

10 Candy:	But **la** [**st** year. Whoo!
11 Chuck:	[°mm
12	[In the l [ast year-
13 Chil:	[°yeah- [**No No. No:.**
14 Candy:	er the year before la [st.
15 Chil:	[Yes.

Figure 2.5. Extract (2)

talk in line 14 is semantically and syntactically far beyond anything that Chil could say on his own.

Though not only spoken, but constructed by Candy, it would be clearly wrong to treat line 14 as a statement by her. First, just a moment earlier, in lines 10 and 12 she voiced the position that is being contradicted here. Second, as indicated by Chil's agreement in line 15, Candy is offering her revision as something to be accepted or rejected by Chil, not as a statement that is epistemically her own. Line 14 thus seems to require a deconstruction of the speaker of the type called for by Goffman in Footing, with Candy in some sense being an animator, or 'sounding box', for a position being voiced by Chil. However, the analytic framework offered in Footing does not accurately capture what is occurring here. Though Candy is in some important sense acting as an Animator for Chil, he is not a cited figure in her talk, and no quotation is occurring. Intuitively the notion that Chil is in some sense the Author of line 14, and its Principal, seems plausible (what is said here would not have been spoken without his intervention, and he is treated as the ultimate judge of its correctness). However, how could someone completely unable to produce either the semantics or the syntax of line 14 be identified as its Author?

Clarifying such issues requires a closer look at the interactive practices used to construct the talk that is occurring here. Chil's intervention in line 13 is an instance of what Schegloff et al. (1977)

describe as Other Initiated Repair. With his *'No No. No:.'* Chil forcefully indicates that there is something wrong with what Candy, the prior and still current speaker, has just said. She can re-examine her talk to try and locate what needs repair, and indeed here that process seems straightforward. In response to Chil's move, Candy changes *'last* year', the crucial formulation in the talk Chil is objecting to, to an alternative 'the year before last'.

Such practices for the organisation of repair, which are pervasive not only in Chil's interaction, but in the talk of fully fluent speakers as well (Schegloff et al., 1977), have crucial consequences for both Chil's ability to function as a speaker in interaction, and for probing the analytic models offered by Goffman and Volosinov. First, through the way in which Chil's instances of 'Yes' and 'No' are tied to specific bits of talk produced by others (e.g. what Candy has just said), they have a strong indexical component which allows him to use as a resource detailed structure in the talk of others, and in some sense incorporate that talk into his own, linguistically impoverished utterances. Thus in line 13 he is heard to be objecting not to life in general, but to precisely what Candy said in line 12, and to be agreeing with what she said in line 14. Second, such expansion of the linguistic resources available to Chil is built upon the way in which his individual utterances are embedded within sequences of dialogue with others, or more generally the sequential organisation of interaction. However, this notion of dialogue, as multi-party sequences of talk, was precisely what Volosinov (1973: 116) worked to exclude from his formulation of the dialogic organisation of language. Nonetheless, Chil's actions here provide a clear demonstration of the larger Bakhtinian argument that speakers talk by 'renting' and reusing the words of others.

Third, what happens here requires a deconstruction of the speaker that is relevant to, but different from, that offered by Goffman in Footing. What Chil says with his 'No' in line 13 indexically incorporates what Candy said in line 11, though Chil does not, and cannot, quote what she said there. Instead of the structurally rich single utterance offered in Goffman's model of multiple voices laminated within the complex talk of a single speaker, here we find a single lexical item, a simple 'No', that encompasses talk produced in multiple turns (e.g. both lines 11 and 13) by separate actors (Candy and Chil). Unlike Ann's story in Figure 2.1, Chil's talk cannot be understood or analysed in isolation. Its comprehension requires inclusion of the utterances of others that Chil is visibly tying to.

Rather than being located within a single individual, the speaker here is distributed across multiple bodies and is lodged within a sequence of utterances. Chil's competence to manipulate in detail the structure of emerging talk by objecting to what has just been said – that is, to act in interaction – constitutes him as a crucial Author of Candy's revision in line 14, despite his inability to produce the language that occurs there. Though not reporting the speech of another Candy speaks for Chil in line 14, and locates him as the Principal for what is being said there. All of this requires a model of the speaker that takes as its central point of departure not the competence to quote the talk of another (though being able to incorporate, tie to and reuse another's talk is absolutely central), but instead the ability to produce consequential action within sequences of interaction.

Fourth, the action occurring here, and the differentiated roles parties are occupying within it, are constituted not only through talk, but also through participation as a dynamically unfolding process. As line 13 begins Candy has turned away from Chil to gaze at Chuck. Chil's talk in line 13 pulls Candy's gaze back to him (her eyes move from Chuck to Chil over the last of his three uses of 'No'). Such securing the gaze of an addressee is similar to the way in which fluent speakers use phenomena such as restarts to obtain the gaze of a hearer before proceeding with a substantive utterance (C. Goodwin, 1980, 1981).

In this case, however, it is the addressee, Candy, rather than Chil, the party who solicited gaze, who produces the talk that follows. Nonetheless, through the way in which he organises his body Chil displays that he is acting as something more than a recipient of Candy's talk, and instead sharing the role of its speaker. Typically gestures are produced by speakers. Indeed the work of McNeill (1992) argues strongly that an utterance and the gesture accompanying it are integrated components of a single underlying process. Line 14 is accompanied by gesture. However, it is performed not by the person speaking, Candy, but instead by Chil (see Figure 2.6).

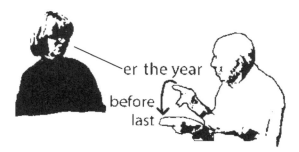

Figure 2.6. Extract (2), Detail

Chil thus participates in Candy's utterance by performing an action usually reserved for speakers, and in so doing visibly displays that he is in some way acting as something more than a hearer. The gesture seems to provide a visual version of what Candy was saying, and specifically to illustrate the notion that one unit (which can be understood as a 'year' through the way in which the gesture is temporally bound to Candy's talk) has another that precedes it. As Candy says 'the year', Chil raises his hand toward her with two fingers extended. Then, as she says 'before last', he moves his gesturing hand down and to the left (see Figure 2.6). Even if this interpretation of the gesture must remain speculative (for participants as well as the analyst) because of Chil's inability to fully explicate it with talk of his own, the gesture is precisely coordinated with the emerging structure of Candy's talk, and vividly demonstrates Chil's participation in the field of action being organised through that talk. Note once again that Participation is being investigated here, not as static categories constructed by the analyst (addressee, speaker, hearer, etc.), but instead as forms of temporally unfolding, interactively organised action through which participants demonstrate with precision (as Chil does here word by word as Candy's talk emerges) their understanding of the events in progress by building action that helps to produce these very same events.

The following provides another example of how the position of speaker is distributed across multiple bodies, and lodged within the sequential organisation of dialogue. Here Chil's daughter Pat and son Chuck are planning a shopping expedition. Once again Chil intercepts a speaker's talk with a strong 'No' (lines 6–7 in Figure 2.7). Pat is talking about the problem of finding socks that

```
 1   Pat:        So  you always need the black socks:
 2   Chuck:      °umm.
 3               (1.7)
 4   Pat:        It's too bad we found those there too
 5               at the store that went outa busi[ness.
 6   Chil:  →                                   [Na-dee No:=
 7               =dih dih dih-
 8               (0.5)
 9   Pat:   →    Yeah=you went to Bergenfield.
10   Chil:       Ye:s.
```

Figure 2.7. Extract (3)

fit over Chil's leg brace, since the store where she bought them last went out of business.

What occurs here has is structurally similar to the 'year before last' sequence examined in Figures 2.5 and 2.6. After Chil uses a 'No' to challenge something in the current talk, that speaker produces a revision, which Chil affirms. Once again Chil is operating on the emerging sequential structure of the local dialogue to lead another speaker to produce the words he needs. However, while Candy in Figure 2.5 could locate the revision needed through a rather direct transformation of the talk then in progress (changing 'last year' to 'the year before last'), the resources that Pat uses to construct her revision are not visible in the transcript. How is she able to find a completely different store and, moreover, locate it geographically? When a visual record of the exchange is examined, we find that in addition to talk Chil produces a vivid pointing gesture as he objects to what Pat is saying. Pat treats this as indicating a particular place in their local neighbourhood, a store in an adjacent town in the direction Chil is pointing (see Figure 2.8).

Chil constructs his action in lines 6–7 by using simultaneously a number of quite different meaning-making practices that mutually elaborate each other. First, as was seen in the 'last year' example in Figures 2.6 and 2.7, by precisely placing his 'No' (again overlapping the statement being challenged), Chil is able to use what is being said by another speaker as the indexical point of departure for his own action. His hearers can use that talk to locate something quite specific about what Chil is trying to indicate (e.g. that his action concerns something about the place where the socks were

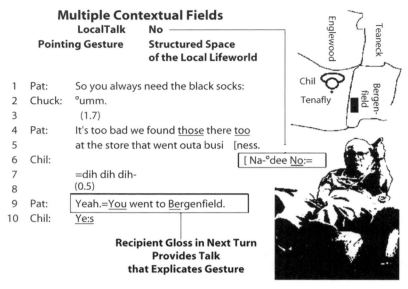

Multiple Contextual Fields

| LocalTalk | No |
| Pointing Gesture | Structured Space of the Local Lifeworld |

1	Pat:	So you always need the black socks:
2	Chuck:	°umm.
3		(1.7)
4	Pat:	It's too bad we found <u>those</u> there <u>too</u>
5		at the store that went outa busi [ness.
6	Chil:	[Na-°dee <u>No</u>:=
7		=dih dih dih-
8		(0.5)
9	Pat:	Yeah.=<u>You</u> went to <u>B</u>ergenfield.
10	Chil:	<u>Ye:s</u>

**Recipient Gloss in Next Turn
Provides Talk
that Explicates Gesture**

Figure 2.8. Multiple Complex Fields

bought). Nonetheless, as this example amply demonstrates, such indexical framing is not in any way adequate to specify precisely what Chil is attempting to say (e.g. in lines 4–5 there is no indication of a store in Bergenfield). However, Chil complements his 'No' with a second action, his pointing gesture. In isolation such a point could be quite difficult for an addressee to interpret. Even if one were to assume that something in the environment was being indicated, the line created by Chil's finger extends indefinitely. Is he pointing toward something in the room in front of them or, as in this case, a place that is actually miles away?[6] However, by using the co-occurring talk a hearer can gain crucial information about what the point might be doing (e.g. indicating where the socks being discussed were bought). Simultaneously, the point constrains the rather open-ended indexical field provided by the prior talk by indicating an alternative to what was just said. By themselves both

[6] The task of locating what is being pointed at is not simply a theoretical problem, but a genuine practical one for those who interact with Chil. On occasion they searched for something in the room when in fact he was pointing well beyond the wall, and vice versa (Goodwin, 2000b, 2003b).

the talk and the pointing gesture are partial and incomplete. However, when each is used to elaborate and make sense out of the other, a whole that is greater than the sum of its parts is created (see also Wilkinson et al., 2003).

The ability to properly see and use Chil's pointing gesture requires knowledge of the structure of the environment being invoked through the gesture. As someone who regularly acts and moves within Chil's local neighbourhood, Pat can be expected to recognise such a structure. A stranger would not. Chil's action thus encompasses a number of quite different semiotic fields (C. Goodwin, 2000a) including his own talk, the talk of another speaker that Chil's 'No' is tied to, his gesturing arm, and the spatial organisation of his surroundings. Though built through general practices (negation, pointing, etc.), Chil's action is situated in, and reflexively invokes, a local environment that is shaped by both the emerging sequential structure of the talk in progress, and the detailed organisation of the lifeworld that he and his interlocutors inhabit together.

One pervasive model of how human beings communicate conceptualises the addressee/hearer as an entity that simply decodes the linguistic and other signs that make up an utterance, and through this process recovers what the speaker is saying. Such a model is clearly inadequate for what occurs here. To figure out what Chil is trying to say or indicate, Pat must go well beyond what can actually be found in either her talk or Chil's pointing gesture. Rather than in and of themselves encoding a proposition, the signs Chil produces presuppose a hearer who will use them as a point of departure for complex, contingent inferential work. Chil requires a cognitively complex hearer who collaborates with him in establishing public meaning through participation in ongoing courses of action.

The participation structures through which Chil is constituted as a speaker are not lodged within his utterance alone, but instead distributed across multiple utterances and actors. In line 9 Pat responds to Chil's intervention by providing a gloss of what she takes him to be saying: 'You went to Bergenfield'. Chil affirms the correctness of this with his 'Yes' in line 10. If this action is analysed using only the printed transcript as a guide it might seem to constitute a simple agreement with what Pat said in line 9. However, when a visual record of the interaction is examined Chil can be seen to move his gaze from Pat to Chuck as he speaks this word.

```
 4   Pat:      it's too bad we found those there too
 5             at the store that went outa busi [ness.
 6   Chil:                                      [Na- °dee No:=
 7             =dih dih dih-
 8                  (0.5)
 9   Pat:      Yeah.=You went to Bergenfield.
10   Chil      Ye:s.
11   Chuck:    [°uh huh. uh huh.((Nods to Chil))
12   Pat:      [To the men's shop.
```

Figure 2.9. Extract (3), Detail

Chuck, who is visiting, lives across the continent. He is thus not aware of many recent events in Chil's life, including the store in Bergenfield that Pat has just recognised (though Chuck, who grew up in this town, is familiar with its local geography). With his gaze shift (and the precise way in which Chil speaks 'Yes', which is beyond my abilities to indicate appropriately on the printed page), Chil visibly assumes the position of someone who is telling Chuck about this store. He thus acts as not only the author, but also the speaker and teller, of this news. He has of course excellent grounds for claiming this position. A moment earlier, in lines 4–5, Pat said something quite different, and it was only Chil's intervention that led her to produce the talk he is now affirming. Within the single syllable of line 10 Chil builds different kinds of action for structurally different kinds of recipients: first, a confirmation of what Pat (someone who knows about the event at issue and now recognises it) see Figure 2.9, has just said and, second, a report about that event to Chuck, an unknowing recipient.[7]

---

[7] For other analysis of how utterances can be built to include both knowing and unknowing recipient, see Goodwin (1979, 1981, 1987).

Both Volosinov's analysis of reported speech and Goffman's deconstruction of the speaker focused on the isolated utterance of a single individual who was able to constitute a laminated set of structurally different kinds of participants by using complex syntax to quote the talk of another. By way of contrast the analytic frameworks necessary to describe Chil's speakership in line 18 must move beyond him as an isolated actor to encompass the talk and actions of others, which he indexically incorporates into his single-syllable utterance in line 10. Moreover, grasping his action requires attending not only to structure in the stream of speech but also to his visible body, and relevant structure in the surround. Chil's speakership is distributed across multiple utterances produced by different actors (e.g. Pat's talk in both lines 13 and 17 is a central part of what is being reported through his 'Yes'), and encompasses non-linguistic structure provided by both his visible body and the semiotic organisation of the environment around him. His talk is thoroughly dialogic. However, analysis of how it incorporates the talk of others in its structure requires moving beyond the models for reported speech and the speaker provided by Volosinov and Goffman.

2.9 Conclusion

In *Marxism and the Philosophy of Language*, Volosinov offered, in opposition to what he termed the 'abstract objectivism' of Saussure, a powerful vision of language as something thoroughly lodged within human dialogue, e.g. 'A word is territory shared by both addresser and addressee, by the speaker and his interlocutor' (Volosinov, 1973). However, at the same time Volosinov was careful to situate the 'dialogic' play of multiple voices, not in sequences of talk by different participants (e.g. the most straightforward notion of dialogue), but in reported speech, talk in which a speaker incorporates in some fashion the talk of another. Volosinov's insights into reported speech constituted the point of departure for a large, diverse and important body of research by subsequent scholars that shed important new light on a host of issues implicated in the organisation of language structure, stance, metalanguage, story organisation and the sedimentation of historically shaped social phenomena in the details of language structure.

However, by restricting investigation to the interplay of voices within the talk and consciousness of a single speaker, the phenomenon of reported speech renders inaccessible to analysis a host of social practices that are crucial to the dialogic organisation of language and action that Volosinov discusses with such insight in the first half of his book. This chapter has attempted to demonstrate the importance of the task posed by Volosinov of working to disentangle the different voices within a single strip of talk, while at the same time expanding such analysis to incorporate genuine multi-party interaction within the organisation of the utterance, and to explore, as an alternative to quotation, sequential practices for assimilating another's talk into a current utterance.

Goffman's deconstruction of the speaker in Footing provides powerful analytic tools for specifying the different kinds of speakers who can co-exist with a strip of reported speech. Indeed, Footing was the most influential article of Goffman's later career. It constituted one point of departure (with Volosinov and Bakhtin) for important lines of research on phenomena such as reported speech, participation, and the dialogic organisation of language and culture. The frameworks developed by Goffman in Footing continue to shape how crucial phenomena that are central to the organisation of language as a social process are analysed. However, as analysis of the story in Figures 2.1–2.4 demonstrated, parties whose talk is being quoted can exist not only as cited figures within the talk of the current speaker, but also as actual present participants. Through the way in which he visibly organized his body the principal character whose talk was being quoted helped to co-construct the multi-party, dialogic field constituted through the reporting of his speech.

Coming to terms with this analytically requires expanding the framework provided by Volosinov in at least two ways. First, rather than being constituted entirely within the stream of speech, the actions constructed within an utterance can incorporate other semiotic modalities as well, such as visible, embodied displays. One crucial consequence of focusing on this larger ecology of sign systems (C. Goodwin, 2000a) which can encompass speech without being restricted to talk, is that the relevant actions of parties who don't speak, such as hearers of various types, can be taken into account analytically. Second, participation is central to the organisation of this multi-party interactive field. Footing actually contains a framework for the analysis of participation that has had enormous influence. However, with respect to the phenomena being investigated here, the framework Goffman offered has major problems. The model of participation in Footing consists of a typology of participant categories that are not linked to the model of the speaker presented in a different section of the article. It thus cannot provide the analytic resources necessary to describe how participants build utterances and action by taking each other into account within an unfolding process of interaction as talk unfolds, i.e. the essential mutual reflexivity of speaker and hearer(s). In this chapter an alternative view of participation is offered. Participants demonstrate their understanding of what each other is doing and the events they are engaged in together by building both vocal and non-vocal actions that help to further constitute those very same events. One consequence of this is a multi-party, interactively sustained, embodied field within which utterances are collaboratively shaped as meaningful, locally relevant action. Within such a framework the speaker is no longer positioned as the locus of all semiotic activity, and the cognitive life of the hearer – including his or her analysis of the details of emerging language structure – is recovered.

Both Volosinov's view of reported speech, and Goffman's speaker, require an actor capable of producing rich, complex language structure. To probe such assumptions, the utterances of a man able to say only three words ('Yes', 'No' and 'And') because of a stroke that left him with severe aphasia were examined. Despite his restricted vocabulary, and almost complete lack of syntax, this man was not only able to act as a powerful speaker in conversation, but also to incorporate the talk of others in his own catastrophically impoverished utterances. Clearly he could not do this with grammatical structure signalling that another party's talk was being quoted. However, he could indexically tie his own limited talk to rich structure in the talk of others and, moreover, position himself, and not that other speaker, as the ultimate author and principal of what was being said. Though not reported speech, this process would seem to constitute a clear example of action built through 'an *active relation* of one message to another' (Volosinov, 1973: 116), and to have strong relevance to the dialogic organisation that Volosinov was trying investigate through reported speech.

However, analysing this process requires moving beyond the domain of scrutiny of both Volosinov and Goffman, the talk of a single speaker, to focus instead on multi-party sequences of talk. Moreover, the interactive construction of meaning and action that occurs here requires a reflexive, cognitively complex hearer and frequently orientation to semiotic structure that extends beyond the stream of speech. Goffman deconstructed the single speaker, and the isolated utterance of that speaker, into multiple entities. Here, by way of contrast, we find a speaker who is distributed across different participants and turns (e.g. the aphasic man prompts, incorporates and claims authorship for things said by others).

Both Volosinov and Goffman offer us powerful insights into the intrinsically dialogic organisation of human language. However, both restrict their analysis to the talk and consciousness of a single speaker. In this chapter I have attempted to demonstrate that the phenomena they draw our attention to can be investigated more richly by focusing instead on how separate parties build meaning and action in concert with each other through their mutual participation in embodied sequences of talk- and action-in-interaction.

'I'm eyeing your chop up mind': reporting and enacting

Elizabeth Holt

3.1 Introduction

In interaction reported speech can be used to portray what a current speaker, or someone else, said on a former occasion. However, it is by no means restricted to the accurate portrayal of prior locutions. In fact there is growing evidence to suggest that it rarely is this (Lehrer, 1989; Tannen, 1989; Clark and Gerrig, 1990; Wooffitt, 1992; Holt, 1996, 2000). Exploring reported speech in naturally occurring interaction reveals that it can, on occasion, be used to portray the words of invented (often stereotypical) characters and to suggest what someone might say/have said on some (often hypothetical) occasion. This chapter explores sequences involving this kind of reported speech. The analysis raises questions relating to the efficacy of approaches to the investigation of these hypothetical 'enactments', considering Goffman's observations on participation structure in comparison to a sequential approach.

Goffman's (1981) work on participation structure has important implications for the analysis of reported speech. His interest in the nature of participation in social encounters led him to criticise the simplistic concepts of 'speaker' and 'hearer' widely used in approaches to the study of language and communication. He sought to explore the complexity of the nature of participation by breaking down the roles into their constitutive concepts. In considering the speaker role he decomposed it into the three constituent categories of 'animator' (the person who utters the words), 'author' (who 'selected the sentiments that are being expressed and the words in which they are encoded' (1981: 144)) and 'principal' (whose 'position is established by the words that are spoken' (1981:

144)). For perhaps much of the time in interaction a speaker plays all three roles at once, but recurrently he or she shifts footing, changing the alignment taken to themselves and other participants in the production of an utterance (1981: 128). Thus, when a speaker uses reported speech to portray the words of another, he or she is the animator of the utterance, but no longer the author or principal. For example, in the following extract Lesley shifts footing to recount the words of someone she refers to earlier as 'Mr R' (see Holt (2000) for a more detailed analysis of this extract).

(1) [Holt:C85:4:2–3]
```
1   Lesley:   AND uh ↑we were looking rou-nd the
2                   ↓sta:lls 'n poking about 'n he came
3        →    up t'me 'n he said Oh: hhello Lesley, (.)
4        →    ↑still trying to buy something f'nothing,
```

In order to report what the man said, Lesley shifts footing to portray herself as merely the animator of an utterance, but not the author or principal. In such instances Goffman's (1981) analysis of the speaker role (and Levinson's (1988) elaboration of Goffman's participation structure) provide valuable insight into how Lesley initiates a change in the production format to produce the reported speech.

However, other naturally occurring instances are less effectively analysed according to Goffman's categories. Take the following extract, where both participants to the interaction collaboratively produce reported thought.

(2) [PT:13–14]v
```
1   Margy:    oh:- Edna I've gott'n in s'many a'those
2                  proj [ects where you] gid in half way then
3   Edna:           [U h : h h h h.]
4   Margy:→   y' think °oh: ghho:d. what'v I[: ↑do]:ne.=
5   Edna: →                              [what-]
6   Margy:    =y' [k n ow].hhh]
7   Edna: →   [What'v]we d]o:ne.=
8   Margy:    =B't it a : : ll wo:rks ou:::t.
```

In line 4, Margy shifts footing to directly report a thought. She is the animator of this thought, she is also the author and principal, but not on the current occasion. She is embedding (Goffman, 1981) a thought portrayed as occurring previously, and therefore the author and principal is her former self.[1] Edna co-completes Margy's reported thought (lines 5 and 7), but it is unclear whether she is animating a thought previously authored by her or is animating Margy's thought. What is clear is that it is designed to collaborate with Margy by also shifting footing to report having the 'same' thought. Further, by timing her contribution to overlap Margy's, and consequently co-completing her utterance, Edna affiliates with her by conveying that she has the same thought at the same time.[2] So, while distinguishing the author and principal of this reported thought is problematic, what is significant (for the participants and therefore for the analyst) is how the turn containing the reported thought is designed to contribute to the ongoing action sequence; how it is designed to display strong affiliation with Margy's point of view.

Thus, problems arise in using Goffman's categories to analyse specific instances of reported speech in interaction. Further, identifying which of the constituent roles the speaker is playing at any time can be of limited use in providing detailed analysis of reported speech in talk-in-interaction. The decompositional approach advocated by Goffman tends to lead to creating further categories as new instances are encountered and analysed (Irvine, 1996: 133). (Thus, for example, Levinson (1988: 172) adds the following 'participant producer roles': 'ghostee', spokesperson, relayer, deviser, sponsor and 'ghostor'.) Yet participants rarely overtly orient to issues to do with the production format (except by displaying that they understood a turn to be footed). An alternative approach is to focus on the procedures participants employ to take different stances within their talk, and on how recipients understand and contribute to the ongoing series of action this involves as displayed in subsequent contributions. Thus, analysis is shifted 'from the elaboration of typologies for participants, to study of the activities that parties must perform in order to

---

[1] However, within the frame of the reported thought she is animator, author and principal (cf. McCawley, 1999).

[2] On the anticipatory completion of reported speech, see Lerner (1991).

participate appropriately in the events of the moment by building relevant action' (See Chapter 2 of this volume).

In this Chapter I focus on sequences of reported speech in telephone conversations that are the product of collaboration by both participants. While Goffman (1981) demonstrated the complexity of the speaker role, he paid less attention to the hearer, attributing to him or her a relatively passive role and failing to recognise that interaction is through and through a product of the activities of all participants (again, see Chapter 2). In the instances that constitute the current corpus the participants shift footing to enact characters, specific people, or themselves on another occasion. The ensuing enacted interactions are the product of collaboration by both participants. They demonstrate the necessity of seeing sequences of reported speech, not as emanating from a speaker aimed at a hearer, but as arising out of the activities of both participants, and as evincing an understanding of what activities the participants are engaged in, and of what constitutes an appropriate contribution to that series of actions.

3.2 Enactments

In many previous studies of reported speech authors based their analysis on invented examples, or ones taken from literary texts to substantiate their claims (e.g. Wierzbicka, 1974; Halliday, 1985; Coulmas, 1986; Li, 1986; Haiman, 1985). One consequence of this is that analysis tended to focus on prototypical instances. It was recognised that there are different kinds of reported speech – authors focused on the differences between direct and indirect forms, and some included free indirect speech (see Thompson, 1984). However, the true complexity of the category generally referred to as 'reported speech' is now beginning to be revealed as a result of a recent move towards investigating naturally occurring instances drawn from interaction (see, for example, Mayes, 1990; Mathis and Yule, 1994; Holt, 1996; Günthner, 1996; Klewitz and Couper-Kuhlen, 1999; Buttny and Williams, 2000).

One element of the device where this complexity has been demonstrated by recent research is in terms of the introductory component. It has long been recognised that reported speech is generally framed by a *verbum dicendi*, a verb of speaking, plus a pronoun or name (e.g. 'John said', 'she thought'), and that indirect reported speech is commonly also preceded by 'that'. Recent research has begun to reveal the wide range of phenomena that can function as an introductory component; for example, sociolinguistic studies highlight regional differences and temporal changes. Macauley (2001) found that Glaswegian adolescents often use forms of 'be like' and 'be' in the framing clause, and according to Romaine and Lange (1991) the increasingly widespread use of 'like' in American English blurs the boundaries between direct and indirect reported speech (see also Ferrara and Bell, 1995; and Tagliamonte and Hudson, 1999). Further, research into English and other languages has revealed that a significant proportion of reported speech is not accompanied by a prefatory framing component. Tannen (1989) found that 26 per cent of the 'constructed dialogue' in her collection of conversational narratives were without an introductory clause. McGregor (1994), in a study of reported speech in Gooniyandi, found that a third of the instances in his collection were free-standing (see also Romaine and Lange, 1991; Mathis and Yule, 1994; Klewitz and Couper-Kuhlen, 1999).

In previous research (Holt, 1996, 2000) into reported speech, based on a large corpus drawn mainly from telephone conversations, I discovered that most instances are preceded by a pronoun-plus-speech-verb (in a few instances the pronoun-plus-speech-verb follows the reported speech). However, a number are not accompanied by any kind of component explicitly flagging other components in the turn as reported speech. This chapter focuses on a collection of those instances of reported speech without an introductory clause. The ones in the current corpus also share elements concerning their sequential position, the conversational environments in which they occur and the actions they perform. For example, most are used in the context of hypothetical scenarios and all contribute towards expanding a joke initiation. I refer to them as 'enactments' (Jefferson et al., 1987; see also Goodwin, 1990; Beach, 2000 for somewhat different, though overlapping, usages of the term). What precisely I mean by this term will become clear based on analysis of the sequential position and design of these instances of reported speech. Here are some instances.

(3) [TCI(b):16:64–65]
(J has bought extra Christmas presents for the children. She proposes to
prevent her husband from finding out by paying the bill when it comes.)

```
 1   J:    But I thought well I'll go ahea:d,
 2         and, .hh and pay for it when it comes
 3         and °he'll never kno:w°,=
 4   L:    =°Yeh, °=
 5   J:    =(we, [got anything))heh-heh-huh=
 6   L:         [hheh huhehhuh]
 7   L:    =[°uhhhh  .uhhhhhhh]hh[hhh°
 8   J:    =[huh e-huh huh huh]   [.hhehh
 9   J:    Ex [cept when Christmas co[:mes a-a-]and=
10   L:        [°°Oh°°              [Y e a h h]
11   J:    =.hhhh he says where'd you get all
12         thahheh heh [hn huh] huh=
13   L:                [mehheh]
14   J:    =hu [h huh °huh°]°hn°
15   L:→      [ .h h h h h ]Santa Claus.=
16      →  =hhheh-h[eh
17   J:→           [.hh ↑Santa Claus brou:ght it.
18      →  (in his sle::d).=
19   J:    =hn[hih [hn-hn-[hen huh=
20   L:        [ Ye:[ah     [.hh
21   L:    =Uh: :[:m
22   J:         [.hhhhhehhhhh    °(   [   ).°
23   L:                              [I found a
24         recipe:  that I'm gonna try:,
```

(4) [Holt:Nov2000:2:3]
(P suggests that, even if D 'makes it big', he won't change. They then recall
an incident where D asked for the remains of a fellow diner's meal.)

```
 1   P:    *ih y- yuh kno:w if you ma::ke it big
 2         time babe you'll ↑NEVUH
 3         CHA::nge:: [will yuh.]
 4   D:               [↑Ahhhhhhh]h
 5         (0.5)
 6   D: →  .hhh  ↑UH you fi:nished with that ch↑o::p
 7      →  p↓et eehh he he he [he he he
 8   P: →                     [I'm (h)eyeing your
 9      →  cho:p up [mi:nd.
10   D:            [hah hah hah hah .hhh it's cool
```

11   (.) .hhh it's cool. (.) so:
12   (0.6)
13   D: your uh: (.) you're all done un dusted
14   you're all uh
15   (0.2)
16   ( ):   (   )
17   P: [I've got my tr]ee up...
18   D: [.hhhhhhhhhhhhhh]

(5) [Holt:F/M:03:1:1:1]
(D has invited P and his wife, Sian, to come and stay. Prior to this they have
been talking about P's central heating breaking down.)
1   D: .hhh Wul mayb- maybe *uh- uh good thing
2   babe would be::uh:: (0.3) if you un Sianes
3   >settl'd< down un had a look at your di:ary
4   i:rius .hhh u [nd
5   P: [>Come down to your house
6   to get wa:rm<
7   (0.4)
8   D: (Y)hehh huh huh huh huh huh [huh
9   P: →   [>Do you two
10   →   want come out for a pi:nt< No:
11   →   can't y[ou see we (want) to get] w(h)a:rm(h)<
12   D: [.hhh ↑N O : : : : : : :]
13   D: [↑PUT THE FI:RE ON eh eh eh heh heh
14   P: [(huh)
15   D: .hhh Wul babe it's not too bloody warm I mean
16   .hhh we've- we've only ju:st got rid of the
17   s:no:w.

In the arrowed turns in each of these extracts, the participants
produce talk that is portrayed as originating from another author,
or authored by themselves, but on a different occasion. At the start
of extract (3) J suggests that if she pays the bill for the Christmas
presents when it comes her husband will never know that she bought
them. In lines 9, 11 and 12 she uses reported speech to portray
what he might say on Christmas Day: 'where'd you get all thahheh'.
This reported speech is preceded by a pronoun-plus-speech-verb:
'he says'. In line 15 L adds a hypothetical reply to the question:
'Santa Claus'. J then repeats this and adds to it: '↑Santa Claus
brou:ght it. (in his sle::d).' (lines 17–18). The enactments in these

two turns are not accompanied by a pronoun-plus-speech-verb. In excerpt (4), prior to the beginning of the extract the participants have been talking about D being rather offhand with some fellow diners (extract (4) is a continuation of (7) below). In lines 1–3 P suggests that if D makes 'it b<u>i</u>g t<u>i</u>me' he'll '↑N<u>E</u>VUH CH<u>A</u>::nge::'. D then reports a turn from an incident that both he and P were party to, where D asked a fellow diner for the remains of her meal: '↑UH you f<u>i</u>:nished with that ch↑<u>o</u>::p p↓et'. In the next turn (lines 8–9) P makes a further contribution to the portrayed dialogue: 'I'm (h) eyeing your cho:p up m<u>i</u>:nd.' Neither of these is preceded by a pronoun-plus-speech-verb. In extract (5), prior to the start of the extract, P has been telling D that his heating has broken down. D then suggests that P and his wife Sian should find a date to come to stay. In lines 5–6 P jokingly suggests that they will come in order to get warm. He then produces a hypothetical dialogue involving D asking whether they want to go out for a drink: '>Do you two want come out for a pi:nt< N<u>o</u>: c<u>a</u>n't you see we (want) to get w(h)a:rm(h)<'. In overlap, D begins to produce a response to the hypothetical invitation: '↑NO:::::::'. He completes this in line 13 with '↑PUT THE F<u>I</u>:RE ON'. Again, these are not accompanied by pronoun-plus-speech-verbs.

Given that most instances of reported speech are preceded by an introductory component and that these play a central role in indicating that what is to come is footed, it is pertinent to consider how these instances are recognised as constituting a change of footing so that the speaker is reporting the words of someone else, or himself/herself, on another occasion. (It is apparent that in each of the extracts above the recipient of a first enactment recognises it as such in that they affiliate by responding with another enactment; see section 3.3.) In the following subsections I consider three recurrent features of the design and sequential position of the enactments in the corpus that contribute towards indicating they are part of a reported interaction, before (in section 3.4) focusing on the activity sequence to which these enactments contribute.

3.2.1 *Enactments following reported speech*

First, enactments recurrently add to a reported interaction where a previous contribution is preceded by an introductory component.

The enactments in both the following extracts are preceded by a
single turn of reported speech.

(3) [Detail]

```
 9   J:    Ex[cept when Christmas co[:mes a-a-]and=
10   L:      [°°Oh°°                [Y e a h h]
11   J:    =.hhhh he says where'd you get all
12         thahheh heh [ hn huh] huh=
13   L:                  [mehheh]
14   J:    =hu[h   huh     °huh°]°hn°
15   L:       [.h  h   h   h   h ]Santa Claus.=
16         =hhheh-h[eh
17   J:            [.hh   ↑Santa Claus brou:ght it.
18         (in   his   sle::d).=
```

(6) [Holt:Nov2000:1:3]
(P and his new partner are about to stay with D at his in-laws' house. D's
in-laws have met P's ex-wife, Pam, but not his current partner.)

```
 1   P:    ↑So you will let me kno:w uh- uh- y- you
 2         don't think there'll be kind of any
 3         ha:ss[le.
 4   D:         [↑Oh (f-) th- there won't be any any
 5         hassle at all they'll uh .hh[hhh
 6   P:                                [>In fact
 7         d'yuh think they will< enjo:y co:mpany.
 8   D:    Ye:s uh- I think it'll be a case of the
 9         more the merrier=they- th- the- they know
10         you ve:ry we:ll .hhhh uhh th- they're very
11         happy for you to (.) to be there (th-) >I
12         don't think there's a problem bab[e<
13   P:→                                    [(They'll)
14    →  say .tch↑it's very nice to meet you Pa::m
15   D:    .hh ↑he huh hee hah hah hah hah hah hah
16         .hhhh ↑by:: you've fucking grown a few
17         inches like haven't [yuh
18   P:                        [(  )
19   D:    hah [hah hah hah hah
20   P:        [°huh huh huh°
21         (.)
22   P:    ↑Yuh ti:ts uh bigger [aren't they?
```

```
23   D:                              [.hhh
24   D:    he hu:::h heh heh .hhh in fact you've
25         got ti:[ts heh heh heh heh hah hah hah]=
26   P:          [heh heh heh excellent (        )]=
27   D:    =[hah HAH HAH HAH HAH HAH hah hah hah
28   P:    =[there you go ( ) ba(h)be
```

In extract (3) the reported hypothetical reaction of J's husband to seeing the presents is preceded by 'he says' (lines 11–12). In (6) the proposed reaction of D's in-laws to meeting P's wife is preceded by '(They'll) say'. In both instances the enactments contribute to the reported interaction initially created using reported speech accompanied by a pronoun-plus-speech-verb. Thus, when L says 'Santa Claus' in line 15 of extract (3), it can be heard as an answer to the preceding question that is clearly marked as reported speech. (That the reported speech and the enactment form an adjacency pair adds to the implication that 'Santa Claus' is to be heard as an addition to the reported interaction.) Similarly, in (6) when D says '↑by:: you've fucking grown a few inches like haven't yuh' (lines 16–17), it can be heard as an addition to the reaction to meeting P's wife, portrayed as emanating from D's in-laws through reported speech.

In excerpt (7), D begins this sequence of reported speech by introducing reported turn construction units with a pronoun-plus-speech-verb. However, as the sequence continues, these are omitted.

(7) [Holt:Nov2000:2:2]

```
1    D:    .hhh un then we .hhh said uh (0.5) I
2      →   said to uh the managing director's wife
3      →   I said- I saiduh .hhh >well actually
4      →   Vicky said it< she saiduh (0.3) .hh
5          uh you fi:nished with that stea:k (0.4)
6          cuz my little do:g'll have that
7          st(h)ea(h)khhh heh heh [heh heh .hhh
8    P:                           [(huh)
9    D:→  so we ni:ck the stea:k .hhh >un then we
10     →   said< (0.2) ↓we gotta go: now,
11         (0.5)
12   D:    .hh we've had a nice ti:me (0.1) but
13         we're o:ff.
```

14   (0.4)
15   D: [see y-
16   P: [we've gotta f<u>ee</u>d the b↑<u>i:</u>tch ut
17   h<u>o:</u>[me

The first reported utterance in this sequence is very clearly flagged
as reported speech. D uses two pronoun-plus-speech-verb introductions in 'I said to uh the managing director's wife I said'. However,
he then repairs this to convey that it was his wife who said it:
'actually Vicky said it< she saiduh'. The next reported utterance
is also clearly marked as reported speech. In lines 9–10, D uses
'>un then we said<' before reporting another turn. In lines 12–13,
however, D adds a further turn construction unit without preceding
it by a pronoun-plus-speech-verb: 'we've had a nice ti:me (0.1) but
we're o:ff.'. In line 15 it appears that D begins to produce a further
addition (possibly 'see yuh'), which is also not preceded by a
pronoun-plus-speech-verb. Thus, at the start of the reported dialogue, D uses several pronoun-plus-speech-verb indicators to clearly
mark this as reported speech, but these are then omitted, and new
turn construction units of reported speech are introduced without
them.

   In each of these instances, therefore, the enactment contributes to
a reported interaction begun in a previous turn. The prior reported
turn (or turns, as in (7)) is preceded by a pronoun-plus-speech-verb.
Thus, one clear indication that these enactments are footed (i.e.
intended to be heard as merely animated by the current speaker at
the present time) is that they contribute to this footed interaction,
which is clearly marked as reported speech through a prefatory
component prior to the first turn.

3.2.2 Changes in voice quality or prosody

According to McGregor, reported speech without an introductory
clause in Gooniyandi tends to be 'uttered in a marked voice quality,
frequently employing a higher pitch register' (1994: 76). Mathis
and Yule (1994), based on their analysis of English examples,
suggest that, when 'quotatives' are absent, changes in voice quality
may be used to indicate that another voice is being introduced.

However, a detailed analysis of prosody in reported speech in
English data by Klewitz and Couper-Kuhlen (1999) revealed that
instances of reported speech without a projecting clause are not
characterised by greater prosodic marking. In the current corpus
the majority of the enactments are accompanied by marked shifts in
prosody or voice quality. A number are accompanied by a marked
rise in pitch at the start of the enacted turn. In both of the following
extracts, participants use falsetto to perform enacted turns.

(8) [Holt:Spring02:B:1]
(Prior to the start of this extract, D has been talking about finding his trip
into a pyramid frightening. He recalled entering the narrow passage in a
long queue of people.)

```
 1    P:     .hh I think the worrying thing for me:
 2           would be stuck down there with you:
 3    D:     °huh hu[h°
 4    P:            [cuz if you went a↑pe
 5    D:     huh hee it'd [bust
 6    P:                  [( )
 7    P:     first of all that r-row a'people are gonna
 8           be wre:cked
 9    D:     °hhhhuh[huh°
10    P:            [un- un- [und you [might [$knock a few=
11    D:                     [°huh°    [°huh° [.h h h h h
12    P:     =blocks [out of position$
13    D:            [°huh°
14    D:     .hhhh[hh
15    P:→          [an' all of a sudden ((f))what's happened
16       →   to the ↑pyrami [ds they've got a blu:nt [to:p
17    D:                    [.hhhhh                  [hhe=
18    D:     =hhee hhe[ °he° °he°
```

(9) [NB:III:2:5–6]
```
 1    F:    No we c'm in fr'm the bea:ch'n then we
 2          c'm in en take a ↓na::p you kno::w,=
 3    F:    =hIt's [rilly  [we rilly ge]t=
 4    J:           [Ye:h [ y o u : : ]
 5    F:    =[.hhh
 6    J:    =[screwin arou [n'there uh?]
```

7   F: [Y e : : : :] ah en
8   then we t-t-
9   (0.8)
10   J: [W'n a'those <u>kids</u>] [come]s in 'n deh=
11   F: [<h e v a ↓<u>bee</u> : :]:[:r   ]
12   J:→   =((f)) ↑<u>Da</u>:ddy <u>Mo</u>mmy:
13   (.)
14   J:→   ((f)) ↑<u>Da</u>ddy=
15   J: =he [h heh <u>hheh</u>]heh] (↑<u>r</u>hhi::ght)]
16   F: [e h <u>Y e h</u>]heh]h e h heh-<u>He</u>]:H=
17   =eh [↓h*e:h]
18   J: [heh eh]
19   F: .hhh hu:h
20   (.)
21   J: °he:h [heh°].hh
22   F:→   [e   e]((f)) Git ↑<u>ou</u>:dda there=
23   J: =<u>he</u>:h <u>heh</u>=

The entire enactment in lines 15–16 of extract (8) is said with
noticeably higher pitch. In (9) both the participants produce enactments using falsetto (lines 12, 14 and 22). Thus, marked shifts in
prosody can contribute towards indicating that the speaker has
shifted footing to enact the words of another.

In *Frame Analysis*, Goffman notes that speakers may use a stereo-
typed accent (he mentions 'baby talk, ethnic and racial accents,
national accents, and gender role expressions' (1974/1986: 535))
to attribute their words to a categorically defined figure. In so doing
speakers tend to avoid using 'connectives' (or 'devices which tell us
who is saying or doing whatever is being said or done' (1974/ 1986:
537)) because 'something closer to stage acting than reporting is
occurring' (1974/1986: 535). In an excerpt from an interaction analysed by Beach (2000), the speakers enact uneducated southern
males by adopting stereotypical accents. They shift footing without
including pronoun-plus-speech-verbs or any other kind of explicit
introductory component to the footed speech. Enactments may be
accompanied by a change in voice quality to convey a regional or
some other kind of accent (see also Mathis and Yule, 1994). In the
extracts in the current corpus regional accents are sometimes

employed. These are always accompanied by dialect forms and so will be considered along with other design features in the next subsection.

3.2.3 *The design of the enactments*

A third set of features concern the design of the enactment. Like other instances of direct reported speech, personal, spatial and temporal deixis fit the reported/portrayed situation (Holt, 1996). However, in enactments, other features of the design may help to indicate that the speaker has shifted footing to play a character, or a particular person. In several instances participants include highly colloquial or dialect terms, and swearing in the enacted turn. In extracts (4) and (8) dialect forms and regional accent are combined.

(4) [Detail]
```
6   D: → .hhh ↑UH you fi:nished with that ch↑o::p
7      → p↓et eehh he he °he [he he he°
8   P: →                    [I'm (h) eyeing your
9      → cho:p up [mi:nd.
```

(8) [Continuation]
```
19  P: → [>it's fair lean' o' er<
20  D:→ hhe [ehh↑oh look °hh the pyramids she:cking heh=
21  P:      [hah
22  D:  =heh heh heh heh heh
```

In extract (4), D uses the Geordie dialect term 'p↓et' at the end of the enacted turn to address the imagined recipient. The inclusion of 'mi:nd' and the stress on this word and 'cho:p' also suggest P's contribution is being delivered using a hearably Geordie accent and dialect. In (8), P uses a Geordie accent in line 19 to say '>it's fair lean' o'er<'. Adopting this accent seems also to account for D's unusual pronunciation of 'shaking' as 'she:cking' in line 20 as it appears he is echoing P's use of the accent in the previous enactment.

In (6) dialect and profane forms are included in the enactments:

(6) [Detail]

```
16    D:→ .hhhh ↑by:: you've fucking grown a few
17        → inches like haven't [yuh
18    P:                        [(  )
19    D:    hah [hah hah hah hah
20    P:         [°huh huh huh°
21            (.)
22    P: → ↑Yuh ti:ts uh bigger [aren't they?
23    D:                        [.hhh
24    D:→ he hu:::h heh heh .hhh in fact you've
25        → got ti:[ts heh heh heh heh hah hah hah]=
```

D begins the enactment in line 16 with '↑by::', a dialect term. Then both P and D use the term 'tits' in their subsequent enactments. In line 16 of (6), D also uses the profanity 'fucking'.

Thus, profanity, regional accents and dialect forms may contribute towards portraying these turns as from a different footing, and forming part of an enacted interaction.

3.3 The environment and sequence of enactments

A further, and major, set of indications that these turns are footed is that they contribute to a sequence of activities initiated in a previous turn (or turns) and, as demonstrated in section 2.1, this often means that they contribute to a previously begun reported interaction. The design of the first enactment in each of the extracts in the current corpus evinces an understanding of the nature of the sequence of activities to which it contributes. It also embodies an attempt to contribute to and extend that sequence of activities. Further, subsequent turns – including second, and sometimes further, enactments – also display an understanding of prior turns and contribute to the ongoing action sequence. Consequently, rather than analysing these turns in isolation, it is necessary to explore the sequence of turns to which they contribute in order to appreciate how these enactments arise out of the activities by both participants, how they evince an understanding of the action sequence they are engaged in, and what they take to be appropriate contributions to that sequence. I start by focusing on turns prior to the first enactment, where the participants begin the sequence by initiating a joking scenario. I will then turn to consideration of the first enactment, exploring how it demonstrates understanding of, and contributes to, this joking scenario.

3.3.1 The joke initiation

In all the instances that constitute the current corpus the enactments occur in the environment of some kind of joke (or tease – see (4), (8) and (9)) made by one of the participants. In the majority of instances the enactments follow the introduction of a hypothetical situation involving one of the participants suggesting something that could happen, or is happening, but which is not a serious proposal. This is often accompanied by laughter. Extract (3) is a case in point.

(3) [Detail]

```
 1   J:    But I thought well I'll go ahea:d,
 2         and, .hh and pay for it when it comes
 3         and °he'll never kno:w°, =
 4   L:    =°Yeh,°=
 5   J:    =°(we, [got anything)  °] heh-heh-huh=
 6   L:          [hheh huhehhuh]
 7   L:    =[°uhhhh  .uhhhhhhh] hh [hhh°
 8   J:    =[huh e-huh huh huh]    [.hhehh
 9   J:    Ex [cept when Christmas co[:mes a-a-]and=
10   L:       [°°Oh°°              [Y e a h h]
11   J:    =.hhhh he says where'd you get all
12         thahheh heh [hn  huh] huh=
13   L:                [mehheh]
```

In lines 1–3 and 5, J completes her telling about purchasing the gifts by saying that if she pays the bill when it comes, her husband will never know she bought them. In line 6, L overlaps the end of this with laughter, and J also laughs at the completion of her turn (line 5), followed by both participants laughing together. J then continues by suggesting a hypothetical scenario where her husband sees all the gifts and questions her about them: 'Except when Christmas co:mes a-a-and .hhhh he says where'd get all thahheh'. J follows this by laughter, which acts as an invitation to laugh (Jefferson, 1979), and L briefly joins in.

   In some instances the initiation of the joking hypothetical scenario is brief; sometimes consisting of a single turn, as in the following two excerpts.

(5) [Detail]

```
1   D:    .hhh Wul mayb- maybe *uh- uh good thing
2         b̲a̲be would be::uh:: (0.3) if you un Sianes
3         >settl'd< down un had a look at your di:ary
4         i:rius .hhh u [nd
5   P:  →              [>Come down to your house
6       → to get wa:rm<
7         (0.4)
8   D:    (Y) hehh huh huh huh huh huh [huh
```

(6) [Detail]

```
8    D:    Ye̲:s uh- I think it'll be a case of the
9          more the merrier=they- th- the- they know
10         you ve̲:ry we:ll .hhhh uhh th- they're very
11         h̲a̲ppy for you to (.) to be there (th-)>I
12         don't think there's a pr̲o̲blem b̲a̲b [e<
13   P:  →                          [(They'll)
14       → say .tch ↑it's very nice to meet you P̲a̲::m
15   D:    .hh ↑he huh hee hah hah hah hah hah hah
```

In (5), P enters the realms of the non-serious by suggesting that the reason he will visit D is to get warm. This is followed by a pause, then D's agreement and laughter. In (6), P uses reported speech to initiate a hypothetical scenario where he suggests D's in-laws mistakenly address his new partner using the name of his ex-wife. This is followed by D's laughter.

In other instances the portrayal of the hypothetical situation preceding the enactment is highly elaborate, as in (8).

(8) [Detail]

```
1   P:  →.hh I think the worrying thing for me̲:
2       →would be stuck down there with you̲:
3   D:    °huh hu [h°
4   P:  →         [cuz if you went a↑pe
5   D:    huh hee it'd [b̲u̲st
6   P:              [( )
7   P:  →first of all that r-row a'people are gonna
8       →be wre̲:cked
```

```
 9   D:     °hhhhuh [huh°
10   P:  →         [un- un- [und you [might [$knock a few=
11   D:                  [°huh°   [°huh° [h h h h h
12   P:  →=blocks [out of position$
13   D:              [°huh°
14   D:   .hhhh [hh
15   P:          [an' all of a sudden ↑↑((f))what's happened
16          to the ↑pyrami[ds they've got a blu:nt[to:p
```

Here, over several turns, P invents a joking hypothetical scenario in
which D is portrayed as panicking inside the pyramid. There is
some quiet laughter from D at several points during this joking
scenario (at lines 3, 5, 9, 11 and 13) and hearable smile voice as
P speaks in lines 10 and 12 (marked by the dollar symbols).

In these instances, prior to the enactment, a participant makes a
joke, usually involving creating a hypothetical scenario. This is
accompanied by laughter by one, or both, of the participants.
Following this, the first enactment occurs.

3.3.2 The first enactment

In several instances the first enactment is produced by the recipient
of the prior joking scenario. Extracts (3) and (6) are cases in point.

```
(3) [Detail]
 9   J:    Ex [cept when Christmas co[:mes a-a-] and=
10   L:       [°°Oh°°              [Y e a h h]
11   J:    = .hhhh he says where'd you get all
12          thahheh heh [hn  huh] huh=
13   L:                 [mehheh]
14   J:    =hu[h huh °huh°] °hn°
15   L: →      [.h  h  h  h h] Santa Claus.=
16      →    =hhheh-h [eh
```

```
(6) [Detail]
13   P:                              [(They'll)
14          say .tch ↑it's very nice to meet you Pa::m
15   D:    .hh ↑he huh hee hah hah hah hah hah hah hah
16      → .hhhh ↑by::you've fucking grown a few
```

```
17        → inches like haven't [yuh
18   P:                        [(   )
19   D:    hah [hah hah hah hah
20   P:         [°huh huh huh°
```

In (3), J jokes about her husband seeing all the gifts on Christmas Day and asking where they came from (thus foiling her plan to keep their purchase secret). L responds to this with laughter (briefly) in line 13. Laughter is an appropriate response to, and appreciation of, the joke. However, rather than limiting her response to laughter, L then adds to the joke by enacting a response to the hypothetical dialogue. Thus, she demonstrates that she understood the joke by extending it further, creating another opportunity to laugh. Following her enactment she laughs, thus inviting J to do the same. Similarly, in (6), P makes a joke by reporting what D's in-laws might say when they meet his new partner. D's initial response is laughter, thus appreciating P's joke. However, he then goes on to contribute to the joke by enacting another observation by his in-laws: '↑by:: you've fucking grown a few inches like haven't yuh'. D then laughs, and P overlaps with laughter.

In these instances the enactments extend a joke initiated by a co-participant. Rather than simply appreciating the joke through, for example, a response of laughter, the recipient of the joke initiation contributes to it further, thus creating another opportunity for the participants to laugh. Both the enactments in the extracts above are followed by invitations to laugh in the form of the speaker continuing the turn with laughter. The enactments, then, display the recipients' understanding of the joke initiation, and their willingness to go along with it by contributing to it further. They display the participants' understanding of the activity they are engaged in through their shift of footing to contribute to the hypothetical dialogue initiated in a prior turn.

In a number of instances in the corpus, however, the participant who initiates the joking scenario proceeds to produce an enactment. Extracts (5), (8) and (9) are cases in point.

(5) [Detail]

```
5   P:                   [>Come down to your house
6        to get wa:rm<
7        (0.4)
```

```
 8    D:     (Y)hehh huh huh huh huh huh [huh
 9    P: →                                     [>Do you two
10        →  want come out for a pi:nt< No:
11        →  >can't y[ou see we (want) to get] w(h)a:rm(h)<
```

(8) [Detail]
```
10    P:        [un- un- [und you [might [$knock a few=
11    D:                  [°huh°    [°huh° [.h h h h h
12    P:    =blocks [out of position$
13    D:            [°huh°
14    D:    .hhhh [hh
15    P:→         [an' all of a sudden ↑↑((f))what's happened
16        →  to the ↑pyrami [ds they've got a blu:nt [to:p
17    D:                    [.hhhhh                  [hhe=
18    D:    = hhee hhe[ °he° °he°
19    P:              [>it's fair lean' o'er<
20    D:    hhe [ehh↑oh look °hh the pyramids she:cking heh=
21    P:        [hah
```

(9) [Detail]
```
 4    J:                  [Ye:h [ y o u : : ]
 5    F:    =[.hhh
 6    J:    =[scre̲win arou[n'there uh?]
 7    F:                  [Y e : : : :]ah en
 8          then we t-t-
 9          (0.8)
10    J:    [W'n a'those ki̲ds] [come]s in 'n deh=
11    F:    [<h e v a ↓ bee:: ]:[:r     ]
12    J: →  =((f)) ↑Da:ddy Mo̲mmy:
13          (.)
14    J: →  ((f)) ↑Da̲ddy=
```

In extract (5), P makes the joking suggestion that he will visit
D in order to warm up. After a pause, D responds with laughter.
P then overlaps the laughter with an enactment that expands the
joke by enacting the interaction that might take place between them
on that hypothetical occasion. In (8), P creates a hypothetical
scenario in which D panics inside the pyramid. He then proceeds
to enact the reaction of onlookers. In (9), J initiates a joke by

suggesting that F and his wife are 'scr<u>e</u>win a<u>roun</u>" (line 6). He continues by creating a hypothetical scenario in which the kids catch them in the act, enacting what they might say.

Thus, the first enactment is not necessarily a recipient activity. It can also be used by the initiator of the joke to extend it further. However, whether the joke initiator or the recipient of the joke initiation does the first enactment, in all the instances in the current corpus the recipient of the first enactment produces a second enactment.

3.3.3 The second enactment

The second enactment displays the speaker's understanding and appreciation of the first enactment, as well as their willingness to go along with it further by adding to it and thus creating another opportunity to laugh or appreciate it in some other way. Thus, in (3) J repeats and adds to the first enactment.

```
(3) [Detail]
15   L:          [.h h h h h ] Santa Claus.=
16               =hhheh-h[eh
17   J: →                 [.hh ↑Santa Claus brou:ght it.
18        →      (in his sle::d).=
19   J:    =hn[hih [hn-hn-[hen huh=
20   L:       [ Ye:[ah      [.hh
21   L:    =Uh::[:m
22   J:          [.hhhhhehhhhh °( [ ).°
23   L:                         [I found a
24               recipe: that I'm gonna try:,
```

J repeats and adds to L's enacted response to her husband's hypothetical question. The repetition of 'Santa Claus' indicates that J is adopting L's suggested response, entering the enacted interaction by playing the role that L has introduced. Thus, both participants collaborate to play a single speaker, J, within this hypothetical, joking interaction. J's enactment in lines 17–18 demonstrates that she understands L's previous continuation of the joke (and that L was enacting what she 'should' say). It also extends the joke further, providing another opportunity to appreciate it. Following her enactment, J laughs, L overlaps with an agreement and response token, then initiates a new topic in lines 23–24.

In (3), J initiates the joke, L does the first enactment, then J does the second enactment. Thus, there is an A,B,A configuration:

Configuration 1

1   A: Joke initiation
2   B: First enactment
3   A: Second enactment.

A further instance of this configuration is extract (4) (arrows labelled 1 indicate the joke initiation; arrows 2, the first enactment; and arrows 3, the second enactment).

(4) [Detail]

```
1       P: 1→    *ih y- yuh kno:w if you ma::ke it big
2          1→    time babe you'll ↑NEVUH
3          1→    CHA::nge:: [will yuh.    ]
4       D:                  [↑Ahhhhhhh]h
5                (0.5)
6       D: 2→    .hhh  ↑UH you fi:nished with that ch↑o::p
7          2→    p↓et eehh he he °he [he he he°
8       P: 3→                        [I'm (h)eyeing your
9          3→    cho:p up [mi:nd.
```

In lines 1–3, P does the joke initiation; in lines 6–7, D does the first enactment; and in lines 8–9, P produces a second enactment.

In the following extracts the joke initiation and the first enactment (in fact, in extract (7) D produces several enactments in succession) are produced by the same speaker, resulting in an A,A, B pattern of contributions:

Configuration 2

1   A: Joke initiation
2   A: First enactment(s)
3   B: Second enactment.

In configuration 1, the first enactment in line 2 constitutes the joking initiation recipient's opportunity to display that he or she understood the joke and is willing to go along with it by expanding it further (this often occurs after he or she has already appreciated the joke through laughter). In configuration 2 the same participant produces the joking initiation and the first enactment (sometimes they are one and the same), so the second enactment is where the recipient expands on, and displays, their collusion in the joke (again, sometimes after laugh appreciation). Analysis of extracts evincing the second configuration illustrates how second enactments show understanding of, and contribute towards, the joke initiated and expanded in previous turns.

(7) [Continuation]
```
 7   P:     st(h)ea(h)khhh heh heh [heh heh, hhh
 8   P:                            [(huh)
 9   D:     so we ni:ck the stea:k .hhh >un then we
10          said< (0.2) ↓we gotta go: now,
11          (0.5)
12   D:     .hh we've had a nice ti:me (0.1) but
13          we're o:ff.
14          (0.4)
15   D:     [see y-
16   P: →   [we've gotta feed the b↑i:tch ut
17      →   ho:[me
18   D:        [>eh eh eh eh eh[eh eh eh[eh eh eh<
19   P:                        [hhhh    [eh huh hh=
20   D:     =.hh[hh so::]
21   P:         [(°excel]lent ba[be)°
22   D:                         [it wuz coo:l
23          (0.8)
```

(8) [Continuation]
```
10   P:                 [un- un- [und you [might [$knock a few=
11   D:                          [°huh°   [°huh° [.h h h h h
12   P:     =bl<u>ocks [out of position$
13   D:               [°huh°
14   D:     .hhhh[hh
15   P:          [an' all of a sudden    ((f))what's happened
16          to the  ↑pyrami[ds they've got a blu:nt[to:p
17   D:                    [.hhhhh                  [hhe=
18   D:     =hhee hhe[ °he° °he°
19   P:              [>it's fair lean' o'er<
```

```
20   D:→   hhe[ehh ↑oh look .hh the pyramids she:cking heh=
21   P:         [hah
22   D:    =heh heh heh heh heh
23   P:    hheh heh heh [( ) sh:i̲:t
24   D:                  [( )
25   P:    [heh heh heh heh heh heh
26   D:    [heh heh heh heh heh heh huhr
27   D:    what's that canny roof ↑like
28   P:    ee:[:::::[:
29   D:          [.hh [it wuz- it is it is dead frightening
30         because once yu- .hhhh uh as I say yu- yuh go
31         down steep...
```

In extract (7), D reports a number of turns from his interaction
with his fellow diners. He begins by making a joke about asking the
managing director's wife for the remains of her meal to feed to his
dog. This is followed by laughter in line 7 and possibly overlapping
laughter from P in line 8. He proceeds to enact turns in which he
announces that they are leaving. P then enacts a further contribution to D's 'reported' turns.[3] It contributes to D's previous turns by
purporting to be by D, and to add to his leave-taking. It follows a
similar format to D's 'reported' turns, beginning with 'we' (as in
lines 10 and 12). It also repeats 'gotta' from line 10. It picks up on
D's earlier mention of collecting scraps for the dog by suggesting
the reason they have to leave is to feed it. Further, it manifests the
irreverent attitude implicit in D's 'reported' turns, emphasising
the term '↑bi:tch' and suggesting that their reason for leaving is
merely to feed the dog. Thus, P demonstrates his understanding and
appreciation of D's prior reported speech and enactment by adding
to them, thus expanding the joke. Following this, both D and
P laugh.

In extract (8), P creates a hypothetical scenario portraying D as
panicking when stuck inside the pyramid. He proceeds to enact

---

[3] In this instance the reported speech and enactments are based on
real events rather than a hypothetical scenario. However, even so, it
seems that D's portrayal of what was said is built to communicate his
offhand attitude rather than represent an accurate depiction of what was
said.

the reaction of the onlookers. D first laughs (lines 17–18), thus appreciating the joke. He then adds a further enacted observation of the pyramid. Like P in the previous enactment, he adopts a high pitch. He also echos P's hearably Geordie accent and dialogue by pronouncing 'shaking' as 'she:cking'. So, like P, D shifts footing to enact an observer at the pyramids witnessing the events take place, and in doing so he adopts a similar pitch and accent. The enactment contributes to, and expands, the joke and provides another opportunity to laugh, which both participants do in lines 22–23.

So, in extracts (7) and (8) the recipient of a joke initiation and enactment adds a further enactment to the sequence. The next extract illustrates that the producer of a second enactment may deliberately overlap the first (in this case, a question and answer pair) in order to concurrently produce an enactment.

(5) [Continuation]
```
 9  P:                        [>Do you two
10      want come out for a pi:nt< No:
11      >can't y[ou see we (want) to get] w(h)a:rm(h)<
12  D:→         [.hhh ↑N O : : : : : : ]
13  D:→ [↑PUT THE FI:RE ON eh eh eh heh heh
14  P:  [(huh)
15  D:  .hhh Wul babe it's not too bloody warm I mean
16      .hhh we've- we've only ju:st got rid of the
17      s:no:w.
```

In line 12, D overlaps P's enactment with a further enactment. D's repeats P's 'no'. Given the timing of the enactment – beginning after 'can't you' (line 11) – and the way 'no' is stretched, it seems that D is intending to overlap P's enactment. Thus, both speakers shift footing to enact the role of a single speaker (presumably P) at the same time. D then proceeds to add to his enacted turn in line 13, followed by laughter.

3.3.4 The joke initiation–enactment sequence

In the extracts analysed above, the participants collaborate to appreciate and build on a joke initiation through enacting a

character or one of the participants. Subsequent enactments extend
the joke by collaborating with the previous enactment, thus displaying the producer's understanding and appreciation of the joke
by expanding it and providing further opportunities to laugh. In
most instances, following laughter and sometimes assessments and
agreements, the sequence is brought to a close, the participants
either return to the topic prior to the joking scenario or initiate a
new topic, as in the following two extracts.

(3) [Detail]

```
15   L:              [.h h h h h ]Santa Claus.=
16        =hhheh-h[eh
17   J: →                [.hh >Santa Claus brou:ght it.
18      →   (in his sle::d).=
19   J:   =hn[hih [hn-hn-[hen huh=
20   L:        [ Ye:[ah     [.hh
21   L:   =Uh::[:m
22   J :        [.hhhhhehhhhh °( [   ).°
23   L:                        [I found a
24        recipe: that I'm gonna try:,
```

(5) [Detail]

```
 9   P:                    [>Do you two
10        want come out for a pi:nt< No:
11        >can't y[ou see we (want) to get] w(h)a:rm(h)<
12   D:→          [.hhh ↑N O : : : : : : : ]
13   D:→   [↑PUT THE FI:RE ON eh eh eh heh heh
14   P:   [(huh)
15   D:   .hhh Wul babe it's not too bloody warm I mean
16        .hhh we've- we've only ju:st got rid of the
17        s:no:w.
```

In (3), the second enactment in lines 17–18 is followed by
laughter (line 19), agreement (line 20) and the initiation of a new
topic (lines 23–24) (this may be touched off by talk of Christmas,
see Jefferson, 1984). In (5), there is laughter from D following the
enactment in line 13, then he initiates a shift (also touched off by
the prior talk) by discussing the weather in a serious manner – in
fact, he complains about how cold it is.

Through the joke initiation, the enactments, the laugh appreciation, and sometimes agreements and assessments, participants
depart from serious talk (or build on talk that is already a departure
from serious talk, as in (3) and (4)) before returning to it once more.
Consideration of the activities the participants engage in to achieve
this transition from serious talk to these joking scenarios demonstrates the high degree of collaboration and affiliation they display
in the face of actions that could be seen as potentially tricky. In the
extracts one participant is portrayed as engaging in an activity that
could potentially be seen as improper, or is being gently teased by
the other participant. In (3), J and L joke about J lying to her
husband about her purchase of the extra gifts; in (4), D and
P joke about D's lack of manners; in (5), P jokes about coming to
visit D simply to warm up; in (7), P and D joke about D's offhand
attitude at his firm's event; and in (8), P teases D about the potentially disastrous consequences of him panicking inside the pyramid.[4] Yet in each instance both participants collaborate to create
these enacted scenarios.[5]

Extract (6) is a little different. Here, it is not one of the participants that is joked about, but D's in-laws. The enactments are also
derogatory to P's ex-wife. Thus, although neither of the participants is explicitly teased, the sequence is potentially tricky, as the
scenario portrays D's in-laws as stupid and socially inept and D's
ex-wife as physically deficient. Again, however, it is not treated as
problematic by either participant, but is marked by a high degree of
affiliation and collaboration. The participants collaborate to produce an extended sequence of enactments after the joke initiation;
thus it takes the following configuration (an expanded version of
configuration 1 above):

1   A: Joke initiation (lines 13–14)
2   B: First enactment (lines 16–17)
3   A: Second enactment (line 22)

---

[4] In the small corpus of calls from which this extract is derived, P frequently teases D about his size, strength and clumsiness. P's attempted
co-completion of 'cuz if you went a↑pe' with 'It'd bust' (line 5) seems to
anticipate this kind of tease.
[5] In Drew's (1987) analysis of teases in interaction he was struck by the fact
that most received a serious or 'po-faced' response from the recipient.

4   B: Third enactment (lines 24–25).

Analysis of this sequence illustrates just how closely the participants work together to produce the enacted scenario.

(6) [Continuation]

```
13    P:                                        [(They'll)
14          say .tch ↑it's very nice to meet you Pa::m
15    D:    .hh ↑he huh hee hah hah hah hah hah hah
16    →     .hhhh ↑by:: you've fucking grown a few
17    →     inches like haven't [yuh
18    P:                         [( )
19    D:    hah [hah hah hah hah
20    P:        [°huh huh huh°
21          (.)
22    P: →  ↑Yuh ti:ts uh bigger [aren't they?
23    D:                          [.hhh
24    D:→   he hu:::h heh heh .hhh in fact you've
25    →     got ti:[ts heh heh heh heh hah hah hah]=
26    P:           [heh heh heh excellent (      )]=
27    D:    =[hah HAH HAH HAH HAH HAH hah hah hah
28    P:    =[there you go ( ) ba(h)be
29    D:    .hhh[hh
30    P:         [(          a chortle) ↑Uhm:
31          (0.2)
32    P:    [( )
33    D:    [°huh°
34    P:    Yeh it's nice to look forward to
35          something.
36    D:    Ye:s (.) it's gonna b[e (top)
37    P:                          [I'm waiting for a
38          phone call...
```

Prior to the reported speech (and joke initiation) in lines 13–14,
P and D are discussing their impending visit to D's in-laws. They do
so in a serious manner; there is no laughter prior to this turn. In
lines 13–14, P initiates a transition by using reported speech to
portray a hypothetical joking scenario. D treats this as an invitation
to laughter by laughing in the following turn (line 15), thus appreciating the joke. He then produces an addition to the interaction

portrayed in P's previous turn: '↑by:: you've fucking grown a few inches like haven't yuh'. This footed turn is not preceded by a pronoun-plus-speech-verb. In a similar manner to P's reported turn, there is a noticeable rise in pitch at the start. It also purports to be by D's in-laws and addresses P's partner. Thus, it displays recognition that the previous turn was footed and that it jokingly suggested the in-laws might mistake the identity of his partner. Besides displaying understanding of the joke, it expands it. It builds on the idea of the mistaken identity, taking it a stage further. It suggests that, rather than simply using the wrong name for someone they realise they have not met before (hence 'nice to meet you' (line 14) in the previous turn), they take P's new partner to be his ex-wife, commenting on her change of appearance.

Following D's enactment (lines 16–17), there is a period of laughing together. Then, in line 22, P adds a second enactment: '↑Yuh ti:ts uh bigger aren't they?'. This displays understanding of D's prior turn by taking the form of a further addition to the hypothetical interaction. It purports to be another comment by the in-laws on her change of physical appearance – this time, the size of her 'ti:ts'. It echoes D's prior enactment by also containing a rise in pitch at the start, and taking the form of an observation followed by a tag question addressed to the hypothetical recipient. D then does a laugh appreciation followed by a third (and final) enactment: 'in fact you've got ti:ts'. This one builds on P's previous enacted observation by also commenting on her 'ti:ts'. In overlap with the end of this turn construction unit, P begins laughing, and D joins in. Then, after several turns in which the participants appreciate the joke through laughter and assessments (lines 27–30), and refer back to the topic out of which the joke developed (lines 34–36), P then introduces a new topic (lines 37–38).

Thus, the participants collaborate to extend the initial joke through their enactments. The enactments both display understanding of, and serve to expand, the joke, providing further opportunities to laugh. Therefore, as well as displaying the participants' understandings of the joke, they also evince what they take to be appropriate contributions to the ongoing sequence. But in this extract the highly collaborative work that participants can perform through their enactments is particularly delicate in that, rather than

simply expanding the joke, the participants work together to escal-
ate an impropriety through the enacted turns.

The term 'impropriety' was used by Jefferson et al. as a 'weak
catchall term' to refer to the 'range of interactional breaches' in
their collection from conversation (1987: 192, n. 4). They pointed
out that improper talk can be indicative of intimate interaction, and
that the introduction of such talk can display that the speaker
understands the conversation to be intimate in nature. Furthermore, such talk may be introduced into an interaction to invite a
co-participant into a display of intimacy when the conversation has
not been intimate so far. Thus, the introduction of improper talk
can be seen as an invitation the recipient accepts, rejects or manages
in some other way. In analysing recipients' treatment of improper
talk, Jefferson et al. suggested that responses 'can be arranged on a
hypothetical continuum ranging from rejection to enthusiastic acceptance, from disaffiliation to escalation' (1987: 160). They analysed extract (9) in detail, identifying a sequence of activities
involving an impropriety followed by disattention, followed by
laugh-appreciation, and finally affiliation.

```
(9) [Continuation]
    1    F:    No we c'm in fr'm the bea:ch'n then we
    2          c'm in en take a ↓na::p you kno: :w,=
    3    F:    =hIt's [rilly  [we rilly ge]t=
    4    J:           [Ye:h [ y o u : : ]
    5    F:    =[.hhh
    6    J:    =[screwin arou[n'there uh?]
    7    F:                  [Y e : : : :   ]ah en
    8          then we t-t-
    9          (0.8)
   10    J:    [W'n a'those kids] [come]s in 'n deh=
   11    F:    [<h e v a ↓bee: :] : [ : r ]
   12    J: →  =((f)) ↑Da:ddy Mommy:
   13          (.)
   14    J: →  ((f)) ↑Daddy=
   15    J:    =he[h heh hheh]heh] (↑rhhi::ght)]
   16    F:       [e h Y e h ]heh]h e h  heh-He]:H=
   17          =eh[↓h*e:h]
   18    J:       [heh eh]
```

```
19   F:     .hhh hu:h
20          (.)
21   J:     °he:h[heh°].hh
22   F:→         [e   e]((f)) Git ↑ou:dda there=
23   J:     =he:h heh=
24   J:     =[heh heh heh]heh hu-uh ].hhhhhhhhhh]=
25   F:     =[hih huh hih]heh-heh-uh] -uh-uh-°uh° ]=
26   F:     =.hh[hhh]
27   J:        [Aah]w[ell (he]v a g'd ↓time)]
28   F:               [N o : :] N o   h a n k ]y
29          pa:nky,h
30          (.)
31   J:     No hanky pan[k y  u h]
32   F:                 [No:: han]°ky panky°.
33          (0.3)
34   J:     We:ll have a good ↓time.
```

The impropriety is in lines 4 and 6, where J suggests the reason they
are in bed during the afternoon is because they are 'screwin'. At
first F disattends this impropriety by saying ' e::::ah en then we t-t-
<hev a ↓bee::::r' (lines 7–8 and 11). At this point J makes an
invitation to laugh by enacting the reaction of the children followed
by laughter (lines 12 and 14–15), and F does a laugh-appreciation
(line 16). F then affiliates by a further enactment (line 22) and then
both participants laugh together (Jefferson et al., 1987).

In (6), the speakers begin by portraying a hypothetical impropriety, but proceed to introduce profanity and crudeness through
the enactments, thus escalating the impropriety. At the start of the
joking sequence, P portrays the in-laws as using the name of his ex-
wife to address his new partner. In the enactment in lines 16–17,
D elaborates the faux pas by suggesting that they actually mistake
his new partner for his ex-wife, commenting on her change of
height. D introduces profanity by including 'fucking' in this enactment. In the next enactment, P escalates the rudeness of the enacted
observation enacting a comment on her 'ti:ts'. Finally D escalates
the implied insult to P's ex-wife by suggesting she has no 'ti:ts'.

Thus, not only is the sequence marked by a high degree of collaboration and affiliation as the speakers work together to expand
the joke through creating an enacted scenario, but it also creates

heightened intimacy. And this is in the face of the fact that what the participants joke about could be seen as potentially problematic for one or both of them (for example, D escalates the insult to P's ex-wife's breasts by implying she has none and, whereas such a comment may be treated as unacceptable in other circumstances, here P shows no indication of finding it at all problematic – in fact, his response is enthusiastic). The fact that the participants are engaged in a joking sequence, and that they have shifted footing to enact characters (the 'reported' speech does not genuinely purport to be what the in-laws might say,[6]) enables them to stand in a position of reduced responsibility for their enacted comments (Beach, 2000: 395).

In this extract, therefore, the participants collaborate to expand the joke while at the same time escalating an impropriety, thus creating a sequence of heightened intimacy. The other extracts in the corpus are also characterised by a high degree of collaboration and affiliation in that the speakers collaborate to create the enacted scenario resulting in laughter, often sequences of laughing together. According to Mathis and Yule, '[m]erging their voices to become that of a character appears to be...[a] way in which the speakers underscore their sameness' (1994: 75). This increased intimacy and collaboration in the extracts in the current corpus is in the face of the fact that the enactments regularly portray one participant as engaged in potentially improper activity, or even constitute a tease.

3.4 Conclusion

Analysis of reported speech in interaction has revealed that some instances are not preceded by a component that frames it as reported speech. The current corpus consists of a collection of these. The enactments in this collection also share the following characteristics: they occur in the conversational environment of joking and often involve creating or adding to a hypothetical scenario,

---

[6] The use of the Geordie accent, the profanity and the crudeness of the enacted comments are very much at odds with what the in-laws might genuinely be expected to say, and thus help to portray this as purely irreverent fun.

and they are collaborative productions – both participants shift footing to produce an extended enacted interaction. Enactments involve speakers shifting footing to play a character (whether a real person – including one of the participants – or invented ones such as onlookers at the pyramids). This analysis suggests that when speakers do not use a prefatory framing component they may do so for systematic reasons and in recurrent environments. In this corpus it is to contribute to enact a character in an ongoing interaction. Using a prefatory component would detract from the suggestion that the participant is 'playing' an attributed speaker and, as section 2.2 demonstrated, this component is redundant as other design features of the turn make it clear that the turn is footed.

Goffman's (1981) work on participation in interaction has demonstrated that several 'speakers' may be present in a single turn; for example, the current speaker or animator of the utterance, but also the original speaker or author and principal. In analysing the extracts that constitute the current corpus, it is evident that participants shift footing to become the animator of a turn portrayed as emanating from another speaker (or himself or herself on another occasion). However, adopting a sequential approach involving analysing these enactments in sequence has revealed how they contribute to the ongoing series of actions, displaying the speakers' understandings of the nature of the activity sequence, and what constitutes an appropriate contribution.

In the current corpus the participants collaborate to initiate and expand a joking scenario. Enactments serve to display their understanding of the joke as well as adding to it and thus creating further opportunities to appreciate it. In each of the instances in the corpus, speakers collaborate to produce the enacted interaction, whether following an A,A,B or an A,B,A configuration (or an expanded A,B,A,B pattern, as in (6)). The enacted interaction is the co-production of the participants: each enactment, while being uttered by a single speaker, arises out of, and contributes towards, a collaboratively produced sequence. Features such as the repetition of words and the continuation of activities manifest in prior enactments demonstrate how the design of subsequent enactments is dependent on the sequence in which it occurs. They demonstrate the importance of seeing interaction as the collaborative achievement of the participants rather than as a series of utterances produced by an active speaker aimed at a recipient.

In two of the extracts the participants initiate or contribute towards expanding or escalating an impropriety: (9) and (6) respectively. However, even when there are no improprieties such as crudeness or profanity in the remaining extracts, nevertheless the enactments portray potentially tricky actions that might be seen as improper in some way. In the extracts the participants collaborate to produce a sequence in which one of them is being gently teased or portrayed as engaged in potentially improper behaviour. But, far from being treated as tricky in any way, these sequences are marked by a high degree of collaboration as both participants shift footing to produce the enacted interaction and are characterised by laughing, often laughing together. Thus, the actions of the participants in these extracts suggest that appropriate contributions to a joking sequence are to expand that sequence through enactments, even when the enactment involves laughing at the (sometimes hypothetical) activities of one of the participants.

4

Assessing and accounting

Elizabeth Couper-Kuhlen

4.1 Introduction

Much research in the past has been devoted to the use of reported speech and thought in fictional writing (Banfield, 1973, 1982; Volosinov, 1973; Leech and Short, 1981; Sternberg, 1982; Fludernik, 1993 – to mention only a few) and in everyday oral story-telling (Tannen, 1989; Mayes, 1990; Holt, 1996). In oral story-telling prosodic dimensions of speech have been shown to be instrumental in marking quotations off from surrounding talk (Klewitz and Couper-Kuhlen, 1999), in constructing enacted scenarios (Yule, 1995; Couper-Kuhlen, 1999) and in conveying multi-voicedness (Maynard, 1996; Günthner, 1999; Holt, 1999). Yet the type of reported speech and thought examined in these studies has as a rule been that found in *narration*, where a sequence of events is recounted in chronological order and participants in these events are animated as story-world figures. Little or no attention has been paid to isolated quotations in conversation which are *not* embedded in a story framework nor are part of any larger narrative context.[1] It is this kind of speech and thought-reporting which the present study sets out to investigate. It will be argued that reported speech in

I am grateful to Susanne Günthner, Gabriele Klewitz, Harrie Mazeland and Sandra A. Thompson for stimulating input on an earlier version of this chapter.
[1] See also Clift, this volume. Günthner (1999), in dealing with 'concealed forms of polyphony', does address a non-narrative use of reported speech in converation, but one which is quite different from the type discussed here precisely because of its concealed nature.

non-narrative contexts is different in design from that in narrative contexts and that it is frequently incorporated into assessments and accounts as a means of heightening evidentiality. In contrast to many forms of narrative reported speech it will be shown that the boundaries between the 'there-and-then' of non-narrative reported speech and the 'here-and-now' are fuzzy. In fact, the former often merges imperceptibly into the latter, thus making the use of quotation outside narration a subtle device for intersubjective negotiation.

The chapter is organised as follows. Section 2 identifies and characterises non-narrative contexts for reporting speech and thought and discusses several of the characteristic features of speech and thought reports in these contexts. Section 3 examines how reporting speech and thought is deployed as a device for building turn-constructional units and turns. Section 4 examines two framing environments for quotative TCUs: assessments and accounts. Finally, section 5 considers sequential follow-ups to reporting speech and thought fragments outside of narration.

4.2 Quoting speech and thought in non-narrative contexts

In order to appreciate what is meant by reporting speech and thought in a 'non-narrative' context, it will be helpful to consider first the use of reporting in a narrative context; for instance, in conversational story-telling. The following is a prototypical case. Edna has called her friend Margy, inter alia to apologise for Edna's husband Bud having kept a power tool which he had borrowed from Margy's husband for too long:[2]

---

[2] This and all following conversational fragments are extracted from recorded conversations which have been meticulously transcribed by Gail Jefferson using a set of notational conventions described inter alia in Schenkein (1978). The original transcripts have been retained here in recognition of their high quality. For ease of reading, more conventional orthography is used when single lines are cited in the running text.

(1) [NBVII: Power Tools:1]

```
13   Edn:          [I:'m sorr [y about that=
14   Mar:                    [nn
15   Edn:          = [da: : [:uh ↑I didn'see that-]
16   Mar:            [. hhh[Oo ::::::::hhhe didn: ]: :need it e-hm-mmm. =
17   Mar:          = .hh [hh ] He jist need'd] it fer that one thing Edna,=
18   Edn:                 [We] : ll Bud'd gah-]
19   Mar:          = hm-mm.=
20   Edn: →        = .hh Yah b'djihknow we took about nine books up there et
21         →       the(p) (.) uh: the↑: e-stamp place'n he got a little pa:r
22         →       tool Fri:dee'n I sz yih better take it do:wn t-Fridee teh
23         →       th-t-Frideez'n'e [sz Oh]: I will Saghturdee=
24   Mar:                          [°whhew]
25   Edn:          = :hhunh[↑unh-↑u[nh-uh]
26   Mar:                  [.hhhhhh[w:We:] ll,=
27   Mar:          =i [h  wz    jist] one [a' tho:se things et nyou, yihknow=
28   Edn:          [ih-hu:nh-hn]        [.hk
29   Mar:          =cu [z↓he-↓I : :] bet hasn' used it since.hhhh Fa:ll(f) nyouknow=
30   Edn:              [Ye: : : :ah.]
31   Mar:          =mayb[e  twi : : ce.]=
32   Edn:               [eeYe: : : ah.]=
```

Focusing our attention from line 20 onwards, we observe that – in order to explain the delay in returning Margy's husband's power tool – Edna produces a report *in story form* of how she and Bud went to the stamp shop ('we took about nine books up there et the... stamp place') and used their stamp books to buy their own tool ('he got a little pa:r tool Fri:dee'). She then reports that she advised Bud to return Margy's tool right away ('yih better take it do:wn t-Fridee teh th-t-Frideez' – a reference to which day of the week the tool should be returned to Margy and her husband, whose last name coincidentally is 'Friday'). But Bud, she reports, procrastinated ('Oh: I will Saghturdee').

Edna's story is constructed and presented as a sequence of four chronologically ordered events – Edna and Bud going to the stamp shop, Bud buying his own tool, Edna admonishing him to return Margy's tool immediately and Bud resisting her admonishment. It is this chronological order of presentation, corresponding to the presumed order of events in the 'real' world, which is a characteristic feature of conversational narration (Labov and Waletzky, 1967; Labov, 1972).[3] Note that the last two events are verbal ones staged as a speech exchange or dialogue, with Edna and Bud taking orderly turns at talk ('I says', 'and he says'...). As in real conversation their turns are sequentially ordered in an adjacency pair relationship of advice/admonishment–(partial) rejection of advice/ admonishment.

Crucially, Edna does not present this dialogue indirectly, as would be the case had she said to Margy, 'I told Bud to bring your tool back on Friday but he said he wanted to wait until Saturday'; instead she demonstrates it (Clark and Gerrig, 1990). Evidence for this is to be seen in the use of second and first person deictic pronouns to refer to Bud, who is not present in the here-and-now of the conversation (Edna's 'you' in line 22, Bud's 'I' in line 23) and the use of a third person term of reference for Margy, who is actually a ratified party to the ongoing conversation ('the Fridays' in line 23). By telling the story this way Edna not only enlivens her talk, but she also succeeds in indirectly assigning responsibility for the delay in returning the power tool. She does so in the words of the characters she portrays: while she herself comes off as a conscientious, morally upright and socially aware person who knows that borrowed tools should be returned immediately if they are no longer needed, Bud emerges as dilatory, lazy and socially inept.

Compare now, by contrast, a prototypical case of reported speech used in a non-narrative context. The following extract comes from a telephone conversation which takes place in Newport Beach between Emma and her sister Lottie. Emma has just come down to the beach for the weekend, where she has an apartment that she rents out during the week. Lottie, who lives at the beach, has been telling her sister about a fishing expedition she went on earlier in the week. We join the conversation as Lottie continues.

---

[3] Conversational narration thus involves by definition more than one event, and typically more than one participant.

(2) [NBII:3:R:5]

```
22   Lot:      En Ru:th uh: this friend a'mi:ne oh:  .hhh well it (.)
23             e-eh sh- I let 'er stay et the. 'waiian hou:se: >over the
24             week<.  So we're goin uh: (.) e:-eh t'morruh morning ou:t.
25             ( . )
26   Emm:      Oh: good. Gunnuh rent a boa : [t? er]
27   Lot:                               [Ye:::]ah=
28   Emm:      =Ah [hah?]
29   Lot:          [Ye : ]ah.
30             ( . )
31   Lot:      Uh hu [ h,
32   Emm:            [W'l: good honey .t.h [hhhhhh]
33   Lot:                                 [Ye : ah,]
34   Emm:      ↑WELL MAYBE AH'LL SEE YUH NEXT ↓week.
35   Lot:      hh hhuh - hu [h↓h] uh huh:    ]huh↓]
36   Emm:                   [e h ]HAH HAH] TI: ]ME goes o:n:,
37   Lot:   →  I:uh I wz ou:t yesterday en I din' wanna ca:ll yuh cuz I
38          →  thought well maybe the people were still there'r something
39             so I didn' ca:ll.
40   Emm:      eeYah,
41   Lot:      .t I din' know what time yih w'r gunnuh get do:wn so I wen
42             ou[t
43   Emm:        [*Oh[::] w e got- ]
44   Lot:            [sh]o:ppin ye]s'°t[ay°
45   Emm:                            [Yah we didn't git↓down til abou:t
46             (0.5) °oh° I °don't know,° (0.3) six uh'clo:ck b't oh::
47             m:ma::n  was it ↓ho::t up there[WO::W.  Th[e wind w ]z=
48   Lot:                                     [(  )      [W h a : t-]
49   Emm:      =blo:win a liddle bih-  .hhhhhhhh Oh but it's pretty,
```

Following Lottie's announcement that she will be going out fishing the next morning with her friend Ruth (lines 22–24), Emma inquires if they will be renting a boat (line 26). Lottie's answer is only minimal, however, nor is she forthcoming with more information about the fishing expedition, to which conceivably she might be expected to invite her sister.[4] So, when Emma now produces a sigh-like in-breath (line 32) and says loudly, '↑WELL

---

[4] In prior talk Emma has expressed reluctance to go out on the jetty herself, since there are so many people.

MAYBE AH'LL SEE YUH NEXT ↓week' (line 34), she is in fact
registering that she won't be seeing her sister the next day. But
she does so in a hyperbolic format which jokingly proposes
that she won't be seeing her sister until 'next week'[5] – in other
words for a long time – and even then only 'maybe'. Lottie's rather
hesitant chuckle in the next turn signals an awareness on her part
that Emma intended her turn to be humorous but also that it was
targeted at her. In fact, line 34 couches a subtle complaint by Emma
that Lottie is too busy to see her. This potential complaint becomes
more pointed when Emma extends her turn with the observation
'TI:ME goes o:n:'

So Lottie now finds herself in the vulnerable position of being
the object of possible blame for not seeing more of her sister, and
she accordingly moves to produce a series of defences: 'I: uh I wz
ou:t yesterday en I din' wanna ca:ll yuh' (line 37) – potential
accounts for why she didn't contact Emma sooner. 'I din' wanna
ca:ll yuh' is at the same time a negative observation about an event
which didn't happen and thus implies that Lottie could indeed
have been *expected* to call Emma (Schegloff, 1988). This admission
calls for another account, which Lottie now provides by saying
she didn't know whether Emma's guests might still be in her apartment. She does this with a fragment of reported thought: 'I din'
wanna ca:ll yuh cuz I thought well maybe the people were still
there'r something so I didn' ca:ll.'

The thought which Lottie quotes here is heralded in by the
discourse marker 'well'[6] and then verbalised with the words 'may
be the people were still there'. Strictly speaking, of course, these are
not *exactly* Lottie's words, as on the occasion Lottie presumably
would have used a present tense form: 'well maybe the people are
still there'.[7] But, despite its tense shift, the reporting makes Lottie's

---

[5] This is presumably a reference to the next time she will be coming down
to the beach.
[6] Discourse markers and other 'expressives' are well-known signs of direct
reported speech and thought (Banfield, 1973, 1982; Coulmas, 1986;
Dubois, 1989). In other words, when a turn-initial discourse marker
such as 'well' appears – as here – in the middle of a turn, it may indicate
a shift in footing to a reported speaker.
[7] This kind of reported speech thus represents a mixture of direct and
indirect reporting forms and is similar to what is called in literary studies

earlier thought process directly tangible and provides a demonstration of her uncertainty at the time, presented in the here-and-now as her reason for not calling Emma. To the extent that it *demonstrates* rather than describes a past situation (Clark and Gerrig, 1990), the reporting of speech and thought in a non-narrative context, as exemplified in (2), is similar to that in a narrative context such as (1).

Yet there are some important differences. First, although both these conversational excerpts contain quotations embedded in turns which are doing telling, the telling in (2) does not contain a chronologically ordered sequence of events with more than one participant. Instead, only one event (or lack of event) – not calling – with only one participant – Lottie – is involved. Moreover, the locutionary agent whose speech or thought is quoted is identical with the current speaker. Admittedly this is also the case in (1), where Edna enacts herself, yet in (1) she additionally enacts Bud, a third party not present in the discourse situation, and the dialogue ensuing between them. Typical for non-narrative speech reporting, on the other hand, is the enactment of a single locutionary agent, who – especially in the case of reported thought – is usually identical with the current speaker himself or herself.

Second, when speech or thought is reported in a non-narrative context, it is routinely introduced by a *verbum dicendi* or quotative marker, e.g. 'I thought' in (2) above. This is a corollary of the principle that only one locutionary agent is involved: there is no dialogue framework which can be relied upon to structure the report of a succession of turns at talk without explicit marking. In story-telling contexts, on the other hand, conversationalists regularly exploit the natural adjacency of turns-at-talk when reporting dialogue and suppress quotative markers after the story figures have been introduced for the first time (Yule et al., 1992; Klewitz and Couper-Kuhlen, 1999).

Third, although the beginning of the quotation in (2) is clearly marked by the use of 'well', its end is much less definite. Rather

free indirect speech (Banfield, 1982; Sternberg, 1982; Fludernik, 1993); see also Polanyi, 1982.

than there being an 'unquote' marker (Golato, 2002b), in Lottie's utterance 'cuz I thought well maybe the people were still there'r something', the status of ''r something' is ambiguous. On the one hand it could be part of what she thought the day before, but on the other it could be a post-possible-completion hedge added to her quotative turn-constructional unit (TCU) in the here-and-now. This kind of ambiguity is not uncommon in non-narrative quoting and may be related to the fact that the quoted and the quoting speaker are often identical.

Summing up the characteristics of non-narrative reported speech and thought observed so far, we note that:

- the locutionary agent quoted is typically the current speaker 'I', especially when thoughts are being reported[8]
- there is an explicit introductory verb of saying or thinking
- the boundaries between the quoted material and *hic-et-nunc* talk are fuzzy, especially towards the end of the quotation.

The following case of reported *speech*, taken from another telephone call between Emma and Lottie, illustrates a further characteristic of quoting in a non-narrative context. This time Emma is talking to Lottie for the first time after having arrived at Newport Beach from 'uptown'. Bud is Emma's husband.

(3) [NBII:1:R:2]

```
46   Emm:     WHAT A MISERBLE WEEKE:ND.
47            (0.2)
48   Lot:     Yea:h en gee it's been: beautiful ↓down here I know
49            you've had it (.) lousy in town have[ncha. ]
50   Emm:                                         [ Yea:h] it rained
51            yesterday,
52            (0.2)
 1   Lot:     mBut the sun wz ou:t here it wz beautiful [yestered]ay.
 2   Emm:                                               [°eeYah.°]
```

---

[8] Alternatively, a generic 'you' may be encountered, as in 'some of that stuff hits you pretty ha:rd and then: °you think we:ll do you want to be° ↑PA:R:T of it' (NBII:2:R:8).

```
 3   Emm:      [(Weh-)]
 4   Lot:      [But it]'s
 5             (0.2)
 6   Lot:      bee:n co::ld.
 7   Emm:   →  I: know it. I edda turn the ↓furnace ↓u:p. I ed tell Bud
 8          →  my Go:d .hh Oh it's cold uptow:n too. It rai:ned yes'day
 9             morning til about ele:ven,
10   Lot:      .t.hh
11             (0.3)
12   Lot:      I:t rai:ned abou:t uh::: u.-let's [see: Thursdee morning=
13   Emm:                                        [°Ye:h.°
14   Emm:      =[°(       )°
15   Lot:      =[real ri:l ha:rd about five uh'clock down here.
16   Emm:       ↑Did it?↑
17   Lot:      Yeah.
18   Emm:      Memorial Da : : y.
19             (0.4)
```

Emma initiates the weather topic here by complaining loudly about the 'MISERBLE WEEKE:ND', presumably in town (line 46). Lottie agrees and then proceeds to proclaim how 'beautiful' the weather has been at the beach (lines 48–49 and 1). At the same time, she acknowledges 'But it's (0.2) bee:n co::ld' (lines 4–6). Emma now professes to know this already and she provides testimony for how she knows: 'I edda turn the ↓furnace ↓u:p' (line 7). She then produces a quotation of what she said to her husband on the occasion: 'I (had to) tell Bud my Go:d' (lines 7–8).[9] The quoted material 'my Go:d' is an exclamation performed as a display of how cold it was. It not only serves to warrant why the furnace had to be turned up but also to demonstrate the effect of the cold, and thus substantiates Emma's concurrence with Lottie's prior assessment.

Emma's self-quote in (3) illustrates a further characteristic of reporting speech outside narration: not only *what* was said on some other speech occasion is portrayed but also – often – to *whom* it

---

[9] As a quote, 'my Go:d' sounds incomplete. We might expect Emma to continue with 'it's so cold I'm going to have to turn the heat up'. In the event, however, she breaks off to reflect on the fact that it's also cold uptown.

was said. This detail is by no means gratuitous. First of all, in contrast to story-telling, where the dramatis personae are known from the outset,[10] it cannot be taken for granted here who the addressee of the isolated quotation is. By specifying that she said 'my Go:d' to Bud, Emma can make it clear that the cold was bad enough to warrant mentioning it to her husband. This detail (together with the stretching on 'my Go:d', which displays a certain degree of affect) enhances the effect the quotation is designed to achieve. Thus a further characteristic of the non-narrative use of reported *speech* – in contrast to narrative uses – is:

- the addressee to whom the quoted speech was originally directed is often mentioned explicitly.[11]

4.3 Quoting speech and thought as a turn-constructional device

We turn now to a closer examination of a set of reported speech and thought fragments in non-narrative contexts. The examples have been culled from two large corpora of English telephone conversations – one British (the 'Holt' collection), the other American (the 'Newport Beach' collection).[12] We begin by asking a pair of questions related to turn construction. How is reporting speech and thought used as a means for building TCUs? How are quotative TCUs used to build turns?

Non-narrative quoting, as we have seen, involves de rigeur two objects: the quotative marker and the material being quoted. Routinely, these two objects are linked together, nexus-like, to build a *single* TCU. In (2), for instance, the words 'cuz I thought well maybe the people were still there'r something' (lines 37–38) are produced all in one breath, without noticeable stretching or

---

[10] In (1), for instance, it is clear that Emma and Bud are the protagonists and are in dialogue with one another.

[11] Further instances in the collection include 'I said to Dwayne' (Holt 5/88:2:4:15,18,20,25), 'we said to them' (Holt 5/88:2:4:24) and 'I was just saying to Leslie' (Holt 5/88:2:4:27).

[12] The initial set comprised approximately eighty examples, several of which were later excluded on the grounds that they were semi-narrative. I am indebted to Gail Jefferson, Paul Drew and Elizabeth Holt for making the transcripts and recordings of these conversations available to me.

pausing in between.[13] By contrast, the prior clauses 'I wz ou:t yesterday' and 'en I din' wanna ca:ll yuh' each have final lengthening, indicative of a phrasing boundary.[14] In (3), 'I ed tell Bud my Go:d' (lines 7–8) is also produced as a single phrase with no stretching or pausing between the two parts. This unit is separated prosodically from surrounding talk by the final lengthening and pitch fall on 'u:p' before it, and by the in-breath and high-pitched new start on 'Oh' immediately following it.

Not only do quotative marker and quotation together typically form a single TCU; fragments of reported speech and thought are overwhelmingly *no longer than* one TCU in non-narrative contexts. Talk which follows a quotative TCU, if related at all, will be hearable as a reformulation, in the *hic-et-nunc*, of the prior quotation. The following extract provides evidence for this. Deena is telling her cousin Mark about the 'horrific' housing prices one has to pay where she lives, a topic occasioned by prior talk about the upcoming marriage of her daughter. Dwayne is Deena's husband.

(4) [Holt: M88:2:4:11]

```
14   Dee:    .p.t.hhh Uh:: but quite honestly the prices that 'ey've
15           'ad to- 'ave to pay up here is absolutely 'orrifi:c you=
16           =kno:[w,
17   Mar:         [Yerah,h So I gather I mean they're .hhhh they're
18           they're fantastic aren't[they  n o : w,]
19   Dee:                            [That's ri:ght,] they're taw-
20           they're payin a hundred 'n ten Mark[
21   Mar:                                        [.tlok↑awhhhhhh,hhh
22           (.) gee:: 'ow do they do it is it- you   sure that's not
23           the telephone ↓number Dee[na         [.hhh
24   Dee:                             [ No: dea [r but it makes you
25       →   cringe, I mean Dwayne 'n I said if we were startin' off
26       →   again today up here we'd u-we: u-wu(.) we'd never get=
```

[13] This kind of prosodic formatting thus stands in marked contrast to that typically found in narrative reported speech, where the quoted material is often set off by a pause or other prosodic break (Holt, 1996; Klewitz and Couper-Kuhlen, 1999).
[14] The following clause 'so I didn't ca:ll' is not clearly separated prosodically from the quotative marker + quote, reflecting the fluid boundary between the end of the quote and the return to the here-and-now.

```
27              → =a↑mor[tgage](would w e )   ]
28   Mar:  →          [ N O]we'd never get]sta:rted would we- no:,
29   Dee:  → I mean with our two even with our two um:n wages
30            →together there's no way Dwayne 'n I could start off
31            → a↑gai↓:n.
32   Mar:  → No.
33            (0.3)
34   Mar:  → No,[.h h h h [h h h h h h h
```

In this fragment Deena informs Mark specifically about the price
of the house which her daughter and future son-in-law have just
purchased: 'they're payin' a hundred 'n ten Mark' (line 20). Mark
registers the information with mock disbelief: 'gee:: 'ow do they
do it is it- you ↑sure that's not the telephone ↓number Deena' (lines
22–23). Yet Mark's subtle attempt at humour is passed over by
Deena in the next turn: ' No: dear'. Her response expands instead on
the exorbitant prices for housing: 'it makes you cringe' (lines 24–25),
now reformulated with a self-quotation: 'I mean Dwayne 'n I said if
we were startin' off again today up here we'd u-we: u-wu (.) we'd
never get a ↑mortgage (would we)' (lines 25–27).

Despite some disfluency partway through, Deena's quotation
comes off as a single turn-constructional unit.[15] Mark responds in
recognitional overlap with an agreeing 'NO we'd never get sta:rted
would we- no:' (line 28), whereupon Deena reformulates her prior
turn with 'I mean with our two even with our two um:n wages
together there's no way Dwayne 'n I could start off a↑gai↓:n'
(lines 29–31). With this revised formulation Deena reasserts and
amplifies her estimation of the housing prices: *although* both she
and Mark work, *still* they could not afford a mortgage. Yet Deena's
second version is not hearable as an extension of the prior quotation, i.e. as something more which she and Dwayne said to
each other on that prior occasion, but rather as a reformulation
(Heritage and Watson, 1979, 1980) of what was said then, now
addressed to Mark in the *hic-et-nunc*.[16]

---

[15] Once again the final object 'would we' has an ambiguous status: it could
be taken as part of the quotation, or it could be a turn completer in post-
possible completion position (Schegloff, 1996c: 91f) addressed to Mark.

[16] Notice that the person reference in the revised version is re-done not
with 'we' but with 'Dwayne and I', an indication of the change in
footing.

Not only is it an observed regularity that reported speech and thought used in non-narrative contexts is maximally one TCU long; this is also a principle to which participants can be shown to orient. Speakers, for instance, regularly reintroduce a quotative marker when the material they are quoting is longer than one unit. This can be seen in the following excerpt, from a later part of Deena and Mark's conversation:

```
(5) [Holt 5/88:2:4:21]
20   Dee:   And eh the other thing Mark if they haven't got a hou:se?
21          (0.8) then there's no way we would be lavi[shing out on=
22   Mar:                                            [.t
23   Dee:   =a ↑wedding ↓for them we'd (.) you kno  [w we would have a=
24   Mar:                                           [No:.
25   Dee:   =very very quiet wedding? .hhh A:nd th[ey would have ) ]=
26   Mar:                                         [then every penny]=
27   Mar:   =[in the ↑hou:se.]
28   Dee:   =[(t h e   money)]and they would have the money [(    )
29   Mar:               [.h h h : h h : h h h h   [hOtherwise
30          it's a sheer waste'v money i'n'it rea[lly,
31   Dee:                                  [Of↑course it is.
32   Dee: →It's no good 'avin' swank- as I- I as I said you know
33        →there['s no point in having a big .hhh (fancy) wedding=
34   Mar:        [.knff
35   Dee:   =eh- an' you goin' off to live in two roo↓:ms
36   Mar:   hhNo:.
37   Dee: →I sai[d no there's js no p]oint at all 'n a' course (0.6)
38   Mar:       [ 'T's pointless.    ]
```

Still talking about her daughter and future son-in-law, Deena now presents the fact that they already have a house as justification for her and her husband 'lavishing out on a ↑wedding ↓for them' (lines 21–22). ('Lavishing' is a formulation from prior talk, where there was explicit detailing of the costs Deena and her husband are incurring in conjunction with the marriage.) Were it not the case that they already had a place to live, Deena claims, 'we would have a very very quiet wedding? .hhh A:nd' (lines 23–25). Mark now co-completes her suspended unit with:'then every penny in the ↑hou:se' (lines 26–27), following which Deena recycles her own (overlapped) completion 'A:nd they would have (the money)' (lines 25 and 28).

In response to this Mark produces a summary assessment concerning weddings in general: 'hOtherwise it's a sheer waste'v money i'n'it really' (lines 29–30), a turn built to initiate sequence and topic closure. Yet Deena uses her next turn as an opportunity to expand the sequence instead. She first concurs adamantly 'Of ↑course it is' (line 31) and then continues, initially in her own words, 'It's no good 'avin' swank-' (line 32). However, this unit is broken off and repaired to be a quotation of something she said on an earlier occasion to her daughter: 'as I- I as I said you know there's no point in having a big .hhh (fancy) wedding eh- an' you goin' off to live in two roo↓:ms' (lines 32–35).

Following only minimal uptake by Mark, Deena now pursues a response to this by recycling part of the prior unit: 'there's js no point at all' (line 37). Although this utterance could be a *hic-et-nunc* reformulation of the prior quotation, as in (4),[17] it is hearable here as a continuation of what she said to her daughter on the earlier occasion due to the reuse of the introductory quotative marker 'I said' (line 37). The fact that speakers regularly repeat a quotative marker before successive utterances in reporting speech non-narratively provides evidence for the fact that they are orienting to the 'rule' of one quotative TCU but no more.[18]

Single-unit reported speech and thought fragments are handy objects for building TCUs. Yet significantly these TCUs rarely stand alone in a turn.[19] Rather they tend to be deployed as follow-ups to a prior TCU in the construction of a multi-unit turn.[20] The TCU

---

[17] Ceteris paribus this is not only a possibility but a strong likelihood, given its position following a response from Mark in the here-and-now.

[18] According to Holt (1996), a tendency to reintroduce a quotative marker for each reported TCU is also found with reported speech in narrative environments.

[19] The collection contains only one example of a stand-alone reported-speech TCU: 'Dwayne said (well) stormy courtship a good ending' (Holt 5/88:2:4:9) – in context a closure-implicative formulation of gist.

[20] There is, however, one case of a single-unit quotation in turn-initial position: 'I WAS JUST TELLING BU:D I WISH I'D GOTTEN MY: BEDS AT (.) SEA:RS' (NBIV:13:R:5). Here the quotative TCU serves to initiate a topic shift.

which immediately precedes a non-narrative quotative TCU is routinely a *frame* for it, projecting or retrospectively informing the subsequent quotation. Recall (2): 'I din' wanna ca:ll yuh cuz I thought well maybe the people were still there'r something'. Lottie's negative report about not wanting to call implies that she should have made an attempt to reach her sister, which in turn (weakly) projects an explanation for why she didn't (Ford, 2001). The subsequent self-quotation, not coincidentally introduced by 'because', provides a demonstration of what is to be taken as this account. And recall (3): 'I ed tell Bud my Go:d'. Emma's quote 'my Go:d' is parasitic for its understanding on the immediately prior TCU 'I edda turn the furnace u:p', itself an account for how she knows that it's been cold. Likewise, in (4), Deena's quotation of what she and her husband Dwayne said to each other about current housing prices is projected by, and serves as a demonstration of, her immediately prior assessment: 'it makes you cringe'.[21] And in (5), Deena's quotation to her daughter is informed by her prior agreement with Mark's assessment that 'it's a sheer waste'v money'. In each case a subsequent (self-)quotation is either projected by, or retrospectively made sense of, in relation to the preceding TCU(s). Such framing is necessitated by the fact that the report is demonstrative rather than descriptive; without a frame its interpretation would be opaque.

To summarise the discussion so far, reported speech and thought fragments comprising quotative marker and quotation are deployed, nexus-like, as devices for the construction of TCUs, which themselves are part of multi-unit turns. The material quoted is seldom longer than one TCU. In the rare case of a series of reported utterances or thoughts, each is introduced with its own introductory quotative marker. Barring this, a next utterance will be hearable, if related at all, as a reformulation of the quoted material in the *hic-et-nunc*. When used outside of story-telling, quotative TCUs rarely form single-unit turns. Instead they are

---

[21] Note that the projective force of 'it makes you cringe' comes in part from the fact that 'it' functions as a so-called 'prospective indexical' (Goodwin, 1996).

typically deployed as follow-ups to prior TCUs which frame them either by projecting or retrospectively informing them.

4.4 Sequential frames for quoting speech and thought

In a conversation-analytically informed approach to reported speech, the analysis does not stop at the TCU or turn. Instead, reported speech TCUs and turns must be seen as situated within a larger sequential context which motivates and frames them. In this section, we pursue the analysis of non-narrative quotation by asking what actions are likely to project or inform quotative TCUs outside story-telling.

4.4.1 Quoting speech and thought in the environment of assessments

In one large group of cases the TCU which serves as a frame for the quotation is an assessing action of one sort or another and the following TCU constitutes a demonstration of something said or thought which is to be taken as supporting this assessment. Consider (4) again in this respect. Deena's quotative TCU about housing prices follows up on her assessment 'it makes you cringe'. Deena's quote of what she and her husband Dwayne said to each other on an earlier occasion is designed to demonstrate the 'cringing' which she has invoked, as well as to reassert her assessment of the housing prices as 'horrific' subsequent to Mark's non-serious response. (Recall that he received her news with mock disbelief and an attempt at humour: 'you ↑sure that's not the telephone ↓number Deena'). It does so by invoking the counter-factual case of her and her husband 'starting off' again at the same time and place as her daughter and son-in-law: even with their double income a mortgage would be out of the question.

The speech fragment which Deena quotes is interpretable as an assessment of the same object (housing prices) on an earlier occasion. Such a quotation accomplishes two things: (i) it substantiates the current assessment by adding supportive detail – detail which provides a measure of just how horrific the prices are; and (ii) it authenticates the here-and-now evaluation by documenting that it is not just a contingent or ad hoc finding but is instead historically valid. Quoting an earlier (congruent) assessment of the object thus substantiates and authenticates its present assessment.

In (5) Deena's self-quotation is similarly framed. In agreeing with Mark's assessment of lavish weddings as 'a sheer waste'v <u>mo</u>ney' if the couple doesn't already have adequate housing, she quotes herself as telling her daughter 'there's n<u>o</u> point in having a b<u>i</u>g .hhh (fancy) wedding eh- an' you goin' off to live in two ro<u>o</u>↓:ms'. This quote details a dramatic contrast between a 'fancy' or 'swanky' wedding on the one hand and 'goin' off to live in two ro<u>o</u>: ms' on the other. The extremes provide a measure for how much of a waste of money an expensive wedding is if the couple doesn't already have proper housing; they end up living in cramped quarters. Yet Deena's quotative TCU does not proclaim concurrence with Mark's assessment as does her 'Of ↑c<u>ou</u>rse it is'. Instead it demonstrates it – with a quote which is a prior congruent assessment of the same assessable. This provides dramatic detail (substantiation) and evidence of its historical veridicality (authenticity).[22]

On other occasions, quotative TCUs are used to build assessing turns which are first assessments mobilized in the service of, for example, complimenting, self-deprecating, etc. (Pomerantz, 1978). For instance, in another excerpt from Edna and Margy's conversation, Margy has just announced that her mother will soon be visiting her together with an old friend. Edna receipts this news, somewhat ironically (Clift, 1999), with the remark 'Open House at the Fridays' (recall that Margy's last name is 'Friday'):

(6) [NBVII:Power Tools:3]
```
4   Mar:   So she's gunnuh come down.u-I:- I don'kno:w how long
5          she'll be 'uhere.[.hh
6   Edn:              [whhh-hhh=
7   Mar:   =B'[t uh
8   Edn:      [n-open House et the Fri[days. ] .hhhhhhhh]=
```

---

[22] See also Clark and Gerrig (1990) and Holt (1996), who make similar points for reported speech in general.

```
 9   Mar:                                    [hhhhh ] hhih-hhih]=
10   Mar:   =[.hhh
11   Edn:   =[Ma:rgy I- I: mar[vel ]atche rilly.eh you fascinate me,=
12   Mar:                   [hhh]
13   Mar:   =hh=
14   Edn:   =I[ve never ]seen a ga:l li[:ke you. ]
15   Mar:    [hOh(h)o]              [°E(h)edn]a, #: : :[↑ah]
16   Edn:                                      [I    ] mean it.
17   Mar:   ((f)) °n No[: no: ((n))no.   ]
18   Edn :             [.hh You do evry]thing so beautif'lly end yer table
19     →  wz so byoo-I told Bud I said ↑honestly. .hhhhh ih wz jis:t
20     →  deli:ghtful t'come down there that day en mee[t these]
21   Mar:                                              [W e :ll]
22             (.)
23   Edn: →  [ga:ls] 'n: ]
24   Mar:   [ I :.] jist  ] wz so:- tickled thetchu di:d,B'[t uh    ] .hh=
25   Edn:                                              [°Mmm]
26   Mar:   =I like tuh do that stu:ff en u-[I he- ]=
27   Edn:                                   [°Ya h]=
```

Prior to the fragment in question, Edna has been thanking Margy for a luncheon at which she was a guest. When Margy now announces the impending visit of her mother and a friend for an unlimited amount of time (lines 4–5), Edna professes admiration: 'Ma:rgy I- I: marvel atche rilly.eh you fascinate me' (line 11). And, in the absence of an immediate response (line 13), she continues with: 'I've never seen a ga:l li:ke you' (line 14). Margy, concurrently with the latter unit, now produces sotto-voce objections: 'Oh', 'Edna' and 'No, no', the latter in falsetto (lines 15 and 17). Yet Edna persists with her compliments, reverting to the luncheon: 'You do everything so beautif'lly and your table wz so byoo-' (lines 18–19). The projected evaluative 'beautiful' is broken off, however, and Edna's turn resumed with a self-quotation: 'I told Bud I said ↑honestly. .hhhhh ih wz jis:t deli:ghtful t'come down there that day en meet these ga:ls 'n' (lines 19–23).[23]

---

[23] Note once again the ambiguous status of 'and' in post-possible completion position. Is it a continuation of Edna's quote or of Edna's *hic-et-nunc* turn?

The quotation of what Edna said to Bud about the luncheon on an earlier occasion – as with other cases of self-quotation in the service of assessing – documents Edna's positive evaluation of the luncheon by way of demonstration. What is demonstrated is the degree of appreciation: the luncheon was memorable enough for Edna to tell her husband about it and to use the descriptor 'delightful' in doing so. In addition, the demonstration includes a detail arguably 'touched off' by prior talk about Margy's Open House, namely that she had 'these ga:ls' at the luncheon as well. This detail retrospectively links talk about the luncheon to the ongoing topic of people visiting Margy's house.

On occasion speakers substantiate and authenticate assessments by quoting a prior evaluation of the assessable by a third party, as in the following extract from another one of Emma and Lottie's phone calls at Newport Beach:

(7) [NBIII:4:R:1]
```
1   Lot:      ...afte[rnoon] yihknow when ih when it isn'so ho:t.
2   Emm:            [ Yea:]h.
3   Emm:      YE : : :s I would tu- It's yis been beautiful though oh
4        →    [it et's:] Bud] seh  its so smoggy uptown it's js terrible=
5   Lot:      [Oh hadn'] it?]  ( )
6   Emm: →    ='n Don came down this morning'e siz it's jis terrible'e
7        →    siz God it's beautiful down here
8   Lot:      Ye::ah.
```

This fragment occurs at the very beginning of the recording and can be presumed to come early in the telephone conversation. In it we hear Lottie referring to the weather as a potential complainable: 'so ho:t' (line 1). Emma responds to this with an assessment of the weather as 'beautiful though' (line 3), comparing it to the terrible smog uptown. The introduction of the weather uptown enhances Emma's appreciation of the weather at the beach. To warrant her evaluation of the weather uptown, she invokes her husband Bud as a witness: 'Bud seh it's so smoggy uptown it's js terrible' (line 4). The smog is thus Bud's experience, and 'terrible' is his choice of descriptor. Yet neither she nor Bud can contrast the weather at the two locations directly. This is where Don comes in. Having been in both places, he is a 'good source' (Pomerantz 1984b: 625) and can provide the clinching testimony: ''e siz it's jis terrible'e siz God it's beautiful down here' (lines 6–7).[24] By quoting a congruent evaluation of the assessable by a third party, Emma can authenticate her assessment, showing it to be warranted not just by her own testimony – under the circumstances this could come off as overly confrontational given the fact that Lottie has just complained about the weather – but by way of the testimony of an independent and objective witness.

In sum, non-narrative quotations are used to substantiate and authenticate assessments. They do this by introducing a congruent evaluation of the same assessable on a prior occasion which is re-enacted to demonstrate the here-and-now assessment and is to be taken as supporting and/or strengthening it.

4.4.2 Quoting speech and thought in the environment of accounts

In a second group the quotative TCUs follow up on units which report dispreferred, disaffiliative or otherwise accountable actions – or implement such actions themselves. The quotation provides a demonstration of something said or thought which is to be taken as explaining why some dispreferred/disaffiliative/accountable action has been taken or not taken. To see this, consider extract (2) once again, presented here in abbreviated form:

(2) (abbreviated)

```
34   Emm:    ↑WELL MAYBE AH'LL SEE YUH NEXT ↓week.
35   Lot:    hh hhuh-hu[h↓h]uh huh:    ]huh↓]
36   Emm:              [e h ]HAH HAH]   TI:]ME goes o:n:,
37   Lot:  → I: uh I wz ou:t yesterday en I din' wanna ca:ll yuh cuz I
38        → thought well maybe the people were still there'r something
39           so I didn' ca:ll.
40   Emm:    eeYah,
```

---

[24] Notice the repeat of the quotative marker 'he says' in line 7, indicating that the following 'God it's beautiful down here' is Don's estimation, not Emma's.

Recall that in the course of explaining why she hasn't contacted her sister earlier, Lottie finds herself reporting the potentially disaffiliative action of not having wanted to call Emma the day before. In the following TCU she quotes her thoughts at that moment in time when she could have been expected to call: 'I thought well maybe the people were still there'r something' (lines 37–38). These thoughts reveal that Lottie had a reason for not calling. In other words she didn't simply *neglect* to call; instead, her not calling was a *reasoned* action warranted by a consideration of the circumstances at the time. Lottie's thoughts portray her as showing not disregard for others, but thoughtfulness instead – she didn't want to bother the guests in Emma's apartment. Quoting these thoughts here transform Lottie's not calling her sister into an act of consideration towards a third party, Emma's guests.

Externalising the interior thought processes which accompany an action or lack of it can reveal hidden intentions, concerns and considerations which extenuate the action or its absence. Furthermore, quoting concomitant thought processes implies that they motivate the action; the action or its absence is thereby transformed into the outcome of a deliberate and rational decision.[25] At the same time, direct quotation of one's thoughts on a prior occasion permits the introduction of strategic detail (e.g. the guests at Emma's house), which can be used to cast a more favourable light on the speaker's character.

A speaker's self-quotation may also be used to justify a past action (or lack of it) which is potentially disaffiliative with respect to a third party. This is the case in the following excerpt from Deena and Mark's telephone call:

---

[25] Cf. Golato (2002), who describes the use of self-quotation in German conversation for rendering past decisions.

(8) [Holt 5/88:2:4:3]

```
20   Dee :                    [Yea:h (.) right. Anyway it's lovely to
21        →   hear from you How- By the way .hhhh Mark now I wuh-
22        →   will: say. I didn't put your mother (.) o:n becuz I
23        →   wasn't sure I mean okay. she should come, but I thought
24        →   .hhh you 'n Leslie are gonna 'av a 'ell'v a day if
25        →   you've gotta cart her abou[t.
26   Mar:                                [.t.hhh iYeah I don't know
27            whether she'd really be A Capable no:w,
28            (.)
```

Prior to this fragment, Deena has been telling Mark about arrangements for her daughter's upcoming wedding. She has just announced that 'only' Mark and his wife Leslie have been invited to the wedding – in other words, not their children, who will not be available for the occasion. In the present excerpt Deena now initiates a move introduced as ancillary – 'By the way' (line 21) – and flagged as undertaken with some reluctance – 'I wuh- will: say' (lines 21–22); she announces that Mark's mother has also not been invited: 'I didn't put your mother (.) o:n' (referring to the list of invitees). As in (2), this is a negative report of an event which didn't occur, and in the case at hand it implies an admission that Deena might have been *expected* to include Mark's mother – an implication borne out by subsequent talk. Following a brief but aborted account of why she didn't include Mark's mother, 'becuz I wasn't sure' (lines 22–23), Deena temporarily reverses position and admits that she should be invited: 'I mean okay. she should come' (line 23). But she continues with a report of her thoughts at the time which led her to decide not to invite Mark's mother.

The ensuing explanation is a demonstration of Deena's reasoning:[26] 'I thought .hhh you 'n Leslie are gonna 'av a 'ell'v a day if you've gotta cart her about' (lines 23–25).[27] As in (2) the quoted

---

[26] Consequently, it contrasts with Deena's earlier aborted account, 'I wasn't sure', which was a description.

[27] Notice that this is not *exactly* the way Deena's thoughts are likely to have run: had they been verbalised at the time, she would presumably have used 'Mark' instead of 'you'. The deictic shift here is indicative of the change in footing associated with the recontextualisation of Deena's thinking.

thought reveals that there was a rational consideration which spoke against taking the expected action. This is now used to retrospectively warrant not taking it. Unlike (2), however, Deena's thought in (8) does not document her concern for some third party (cf. Emma's guests) but instead for her interlocutor, Mark. Not inviting Mark's mother is presented as showing consideration for Mark and his wife's wellbeing. This is accomplished in part through the way she words the quoted material: Deena not only shifts the appropriate referring forms from 'Mark' to 'you' (See fn. 27), but she also subtly aligns with Mark's putative position, so that caring for his mother on the wedding day becomes 'carting <u>her</u> about' and is predicted to mean 'a hell of a day' for him and his wife.[28] The quotative TCU thus allows a demonstration of something which: (a) extenuates the lack of action by revealing its rational basis; and (b) casts a more positive light on its apparent disaffiliation by revealing a hidden concern for the interlocutor's wellbeing.

Quite regularly it is a speaker's *thinking* (rather than their speech) which is quoted in conjunction with accounting for dispreferred or disaffiliative actions. The thoughts are construed as ones which occurred at the moment in time when an expected or otherwise accountable action should have taken place (but didn't). Thus the displayed thinking is implied to motivate the action or lack of it, rendering it a conscious decision. In fragments (1) and (8) it is *past* actions which are portrayed as having been undertaken rationally and deliberately at the time. On occasion, however, the quoted thought can be used to imply an account for a disaffiliative action which is part of the ongoing conversational sequence.[29] To see this, consider the following extract from a telephone call between Emma and her friend Nancy, in which Emma has been telling Nancy about

[28] In the event Mark's reply passes over – uncommented – this dimension of Deena's quotation and does not reciprocate its proposed alignment. Instead Mark engages in next turn with the original question – should his mother be invited or not – subtly shifting focus from his own pleasure or lack of it to whether she would be physically up to the strain.

[29] See Heritage (1988) for a cogent description of the two kinds of accounting.

how she has to clean her apartment because new guests are arriving the following weekend:

(9) [NBII:2:R:14]

```
23   Emm:    Bu:t oh God the ↑windows uhr dir::ty en [ahh
24   Nan:                                            [↑eh heh-heh-heh-
25           °h[eh°
26   Emm:    [I don'know I hate tuh clea:n
27   Nan:    °I do too:.°
28           (.)
29   Emm:    Ghod I hate tih cl- ah seems like ALL I'M DOIN is
30           .hhh[hhhh]h pickin up sump'n er throwin sum[p' n ]
31   Nan:        [Yah, ]                                [°M-h]m,°=
32   Emm:    =e: : : ↑°all ni° I guess we all are that way °arn't we°?
33           (.)
34   Nan:    .pk.hhh We:ll course I:'ve jst gotten disintrested becu:z
35     →     yihknow I sit he[re'n I think,
36   Emm:                    [(Ya:h,)
37   Nan:  → uW'l: wh- what ↓fo:r.h=
38   Emm:    =Ye[ah,
39   Nan:       [Yihknow, w't'm I doing it fo:r, I don't (.) give a
40           da:mn (0.2) so wh(h)y in the Sa-am Hill e[m I(w)]
41   Emm:                                            [°Well° ] yih
42           af[tih do it fe]r yer own pride'n jo[ : y,
43   Nan:      [w a s t i n g]                    [↑↑Wooh, .h-.hhhhhah
44           [(It's the only rintris)]
45   Emm:    [Yih can't live in f i :]lth you woul[dn' li:ke tha:t    ]
46   Nan:                                         [Wul of ↑↑cou:rse] not.
47           (.)
48   Nan:    'v cou:rse that's the only reason I ever do anything tuh
49           clean et a:ll.
50   Emm:    °Ya:h.°
```

Following a brief interlude not shown here, Emma reverts in line 23 to the topic of cleaning her apartment, breaking out into an exclamation of how she hates to clean (line 26). Nancy agrees but in a rather detached fashion (line 27). The fact that her agreement is not hearably upgraded may account for why Emma now begins to recycle her exclamation 'Ghod I hate tih cl-' and then expands it with 'ah seems like ALL I'M D<u>OI</u>N is .hhh hhhhh p<u>i</u>ckin up sump'n er throw<u>in</u> sump' n' (lines 29–30).

As Nancy's (concurrently produced) responses are once again only minimal (line 31), Emma now pursues more substantial uptake by producing an assessment about women and cleaning in general: 'I guess we <u>all</u> <u>a</u>re that way °<u>a</u>rn't we°?' (line 32). Although this turn is built to be easy to agree with, Nancy actually delays in next turn, producing first an in-breath, then a filler 'W<u>e</u>:ll course', and finally the non-committal '<u>I</u>:'ve just gotten disin-trested' (line 34). Her response is thus clearly dispreferred. She then proceeds to explain her disinterest by quoting her thoughts on those occasions when she should be cleaning: 'I sit here'n I think, u<u>W</u>'l: wh- wh<u>a</u>t ↓f<u>o</u>:r' (lines 35 and 37).[30] Since Nancy's thinking implies that there are no good reasons for why one should clean, the quotation can be taken to serve as an account for her disinterest in cleaning and thus for her dispreferred response to Emma's prior turn.

Note, incidentally, that from line 39 onwards Nancy's next utterances – '<u>w</u>'t'm I doing it f<u>o</u>:r', '<u>I</u> don't (.) g<u>i</u>ve a d<u>a</u>:mn (0.2) so <u>wh</u>(h)y in the Sa-am Hill em I (w)...wasting' (lines 39–40) – are ambiguous with respect to their status as *hic-et-nunc* speech or reported thought. Because Nancy's thinking is presented as habitual ('I sit here'n I think' in line 35), these questions could as well be asked in the here-and-now as on single (past) cleaning occasions. In fact, Emma's response shows that she treats them as part of the *hic-et-nunc*; she answers the question of why one cleans, '°Well° yih <u>a</u>ftih d<u>o</u> it fer yer own pride'n jo:y' (lines 41–42) and 'Yih <u>can</u>'t live in f<u>i</u>:lth <u>y</u>ou wouldn' l<u>i</u>:ke th<u>a</u>:t' (line 45).

Habitual thoughts are particularly useful when speakers are accounting for *hic-et-nunc* actions or lack of them which are recurrent. In the following fragment from the closing of Emma and

---

[30] Despite the fact that the quotative marker and the quoted phrase here are in two different lines of transcript, they are produced in one go, with no intervening pause or stretching.

Lottie's conversation, for instance, Emma provides an account for why she will be unable to stay down at the beach as her sister has been encouraging her to do:

(10) [NBIV:1:R:3]

```
  1    Emm:    *ih area .hhh (.) ↑WELL HONEY GOOD LUCK TO YU:?
  2            (.)
  3    Emm:    [a : n d ] uh
  4    Lot:    [°Yi-ah°] Ah wish you were gunnuh STA[:Y ,
  5    Emm:                                         [ha- I: do too:*:.
  6            (.)
  7    Emm: →  But I think oh I've g*ot so damn much t*ih ↓*do. I really
  8            *I ↓g*otta g*et home: fer .hhh ↑Ah may stay n*ext ↓w*eek.
  9    Lot:    ↑Oka:y,
 10    Emm:    .hhh[h
 11    Lot:        [°U[h huh,°]
 12    Emm:          [A : n  ] d uh .h-.hh↑Ah'll: see yih ↓Fri:d*ee
 13            (0.2)
 14    Lot:    Oka: :y,
```

In line 7 Emma quotes herself as thinking 'oh I've g*ot so damn much t*ih ↓*do'. She then reformulates this in the here-and-now as 'I really *I ↓g*otta g*et home:' – hearably providing a reason for not staying down at the beach. Yet Emma's quoted thought is not one which took place specifically on the occasion of her deciding to return home that weekend, but rather one which she habitually has. It can consequently serve as a generic warrant for her leaving the beach and going home on multiple (past, present and future) occasions. In the case of habitual thought, the grounds for an action or lack of it are made to appear not as a one-off decision but as a recurrent consideration. Like past thoughts on single occasions, however, quotations of habitual thought lend themselves well to exclamations, expletives – cf. 'so damn much' in line 7 of (10) – and other expressive elements which demonstrate rather than describe an inner state implied to motivate a dispreferred or otherwise accountable action.

Although the quotative marker 'I thought' is routinely used to introduce quoted thoughts in accounting, note that it is not per se a marker of direct reported speech. Under the appropriate circumstances, it can also introduce the description of a (past) thought process. The distinction between description and demonstration is a very fine one, often dependent on the presence (or absence) of subtle prosodic and paralinguistic effects. This is the case in the next fragment, which contains both a demonstrative and a descriptive 'I thought'.

(11) [NBII:1:R:3]

```
42   Emm:    Well I jis tried tih getta ↑ca:ll through ah wz gunnuh
43           call Nancy: uh Ja:mes she's (0.2) been comin do:wn here
44           once in awhi:le en I: can't get her number so I thou:ght
45           (0.2) .hh ah'll call you ah didn'know whether: (.) uhb
46           uh wz my ↑telephone wz funny. I couldn't uh: .hh I
47           gotta busy si:gn all th'ti:me. So,
48           (0.2)
49   Lot:    From he:r?
50   Emm:    .hh ng-Uh tried tuh get her number then it's: uh busy.
51           (.)
1    Emm:    E[n I hang up'n then it's busy when I pick it u:p.=
2    Lot:     [M-
3    Emm:    =Ah don'know whether'r phone's bih- (.) di:s-c'nnected'r
4            not they'd tell me I'm su:re.
5            (0.7)
6    Emm:    So I trie:d you I thought well now maybe I c'n get
7            Lottie a:nd uh (0.3) by gosh I go↑: tchu.
8            (0.2)
9    Lot:    Y[e : ]ah
10   Emm:     [B't]
11           (.)
```

```
12  Lot:      eh [heh] Yeah yo(h)u di:d.
13  Emm:         [So:]
14  Lot:      [ehhh
15  Emm:      [Y(h)EAH [heh heh heh ]
16  Lot:              [huh huh huh] hu- [uh hu:h
17  Emm:                               [.hhhh
18  Emm: →   So:: anywayay .hh I: thou:ght she always likes tuh go do
19       →   somethi:ng °en: I thought may'we c'd go [↓sh:o:ppin'° =
20  Lot:                                             [wgl
21  Emm:     =°e[r do sump'n,°
22  Lot:         [ml
23  Lot:      u-hOh ye:ah. Gee the May Comp'ny er sure havin a big
24             sale,
25  Emm:      °Are the:y?°
26            (0.2)
27  Lot:      .hh Ye:ah:. Yihknow ther forty fifth annavers'ry.
28  Emm:      °Yeh ah'd like tih get s'm beds- (.) new bedspreads°
```

At the beginning of this fragment Emma is recounting – in story form – how she came to call her sister: she tried to a call her friend Nancy (lines 42–43) but she couldn't get through (line 44), so she decided to call Lottie to see whether her phone was still working (lines 45–46). The latter event is presented in the form of a self-quotation of what Emma thought: 'ah'll call you', recycled again in lines 6–7 as 'well now maybe I c'n get Lottie'. These are examples of the use of direct reported speech within a narrative framework.

Yet interestingly, once the chronological story of Emma calling Lottie is completed at line 7 with 'a:nd uh by gosh I go↑:tchu', Emma reverts to why she wanted to call her friend Nancy in the first place. She now quotes herself – outside of the narrative frame-work – as thinking 'she always likes tuh go do somethi:ng', a demonstration of what is to be taken as motivating her attempt to contact Nancy. Although in syntactic terms it is difficult to decide whether this quotation is direct or indirect, its prosodic delivery marks it as direct. There is a pitch reset on 'she' (see Figure 4.1) and the delivery is in general lively – both features which imply the animation of a different 'voice'.

Yet Emma now continues with: '°°en: I thought may'we c'd go ↓sh:o:ppin'° °er do sump'n°'. Significantly, this thought – despite

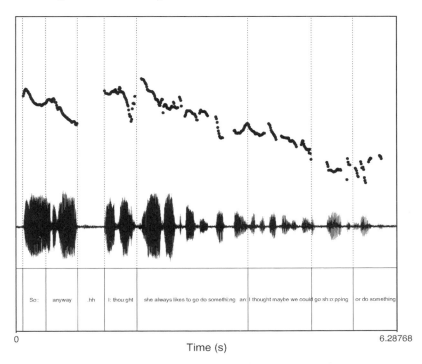

Figure 4.1. An acoustic analysis of the delivery of lines 18–19 and 21 in example (11)[31]

the introductory quotative marker – is not re-enacted in Emma's past voice but is reported indirectly in the here-and-now. This is clear from its unanimated delivery, without pitch reset and with rapidly decreasing pitch and loudness (see Figure 4.1). In addition, the word '↓sh:o:ppin" has a distinctive stylised pitch contour (a drop of a major third from 'go' to a steady tone held on the stretched syllables of '↓sh:o:ppin"), which tags it as addressed to Lottie.[32] And in fact Lottie orients to this by picking up the

---

[31] Figure 4.1 shows an acoustic analysis of lines 18–19 in (11) carried out with the software program Praat. At the top it represents the pitch curve and in the middle the air-pressure waveform (including a rough indication of amplitude), both aligned as indicated with the words at the bottom.

[32] The effect of the prosodic stylisation here is to convey roughly 'This is routine, you know'; cf. Couper-Kuhlen (2003).

shopping theme in next turn and announcing to Emma that the May Company is having a big sale.

Thus, in this telling sequence Emma first demonstrates her past thinking and then describes it as a past thought. Both her direct and indirect reporting strategies are, however, mobilised in warranting a past action or its attempt (calling Nancy), which – because it is implicated in Emma's present call to her sister to check her phone connection – may be felt to require special justification.

In sum, quoting one's own thoughts (or on occasion those of a third party[33]) can be a means to warrant some accountable action, or the report of some accountable action or lack of it. The former calls for justification because of its dispreferred or disaffiliative potential, the latter because negative reports of not doing something amount to admissions and thus necessitate defences. Accounts which involve quoting thoughts are useful because they reveal the accountable action to have been a deliberate decision, undertaken (or not) for a reason. Moreover, because quoted thoughts are imported from another situation, they enhance the authenticity of the reasons provided.[34] If they are past thoughts, they bear the weight of history; if habitual thoughts, the weight of habituality. Quoted thoughts can, and often do, incorporate expressive displays of affect, hallmarking the inner state which accompanies or accompanied the taking of a decision. In conjunction with this, they can reveal unspoken intentions and hidden concern for others which mitigate the severity of the apparent transgression.

4.5 Sequential follow-ups to quoting speech and thought

The final set of questions to be asked concerning reported speech in non-narrative environments relates to its sequential follow-up.

---

[33] For an example of a third-party quote used in accounting, consider NBII:4:R:4, where Nancy asks Emma (with reference to Bud), 'Oh he wasn't going- you didn't go fishing-', to which Emma replies, invoking her doctor, 'Oh I CAN'T go ↑Oh:: God I can't go in a boat for a long time he says ↑no boating or no::, (0.2) GO:LF'.

[34] The use of quotation in accounting thus provides a specific instance of what has been described in the literature more generally as the demonstrative/evidential function of reported speech (Clark and Gerrig, 1990; Holt, 1996; Clift, this volume).

How does the quoting speaker make the transition from a deicti-
cally displaced situation back to the here-and-now? How does his
or her recipient respond to the quotative TCU or turn?

Quotations outside of narration, it will be recalled, are clearly
signalled by quotative markers and they often begin unmistak-
ably with discourse markers such as 'well', 'oh' or 'hey'. Their
endings, however, tend to be fuzzy. As seen in numerous of the
examples above, a post-possible completion stance marker may
be appended which can be either part of the quoted speech or
part of the speaker's *hic-et-nunc* turn. Moreover, in the next TCU
of their turn, speakers often reformulate the quoted speech or
thought with 'their own words', i.e. in the present. Both these
observations suggest that the transition from a displaced deictic
field back to the here-and-now is a gradual one – indeed, that there
may be a benefit to be had from allowing the two worlds to merge
imperceptibly.

When we now examine how interlocutors respond to a quotative TCU or the turn which contains it, we discover that the
merging of the two worlds carries over to next turn. In cases
where a reformulation ensues following the quote, this is perhaps
to be expected. In the following cases, for instance, the next speaker
produces a here-and-now response (shown with a double arrow) to
a prior *hic-et-nunc* reformulation of the quoted material (single
arrow):

(2)

```
37   Lot:      I: uh I wz ou:t yesterday en I din' wanna ca:ll yuh cuz I
38             thought well maybe the people were still there'r something
39             so I didn' ca:ll.
40   Emm:      eeYah,
41   Lot:  →   .t I din' know what time yih w'r gunnuh get do:wn so I wen
42             ou[t
43   Emm: →       [*Oh[:: ]  w e got-]
44   Lot:            [sh]o:ppin ye]s'°t[ay°
45   Emm: →                         [Yah we didn't git ↓down til abou:t
46         → (0.5) °oh° I °don't know,° (0.3) six uh'clo:ck b't oh::
```

(4)
24   Dee: [No: dea[r but it makes you
25   → cringe, I mean Dwayne 'n I said if we were startin' off
26   → again today up here we'd u-we: u-wu(.) we'd never get=
27   → =a↑mor[tgage](would w e)   ]
28   Mar: →   [N O]we'd never get]sta:rted would we- no:,
29   Dee: → I mean with our two even with our two um:n wages
30   →together there's no way Dwayne 'n I could start off
31   → a↑gai↓:n.
32   Mar: → No.
33   (0.3)
34   Mar: → No,[.h h h h [h h h h h h h

(9)
34   Nan: .pk.hhh We:ll course I:'ve jst gotten disintrested becu:z
35   → yihknow I sit he[re'n I think,
36   Emm: [(Ya:h,)
37   Nan: → uW'l: wh- what ↓fo:r.h=
38   Emm: =Ye[ah,
39   Nan: [Yihknow, w't'm I doing it fo:r, I don't (.) give a
40   da:mn (0.2) so wh(h)y in the Sa-am Hill e[m I(w)]
41   Emm: [°Well°] yih
42   af[tih do it fe]r yer own pride'n jo[: y,
43   Nan: [w a s t i ng]   [↑↑Wooh, .h-.hhhhhah
44   [(It's the only rintris)]
45   Emm: [Yih can't live in f i :]lth you woul[dn' li:ke tha:t   ]

(11)
18   Emm: → So:: anywayay .hh I: thou:ght she always likes tuh go do
19   → somethi:ng °en: I thought may'we c'd go [↓sh:o:ppin'° =
20   Lot: [wgl
21   Emm: =°e[r do sump'n,°
22   Lot: [ml
23   Lot: u-hOh ye:ah. Gee the May Comp'ny er sure havin a big
24   sale,

Next speakers may even co-opt wording from the prior reformulation to build their responses: in (3), Lottie's 'what time you were gonna <u>get down</u>' is picked up by Emma's 'we didn't <u>get down</u> till about six o'clock', and in (9) Nancy's 'what am I <u>doing it for</u>' is reprised by Emma's 'you're <u>doing it for</u> your own pride and joy'.

However, it is somewhat more surprising to find cases where recipients respond in the here-and-now (double arrow) to what is reported as said or thought on an earlier occasion (single arrow):

```
(4)
24    Dee:                          [No: dea[r but it makes you
25         →  cringe, I mean Dwayne 'n I said if we were startin' off
26         →  again today up here we'd u-we: u-wu(.) we'd never get=
27         →  =a↑mor[tgage](would w e )   ]
28    Mar:  →     [ N O]we'd never get]sta:rted would we- no:,

(6)
18    Edn:                    [.hhYou do evry]thing so beautif'lly end yer table
19         →  wz so byoo-I told Bud I said ↑honestly. .hhhhh ih wz jis:t
20         →  deli:ghtful t'come down there that day en mee[t these]
21    Mar:  →                                             [W e :ll]
22            (.)
23    Edn:  →  [ga:ls] 'n: ]
24    Mar:  →  [ I :.  ] jist] wz so:- tickled thetchu di:d,B'[t uh] .hh=

(8)
23    Dee:  →  wasn't sure I mean okay. she should come, but I thought
24         →  .hhh you 'n Leslie are gonna 'av a 'ell'v a day if
25         →  you've gotta cart her abou[t.
26    Mar:                              [.t.hhh iYeah I don't know
27            whether she'd really be A Capable no:w,
```

The single-arrowed quotations here are reporting speech and thought from *prior* occasions in the service of assessing and accounting, and yet they are treated by recipients as if they were assessing and accounting in the *present* situation. In (4), for instance, Mark agrees with Deena's quoted assessment 'if <u>we</u> were startin' off again today up here... we'd never get a ↑<u>mortgage</u>' as if it were being said now with reference to him: 'NO we'd never get <u>sta</u>:rted would we', reprising her (quoted) words 'startin' off...we'd never get' with his own 'we'd never get <u>sta</u>:rted'. In (6), Margy responds to Emma's quote '<u>ih</u> wz jis:t de<u>li</u>:ghtful t'come down there that day en <u>m</u>eet these ga<u>:</u>ls' as if it were a compliment being paid to her now, and she builds her response syntactically on its wording: 'we:ll I: <u>j</u>ist wz so<u>:</u>- tickled thetchu <u>di</u>:d' (i.e. come down here that day and meet those gals). And in (8) Mark responds to Deena's quoted account '<u>you</u> 'n Leslie are gonna 'av a ' <u>ell</u>'v a day if you've gotta cart <u>her</u> about' as if it were an explanation proffered in the present for not inviting his mother: 'iyeah I d<u>o</u>n't know whether she'd <u>re</u>ally be A C<u>a</u>pable no<u>:</u>w'.[35]

A further excerpt from Deena and Mark's conversation demonstrates just how thoroughly interwoven past quoting and present talk can become:

(12) [Holt 5/88:2:4:20]

```
16   Dee:      uhh:n You know it (0.3) it really really does mount
17      →      ↑u↓:p.[(   ) moment it (.) b't it- so far I said to=
18   Mar:           [eYea:h
19   Dee:  →  =Dwayne we'll leave that (0.3) I said we'll leave that
20      →      money in the Building Society (until [          )
21   Mar:  →                                    [£gnYeh til the
22      →      la:st minute 'at['s ri:ght£
23   Dee:                        [( )
24           (0.3)
25   Mar:      .hh:hh[hhh
26   Dee:          [an' leave it there until it's you know we have
27           (0.3) [vir-virtually got to pay it. ↓Bu[t
28                 [grrk                              [
29   Mar:                                    [Ye:s
30           (1.4)
```

In prior talk Deena has announced to Mark that she and her husband have already paid out a large sum of money for deposits in conjunction with the upcoming wedding of their daughter. In line 16 she summarises the situation with the assessment 'it <u>re</u>ally really does mount ↑u↓:p'. She now begins to quote what she said to Dwayne on an earlier occasion by way of substantiating how much money is involved: 'we'll <u>le</u>ave that money in the Bu<u>i</u>lding Society

---

[35] 'Capable' is possibly a self-repair of 'A' (= *able*).

(until...)' (lines 19–20). In other words, it is such a sum that the money is more profitably kept in a savings account where it will earn interest. Mark can now anticipate the rest of Deena's quotation and he proceeds to co-complete her TCU: 'Yeh til the la:st minute 'at's ri:ght' (lines 21–22). The fact that Mark co-completes Deena's quotation *as if* it were part of the here-and-now is a telling indication of how easily a past speech or thought event, when quoted directly, can become part of the warp and weft of present talk.

Importing words from a displaced situation as fragments of direct reported speech and thought outside of narration can produce a curious blend of here and there in conversation. On the one hand, the quoted words are flagged via a quotative marker as belonging to another (displaced) deictic field, but on the other they are produced *as if* they were being said now – with all the prosodic and paralinguistic appurtenances of *hic-et-nunc* speech. Syntactically they often fade off into surrounding talk. In fact, this indeterminate status, being neither fully here nor there, can be of benefit to speakers, who can construe assessments and accounts as part of the past and thus veridical but at the same time render them 'negotiable' by reanimating them in the present.

Quoting speech and thought in the service of asssessing and accounting has a further advantage for speakers. It routinely expands the sequence, thereby leading to further negotiation and possibly to reversed speakership roles. To see this, consider (10) once again:

(10)

```
 1    Emm:     *ih area .hhh (.) ↑WELL HONEY GOOD LUCK TO YU:?
 2             (.)
 3    Emm:     [a : n d] uh
 4    Lot:     [°Yi-ah°] Ah wish you were gunnuh STA[:Y ,
 5    Emm:                                         [ha- I: do too:*:.
 6             (.)
 7    Emm: →   But I think oh I've g*ot so damn much t*ih ↓*do. I really
 8             *I ↓g*otta g*et home: fer .hhh ↑Ah may stay n*ext ↓w*eek.
 9    Lot:     ↑Oka:y,
10    Emm:     .hhh[h
11    Lot:         [°U[h huh,°]
12    Emm:            [A : n ] d uh .h-.hh ↑Ah'll: see yih ↓Fri:d*ee
13             (0.2)
14    Lot:     Oka::y,
```

When Lottie expresses her wish that Emma stay down at the
beach (line 4) and Emma joins in this wish, implicitly acknowledging that she won't be staying (line 5), Emma's subsequent quote of
her thoughts – providing an account for why she can't stay –
prolongs the sequence (line 7). Yet it is not only Emma's direct
quote here which contributes to sequence expansion, but also the
reformulation of her account for not staying in the here-and-now
and her weak promise '↑Ah may stay n*ext ↓w*eek' (line 8), which
Lottie acknowledges in next turn. So, whereas Emma went into
this sequence as a recipient – responding to Lottie's expression of a
wish – she emerges as an initiator of its expansion by producing
units which themselves require uptake from her interlocutor.
A quotative accounting TCU can facilitate such a reversal of speakership roles.

Something similar happens with quotative TCUs deployed in the
service of assessing. For instance:

(5)

20	Dee:	And eh the other thing Mark if they haven't got a hou:se?
21		(0.8) then there's no way we would be lavi[shing out on=
22	Mar:	[.t
23	Dee:	=a ↑wedding ↓for them we'd (.) you kno[w we would have
24	Mar:	[No:.
25	Dee:	=very very quiet wedding? .hhh A:nd th[ey would have)]=
26	Mar:	[then every penny]=
27	Mar:	=[in the ↑hou:se.]
28	Dee:	=[(t h e money)]and they would have the money[( )
29	Mar:	[.h h h : h h : h h h h[hOtherwise
30		it's a sheer waste'v money i'n'it rea[lly,
31	Dee:	[Of ↑course it is.
32	Dee:	→ It's no good 'avin' swank- as I- I as I said you know
33		→ there['s no point in having a big .hhh (fancy) wedding=
34	Mar:	[.knff
35	Dee:	→ =eh- an' you goin' off to live in two roo↓:ms
36	Mar:	hhNo:.
37	Dee:	→ I sai[d no there's js no p]oint at all 'n a' course (0.6)
38	Mar:	['T' s pointless.]

Recall that, prior to the quotative TCU in question, Mark
has made an attempt to take over speakership by co-completing
Deena's turn (lines 26–27) and he has produced a summary-assess-
ing turn arguably designed to initiate topic and sequence closing
(<u>Oth</u>erwise it's a sheer waste'v <u>mon</u>ey i'n'it <u>re</u>ally', lines 29–30).
Deena's 'Of ↑c<u>ou</u>rse it is' (line 31) would consequently be closure-
implicative if it were not expanded. Her expansion involves a
hic-et-nunc fomulation of a point in support of her opinion, broken
off midway in favour of a quotation demonstrating the point.
Quoting her prior assessment of the usefulness of lavish weddings
in comparison to proper housing allows a demonstration which
supports her evaluation – and at the same time secures her a
strategic position from which she can initiate further sequence-
and topic-expanding talk. Framed by the *hic-et-nunc* but aborted
evaluation 'It's n<u>o</u> good ' avin' a swank-' (line 32), her subsequent
quotation to her daughter becomes an evaluative object itself –
offered up for agreement (or disagreement) from her interlocutor.
Mark responds by agreeing in the here-and-now with '<u>No</u>:'
(line 36) and, again, in overlap with Deena's reprise, ''T's <u>point</u>less'
(line 38).

In fact, it is because next speakers treat non-narrative quotative
TCUs as assessing and accounting in the here-and-now that sequence expansion results and speakership roles are reversed.
Only minimal uptake would abruptly curtail the sequence. This
is what happens in the following excerpt, where Emma and
Lottie are talking about a foot fungus they have which affects the
toenails.

(13) [NB:IV:10:R:27]
22   Emm: [<u>Is</u>n' this]FUNNY <u>YOU</u>'N <u>I</u>: WOULD <u>HAVE</u> IT.h
23   (0.4)
24   Emm: Th<u>is</u> is re[e↑<u>di</u>cul]ous.]

```
25   Lot:              [E:VRY]BUDDY]'S GOT ih .hh Inna:t funny we were
26              in a p-uh:[↓:
27   Emm:              [Oh: God it's ↑terrible Lottie m:y ↑toenails .hehh
28              ther jis look so sick those big t:oenails it jis u-makes me:
29              sick. Yihknow ther diss (.) u-dea:d. (.) Evrything's dead I
30          →   d- I sat ou:t (.) tihday en I s'd my Go:d em I jis (.)
31          →   DY:ING it's: (.) like I'm ossi↓fied.
32   Lot:    →   NO I- ↑we w'r in: some [pla:ce uh don'know'f ih wz Bullock's=
33   Emm:                              [((sniff))
34   Lot:    =er somepla:ce (0.4) I ↑guess it w'z Bullock's. A:nd
35              somebuddy wz ta:lkin abaht ih a:n' ah: bet ther ↓were .hhh
36              TE:N PEOPLE arou:n'the:re, en they a:ll star'duh say w'l
37              they had the sa:me thing? en I kno:w like Doctor Compton
38              says iss fr'm the damn .p detergent.
39              (1.4)
40   Lot:    It RILLY I:[S.
```

Despite Emma's dramatic demonstration of her thinking earlier that day, 'my Go:d em I jis (.) DY:ING it's: (.) like I'm ossi↓fied' (lines 30–31), produced to substantiate her assessment that the fungus is '↑terrible', Lottie does not deal with her quotation in next turn as making a here-and-now assessment. She does not produce immediate and strong disagreement of the sort 'Oh don't be silly, of course you're not', which would be the preferred response to such a self-deprecatory assessment if it were delivered in the here-and-now (Pomerantz, 1984a). Instead she produces only a minimal 'NO' and resumes the story she began in line 25, discontinued when Emma intervenes.[36] In this case, then, a current speaker's deployment of a quotative TCU does not result in a reversal of speakership roles (Lottie remains primary speaker), precisely because next speaker declines to treat the quoted material as a *hic-et-nunc* action.

[36] Lottie's story is intended to back up her earlier claim that E:VRY BUDDY's GOT ih' (line 25), a mildly disagreeing reply to Emma's remark that it's 'funny' how just she and her sister have the fungus (line 22).

4.6 Conclusion

Importing speech or thought into conversation from a situation removed from the here-and-now is a resource which speakers can use to construct multi-unit turns at talk. Outside of story-telling the reported fragments are typically deployed: (a) as a follow-up TCU to an assessing action; or (b) as a follow-up TCU to a prior dispreferred, disaffiliative or otherwise accountable action, or a report thereof. In the first case the quotative TCU serves to demonstrate something said or thought on an earlier occasion which substantiates and authenticates the assessment by adding strategic detail and attesting to its historicity. In the second case the quotative TCU demonstrates something said or thought earlier which explains or justifies the action taken (or not taken) and reveals it to have been a reasoned act carried out on the basis of a deliberative decision.

At the same time reporting past or habitual speech and thought in a non-narrative context can be a way of proposing an assessment or account in the here-and-now. This merging of the two worlds is facilitated by the fact that non-narrative quoted material is often prosodically and paralinguistically expressive and fades off syntactically into following *hic-et-nunc* talk. Recipients can be observed to orient to the quoted material in next turn *as if* it were an assessment or account in the present. This leads to a prolongation of the sequence, which the quoter – by quoting – initiates. Re-enacted assessments and accounts are thus partly there and partly here. In a curious mixture of past and present, they present assessments and accounts as motivated by the past while at the same time opening up this past for renegotiation in the present.

5

Getting there first: non-narrative reported speech in interaction

Rebecca Clift

The sheer fact of doing quoting can be the expressing of a position.

(Sacks, 1992b: 309)

5.1 Introduction

Research on so-called 'direct reported speech' (henceforth simply 'reported speech') in interaction has hitherto overwhelmingly focused on the most common context for its occurrence, namely story-telling, whether in mundane talk (see, inter alia, the collection in Lucy, 1993 and Holt, 1996, 2000) or in various institutional contexts (e.g. Buttny, 1997; Holt, 1999; Clayman, this volume; Galatolo, this volume; Rae and Kerby, this volume; and Wooffitt, this volume). There are occasions in mundane talk, however, in which reported speech is not used in the service of a more extended story but, as in the following, is deployed fleetingly by a speaker in the course of an exchange with another (arrowed) (see also Couper-Kuhlen, this volume):

(1) [Rahman:B:2:JV(14):4]

```
1  Jenny:  They're [a lovely family now aren't [they.
2  Vera:          [°Mm:.°                      [They are: ye[s.
3  Jenny:                                                   [eeYe[s::,
4  Vera:                                                        [Yes,
```

An early version of this chapter was presented at the Department of Language and Linguistic Science, University of York, UK, in June 2003. My thanks to the audience there, who provided useful comments and observations. I am also very grateful to Elizabeth Holt for her helpful suggestions on the first draft. Any errors remain my responsibility.

```
5   Jenny: → Mm: All they need now is a little girl tih complete i:t.
6   Jenny:   [h e h  h e h ]
7   Vera:    [Well I said t]uh Jean how abou:t it so our Bill (0.2)
8   Vera:    laughingly said 'ey she'll havetuh ask me fir:st no:w.
9   Jenny:   h:ha[:ha:
10  Vera:        [huh huh-u huh-u [uh uh
11  Jenny:                        [ 'Eez 'ad enough 'as 'ee=
12  Jenny:   =heh [heh eh ih huh huh
13  Vera:         [Yea::h hih- Yea:h,
```

In (1), Jenny and Vera have been talking about Vera's son Bill, his wife
Jean, and their children. Vera's report of what she said to Jean at line 7,
and its response from Bill, neither launches an extended story-telling,
nor forms an element of an ongoing story. It is offered as a response to
an assessment from Jenny, 'All they need now is a little girl to complete
it', and in turn gets laughter from her, endorsed by Vera's own laughter
at line 10. Jenny's jocular inquiry at lines 11–12 subsequently provides
a wry commentary on what Vera has reported.

It is evident, then, that the interactional motivations for the
reported speech in such contexts cannot be understood by reference
to a larger interactional unit such as a story-telling. This chapter is a
preliminary investigation of such fleeting uses of reported speech in
an effort to establish what those interactional motivations might
be. An initial sketch of some of the similarities and differences in a
set of cases is followed by a more extended examination of both the
environments in which reported speech occurs – its position – and
the features which provide for its use in those environments – its
composition. In various ways, these particular uses of reported
speech will be seen to be a powerful resource in environments of
competitive assessment. Support for the analysis of this set of cases
is then provided in a comparison with another set, which are also
examples of reported speech but are formatted somewhat differently. One final example, which shows a speaker repairing from
one format to the other, underscores the central claim regarding the
deployment of reported speech.

5.2 An initial sketch

The following extracts show, in a similar manner to extract (1),
reported speech being introduced as a response to another's prior turn:

(2) (From Schegloff, 1997: 173) [MDE:MTRAC:60-1:2:1-2]
(Marsha, who lives in southern California, is separated from Tony, who
lives in northern California. They are discussing the travel arrangements
of their son Joey, who is travelling from mother to father. Joey has had
the top of his car stolen, and so, instead of driving from southern to
northern California, is flying. Tony broaches the issue of how Joey will
retrieve his car.)

```
35    Tony:     W't's 'e g'nna do go down en pick it up later? er
36              somethin like (    ) [well that's aw]:ful
37    Marsha:                      [H  i  s  friend ]
38    Marsha:   Yeh h[is friend Stee-    ]
39    Tony:          [That really makes ] me ma:d,
40              (0.2)
41    Marsha:   .hhh Oh it's disgusti[ng ez a matter a'f]a:ct.
42    Tony:                          [P o o r   J o e y,]
43    Marsha:→I- I, I told my ki:ds. who do this: down et the Drug
44              Coalition ah want th'to:p back.h {.hhhhhhhh/(1.0 )}
45              SEND OUT the WO:RD.hhh hnh
46              (0.2)
47    Tony:     Yeah.
48    Marsha:   .hhh Bu:t u-hu:ghh his friend Steve en Brian er driving
49              up. Right after:: (0.2) school is out.En then hi'll
50              drive do:wn here with the:m.
```

(3) [Holt:X-1-1-6:2]
(Lesley has just announced that her phone had been cut off for non-
payment of a bill, and that this had happened to several people in the area
in the last few days.)

```
53    Mum:    Oh: lo:ve.
54            (0.4)
55    Mum:    That's a nuisance isn't it.
56    Les:    Ye[s.
57    Mum:      [They're getting terrible.
58            (0.3)
59    Les:    We:l [l I- I ↑s a i d  ]
60    Mum:         [ I-I mean↑look what]
61            (0.2)
62    Les:→   I said to them. £↑This is British Telecom for you.(h)£=
```

```
63   Mum:    =Yes. .h An' ↑look what they cha:rge. They charge you
64           .h three pounds (just t' have) this blessed old thing
65           in your hou:se.
66           (0.5)
67   Les:    Yes.
```

Considered together, these three extracts, (1)–(3), appear to show participants engaged in very diverse business: discussing grandchildren, reflecting on a son's misfortune and complaining about the telephone company. Yet closer attention specifically to the turns in reported speech reveals some common characteristics. Briefly glossed, these are as follows:

- The reportings themselves may not initially appear to address the prior turn. The switch to the past tense with 'I said' or 'I told' invokes a relevant past exchange on the same topic. However, the turn-initial 'well' in extracts (1) and (3) and – less obviously, but as we shall see, 'ez a matter a'fact' – serve to link the upcoming turn to the prior in the face of this apparent disjunction.
- They follow assessments. The speaker who produces the reported speech is clearly using it to be responsive to an assessment from the other.
- They occur in the environment of overlap: in (1), the turn in reported speech is launched in overlap with the laughter at the end of its prior turn; in (2), it appears to be launched just after an overlap; and in (3), it is launched in overlap.

Pursuit of the interactional motivations for the reported speech in extracts (1)–(3), then, will focus on these observations and will aim to establish whether – and to what extent – the broad sketch of the apparent commonalities are sustainable. We should, at the same time, however, remain alert to the apparent distinctions between the exemplars. So, while in exemplars (1) and (3) the utterances in reported speech are one turn-constructional unit (TCU) long (and thus support Couper-Kuhlen's proposal (this volume) that such fleeting uses of reported speech are maximally one TCU long), (2) consists of two TCUs, 'I want the top back. Send out the word'. How can we account for this apparent anomaly? And how can we explain the fact that, while (2) and (3) report the utterance of a single speaker, (1) reports the utterances of two – Vera and Bill? We shall explore these issues by noting in the first instance Schegloff's assertion that, with respect to turns-at-talk, 'both *position and composition* are ordinarily constitutive of the sense and import of an element of conduct that embodies some phenomenon or practice' (1993: 121). The observations that the reported speech utterances in our sample follow assessments, and that they occur in the environment of overlap, of course relate to the position of their turns within a given sequence and will be examined later. First, however, we investigate the issue of how the turns in reported speech address their prior turns by examining the composition of those turns.

5.3 The composition of the turns in reported speech

As noted above, one source of an apparent disjunction between the turns in reported speech and their priors is that the former represent a shift into the past tense to report what the speaker herself had said to another or others. But another source of the disjunction lies in the construction of the reported speech itself. What is reported is comprehensible even when removed from its environment of occurrence:

From (1)   I said to Jean, 'How about it?'
From (2)   I told my kids ... down at the Drug Coalition, 'I want the top back. Send out the word'.
From (3)   I said to them, 'This is British Telecom for you'.

Despite their lack of prior context, all three are recognisable as formulaic utterances for doing particular actions. So in (1), what is reported – 'How about it?' – is a familiar colloquial format for making a suggestion or a proposal. In (2), while 'I want the top back' is not similarly formulaic, it recognisably does a demand, and what is subsequently added to that, 'Send out the word', is again a formulaic utterance for issuing an order; and in (3), 'This is British Telecom for you' is again recognisable, this time as doing a complaint. So the reported speech in each is constructed to be recognisable even when standing alone. The recognition of the actions being done is enhanced by the direct and forthright character of the utterances reported; the suggestion, the demand and the complaint are reported as being delivered bluntly, with no mitigation. Indeed, their dramatic quality verges on caricature. They are also clearly reported as initiating utterances in specific contexts, even if they are clearly responsive to particular situations (e.g. the stealing of the top of the car).

The distinctiveness of the turns in reported speech when set against what precedes them does not, however, entail a disattention to the sequential context in which they occur. In these cases, the construction of the reported speech turns themselves shows quite the opposite. In so doing, it illuminates what many (e.g. Clark and Gerrig, 1990; Lehrer, 1989; Mayes, 1990) have noted as the puzzle concerning reported speech: that what is reported is rarely what was originally, in fact, said. It is now possible to see how what is reported is exquisitely fashioned to the context of its reporting. So, in (1), Vera's 'How about it?' is clearly not built to be a first action, since the proform 'it' can only refer to something recoverable from the context. In the case of reported speech, that context is clearly the one in which the speech is reported, rather than that which is being reported. In this respect, it is acutely sensitive to Jenny's prior turn in the current interaction; it is shaped to Jenny's assessment 'All they need now is a little girl…', with 'it' as a subsequent, rather than initial, form referring to a topic already established (see Schegloff, 1996b, for an account of initial versus subsequent reference forms with respect to persons). What Vera actually said (if, indeed, she actually said it) and its proximity to the report, is of course irrecoverable. It is surely the case, however, that its form would have been equally fitted to its own – different – sequential environment. If, for example, Vera's proposal had been produced as a broaching of a topic, it would necessarily have been produced as an initial, rather than subsequent mention; something along the lines of 'Have you ever thought about/How about…?'. Speculation aside, it is evident that what gets reported is shaped by reference to the context in which the reporting is done. So what Vera reports is done from the sequential place she is in with respect to Jenny, and not where she might have been with respect to Jean. 'How about it?' is built to follow Jenny's turn.

In similar vein, Marsha's reporting in (2) shows exquisite sensitivity to Tony's prior turn. Tony's 'That really makes me mad' in the first instance is receipted by Marsha with a second assessment. Marsha's portrayal of what she said, with its unmitigated bluntness, 'I want the top back. Send out the word' thumps the table, figuratively speaking. In the emphatic articulation of the demand, with the raised volume, Marsha effectively enacts what Tony has asserted – 'That really makes me mad' – and is consistent with a display of her own subsequent assessment that 'it's disgusting'. In (3), Lesley's launch of her reported speech is similarly dependent on the prior context. Her proterm reference in 'I said to them' is dependent on the co-referentiality of 'them' with Mum's 'they' in line 57 – a reference to the telephone company. The reported speech itself, 'This is British Telecom for you', is launched upon Mum's assessment that 'They're getting terrible'. As a recognisable format for doing a complaint it picks up and embodies Mum's complaint about the ongoing state of affairs; effectively, 'What can you expect from British Telecom?'

So, in sum, the apparent disjunction between the turns in reported speech and their priors suggested by the switch into reporting a past event is somewhat deceptive. What is reported in fact shows quite extraordinary attentiveness to the prior turn, while still being designed to be recognisable as prosecuting actions independently of its sequential context.

Such are the commonalities – but it is in the composition of the turns that we also see revealed the differences noted earlier with respect to the interactional units being reported, and the number of speakers being reported. We recall that the reported speech in extracts (1) and (3) are one TCU long, while (2) consists of two TCUs, apparently contradicting Couper-Kuhlen's proposal (this volume) that such fleeting uses of reported speech are maximally one TCU long. Attention to the production of the whole turn, however, furnishes some evidence to suggest that the turn in reported speech was originally designed to be a single TCU, 'I want the top back', and that the second TCU, 'Send out the word', is built to be an upgrade of the first. In addition to the pitch peak on 'top' which adumbrates completion (Schegloff, 1996c: 84), suggesting that the turn is designed to be complete after 'back', Marsha's in-breath of a second provides her recipient with ample opportunity to respond – which he chooses not to do. Marsha's comparatively louder 'SEND OUT THE WORD' may thus be hearable as a further attempt to prompt a response. In addition, as noted earlier, the first TCU does not constitute a recognisably formulaic expression in the same way that the examples in (1) and (3) do; 'SEND OUT THE WORD', however, is clearly recognisable as such a formulaic expression. This, then, may be another means alongside the articulatory – a differently designed TCU – of trying to secure uptake. Such an example, then, far from undermining Couper-Kuhlen's claim, would seem to support it. It suggests that, in the first instance, single turns in reported speech are indeed one TCU in length, and that only when uptake is not forthcoming does a turn get expanded beyond the first TCU. A significant exception to this, however, is revealed if we consider the latter of the two differences we noted earlier – the number of speakers being reported. We register again the apparent discrepancy between exemplars (2) and (3) in which the speaker reports herself and the example represented in (1), which reports the speaker and one other. The discrepancy, of course, lies in the *type* of action being reported: while (2) and (3) report a demand and a complaint respectively, what Vera reports in (1), as the first part of an adjacency pair, 'How about it?', makes a response conditionally relevant. The reporting of Bill responding to this (note that as an unaddressed party his response is actually portrayed as an intervention) is therefore motivated by the first pair part. So the reporting of adjacency pairs may be seen as the one exception to the 'one TCU' constraint proposed by Couper-Kuhlen and otherwise largely supported here. If upheld in further data, the constraint more globally appears to relate to units rather than TCUs as such, so that 'one unit' – be it TCU or adjacency pair – is apparently the maximal length of what is reported in such cases. The two main areas of visible difference between the two extracts, then, appear to converge on the issue of the units being reported: both what was initially identified as relating to how much of what is reported (one or two TCUs?) and the number of speakers (one or two?), in fact, have to do with this 'one unit' constraint.

Otherwise the composition of the turns in reported speech shows striking similarities. In the first place, the reporting frame, 'I said'/ 'I told' is fitted to its prior by means of a TCU-initial object, but otherwise appears not to be ostensibly addressing its prior. In each case the reported speech is designed as prosecuting distinct

actions which would be identifiable as such even without the prior
context. Yet paradoxically, what is reported displays careful attention to the prior turn and as such is closely fashioned to the
reporting context.

5.4 The position of the turns in reported speech

As we initially noted, extracts (2) and (3) are similar to (1) in showing the reported speech following assessments. In (2), Marsha's
'I told my kids' follows assessments from both Marsha herself
('Oh it's disgusting') and, in overlap with the end of her assessment,
Tony ('poor Joey'). In (3), Lesley launches her utterance in reported
speech at line 59, following an assessment from Mum, 'They're
getting terrible', and a slight pause. We recall that in (1), too, Vera's
utterance in reported speech follows Jenny's assessment of
Vera's family. So in all three cases, the reported speech utterances
are placed in a distinct sequential position after a prior assessment.
Furthermore, these assessments may themselves be seen to follow
prior assessments and agreements with them. These cases of reported speech, then, all occur in what may be broadly characterised
as assessment environments. To establish what they may be doing
in such contexts, it is necessary to examine more closely what is
being done by means of these assessments.

5.4.1 Epistemic authority and subordination in assessing

Recent work on assessments and their agreements by Heritage and
Raymond (2005) has argued that speakers' differential rights to
assess referents are tacitly encoded in who produces an assessment
first, and who second – an ordering which establishes who is
agreeing with whom. They propose that offering a first assessment
makes a claim to primary rights to evaluate the matter assessed:

(From Heritage and Raymond, 2005: 19)
(4) [SBL 2-2-3:5]
```
1   Chloe:→  We:ll it was [fu:n Clai[re, ((smile voice))
2   Claire:            [hhh     [Yea: : [:h, ]
3   Chloe:                          [°Mm°
```

(5) [SBL:2-1-8:5] (From Heritage and Raymond, 2005: 23)

```
1   Norma:→  I think evryone enjoyed jus sitting aroun'
2           →  ta::lk[ing.]
3   Bea:              [ h h] I do too::,
```

In each case the first position assessments are produced as simple declarative evaluations and receive agreements in second position. However, in some cases, speakers offering first assessments may work to defeat an implication that they are claiming primary rights to evaluate the matter at hand, In the following (from Heritage and Raymond, 2005: 18), Norma evidentially downgrades her assessment of a longtime acquaintance of Bea's with 'seems', and she in turn receives a declaratively asserted agreement from Bea, 'Awfully nice little person':

(6) [SBL:2-1-8:5]

```
1   Bea:   hh hhh We:ll , h I wz gla:d she c'd come too las'ni:ght=
2   Nor:→  =Sh[e seems such a n]ice little [l  a  dy]
3   Bea:       [(since you keh) ]          [dAwf'l]ly nice l*i'l
4          p*ers'n. t hhhh hhh We:ll, I[: j's  ]
5   Nor:                                [I thin]k evryone enjoyed jus...
```

Conversely, speakers in the position of responding to an assessment may work to defeat the implication that their rights to assess are secondary to a first speaker. So, for example, a negative interrogative in a second position assessment can attenuate its second position status by providing a putatively 'new' first pair part for the previous speaker to respond to:

(From Heritage and Raymond, 2005: 22)

(7) [NB VII:1-2]

```
1   Emma:  =Oh honey that was a lovely luncheon I shoulda ca:lled you
2          s:soo[:ner but I:] l : [lo:ved it.Ih wz just deli:ghtfu[: l.  ]=
3   Mar:        [((f)) Oh:::]     [*'(   )                        [Well]=
4   Mar:   =I wz gla[d  y o u ] (came).]
5   Emma:           ['nd yer f:]  friends] 'r so da:rli:ng,=
6   Mar:   =Oh::: [: it wz : ]
7   Emma:         [e-that P]a:t isn'she a do:[ :ll? ]
8   Mar:→                                    [iY e]h isn't she pretty,
```

Table 5.1. *Some practices for indexing relative primacy and subordination of assessments: a summary of Heritage and Raymond (2005)*

First position epistemic downgrading can be indexed by:

- evidential weakening (e.g.'seems', 'sounds')
- tag questions (e.g. 'aren't they' – from extract (1))

Second position epistemic upgrading can be indexed by:

- confirmation + agreement (e.g. 'they are, yes' – from extract (1))
- *oh*-prefaced second assessments (e.g. 'oh it's disgusting', from extract (2))
- tag questions (e.g. 'it is, isn't it)
- negative interrogatives (e.g. 'isn't it beautiful')

Margy's downgraded assessment of her friend ('pretty' in response to Emma's 'a doll') is nevertheless packaged as a negative interrogative, which asserts her primacy in the right to assess her friend. Heritage and Raymond examine a range of such grammatical practices through which the producers of first and second assessments can index the relative primacy and subordination of their assessments relative to that of co-participants. Some of these are summarised in Table 5.1 above.

As the summary shows, a primary resource for indexing secondary access to a referent relative to a co-participant is the use of tag question. In this light, let us consider (1) again:

From (1)

```
 1   Jenny:    They're [a lovely family now aren't [they.
 2   Vera:             [°Mm:.°                         [They are: ye[s.
 3   Jenny:                                                         [eeYe[s::,
 4   Vera:                                                               [Yes,
 5   Jenny:    Mm: All they need now is a little girl tih complete i:t.
 6   Jenny:    [heh heh]
 7   Vera:→    [Well I said t]uh Jean how abou:t it so our Bill (0.2)
 8   Vera:     laughingly said 'ey she'll havetuh ask me fir:st no:w.
 9   Jenny:    h:ha[: ha:
10   Vera:         [huh huh-u huh-u[uh uh
```

We can now see how Jenny's assessment at line 1, 'They're a lovely family now, aren't they' is modulated by means of the tag question as a question to be answered rather than as an assertion to be agreed with. She thereby, as Heritage and Raymond put it, 'cedes epistemic authority in the matter to her coparticipant' (2005: 20), who, after all, is the children's grandmother. This epistemic downgrade by Jenny receives, with some alacrity, the response 'they are, yes' from Vera. As work on responses to 'yes/no' interrogatives has shown (Raymond, 2000), deferral of a 'yes' response, as occurs here, is a marked action. Here, the ordering of elements prioritises confirmation ('they are') over agreement ('yes'). As Heritage and Raymond note, in treating confirming as the priority, a speaker can propose that one held this position prior to and independently of her co-participant (2005: 23), despite having to respond to that co-participant's claim to the same position. So Jenny's initial assessment downgrades her rights to assess, while Vera upgrades hers. Jenny's acknowledging 'yes' and Vera's own responsive 'yes' to her provide for a subsequent termination of that particular assessment sequence. But this is not what happens: Jenny's strong assessment, 'all they need now is a little girl to complete it', continues the sequence. The strength of the assessment is marked by the extreme case formulation (Pomerantz, 1986) 'all they need', and the lack of evidential weakening that characterised the prior assessment. The only slight modulation is apparent after it with a couple of laugh tokens (line 6), which, constituting a post-completion stance marker (Schegloff, 1995), recast the prior TCU as a light-hearted proposal. While laughter has been shown to constitute an invitation to laugh along, in a display of affiliation (Jefferson, 1979), Vera's response – despite starting in overlap with the laughter – displays no subsequent orientation to the laughter at all, and so hearably resists affiliating with Jenny (see Jefferson, (1979: 83–85) for a discussion of such cases). The launch of her turn is designed to pick up precisely at the end of Jenny's assessment in line 5, the turn-initial 'well' indexing what follows as responsive to its prior (Pomerantz, 1984a: 72; Sacks, 1992a: 76). It is, then, in the context of the strong assessment of Jenny's that it is possible to establish what Vera's turn in reported speech is designed to do. It provides, in the face of an epistemically upgraded assessment from her co-participant, *a powerful evidential display of having reached that assessment first*. By reporting a past event, and specifically enacting an utterance that embodies the assessment that the co-participant has made, the speaker lays claim to primary rights to do the assessing. She claims priority – in a sense, pulling rank – on the basis of sheer chronology: she was there first.

The next two examples show reported speech being produced in similar interactional environments to similar evidential ends. Most of extract (2) is reproduced here:

From (2)

```
35   Tony:      W't's 'e g'nna do go down en pick it up later? er
36              somethin like (     ) [well that's aw]:ful
37   Marsha:                    [H i s  friend ]
38   Marsha:    Yeh h[is friend Stee-    ]
39   Tony:           [That really makes] me ma:d,
40              (0.2)
41   Marsha:    .hhh Oh it's disgusti[ng ez a matter a'f]a:ct.
42   Tony:                           [P o o r  J o e y ,]
43   Marsha:→  I- I, I told my ki:ds. who do this: down  et the Drug
44              Coalition ah want th'to:p  back.h {.hhhhhhhhh/(1.0 )}
45              SEND OUT the WO:RD.hhh hnh
46              (0.2)
47   Tony:      Yeah.
48   Marsha:    .hhh Bu:t u-hu:ghh his friend Steve en Brian er driving
49              up...
```

Here, Tony upgrades a negative assessment about Joey's predicament – 'well that's awful' (line 36) – to the more personalised 'that really makes me mad' (line 39). After a post-overlap resolution hitch (Schegloff, 2000b: 34) at line 40, Marsha produces a second assessment, 'oh, it's disgusting'. By dint of the *oh*-prefacing, as marker of second position epistemic upgrading (see Table 5.1), and the upgrade from Tony's 'mad' to 'disgusting', she indexes her own primary rights to assess the situation. There are, of course, clear circumstantial grounds to support Marsha's claim to such priority: she has, after all, related the incident to Tony, an incident which took place outside *her* house. The upgraded assessment 'oh it's disgusting' is then subsequently itself epistemically upgraded by means of the reported speech. In this particular case, the upgrade represented by the reported speech is explicitly marked by 'as a matter of fact'. For, while the transcript represents what is hearable on the tape – final prosody after 'fact' such that Marsha appears to be saying 'oh it's disgusting as a matter of fact' – there are various grounds, as Schegloff notes, for taking 'as a matter of fact' as introducing the reported speech, so that Marsha is saying 'oh it's disgusting. As a matter of fact I told my kids...'.[1] The upgrading capacity of 'a matter of fact' (see Clift, 2003) underscores clearly that the reported speech constitutes an epistemic upgrade of Marsha's own prior upgrade of Tony's assessment. Schegloff, in his observations on this extract, notes that Marsha's 'disgusting' is vulnerable to suspicion that it has been coerced by Tony's interruptive upgrade of his prior assessment in reaction to Marsha's tepid agreement at line 38, 'yeh'; that Marsha is just going along, is saying 'what's necessary' (1997: 178). In this light we can see that while the *oh*-prefacing and the upgrade to 'disgusting' are grammatical resources for claiming epistemic priority, it is the use of the reported speech which *displays* such priority (see Drew, 1992: 485; Sacks, 1992b: 113-114, on the distinction between claiming and displaying). As such, the reported speech may be seen as a form of interactional 'trump card'. Just as in (1), what is reported is acutely sensitive to the assessment it seeks to counter. While Marsha eschews possible agreement with Tony, she is, as we have seen, far from disattending what he says. Her vivid prosodic animation of the reported speech constitutes an insistence on how it was told. Holt's (1996: 241) claim that reported speech provides evidence is instantiated in what Marsha is doing here: providing evidence, as no mere gloss could do, of an independent event which pre-existed the current, here-and-now occasioned reference to it. And indeed

---

[1] Schegloff (1997) notes that the main grounds for this lie in the overlap of Tony's talk ('Poor Joey' at line 42) with Marsha's at line 41. As speakers emerge from an overlap, there is routinely a post-overlap resolution hitch (such as the pause at line 40). In this case that hitch is manifested in the prosody; it happens to come just at a point of possible grammatical completion, which gets it heard as 'final intonation'. As Schegloff notes (p.c), it is problematic to start a new TCU while in a continuing overlap (one reason being that it sounds as if the speaker is dropping out). There is incentive enough for Marsha here not to drop out; she has already been revealed to be insufficiently upset compared to Tony by the incident, and she has – and is about to provide – independent evidence of how upset she was. There is, in short, little reason for her to yield the turn space at this point.

the effect of this is evident in Tony's response: a somewhat lukewarm uptake, with a pause and then a bland acknowledgement,
'yeah'. In contrast to a receipt object such as 'oh', which responds
to prior talk as significant, and marks it as information to be
'foregrounded' from surrounding talk, 'yeah' avoids treating prior
talk as informative (see Heritage, 1984a: 305), on the difference
between 'oh' as an informing receipt and 'yeah' and 'mm'). What
Marsha reports, then, is not receipted as an informing in its own
right. Tony's expressions of indignation and sympathy having been
trumped, Marsha is now in a position to reinitiate her answer to
Tony's 'W't's 'e g'nna do?'

In extract (3), we again see a covert dispute regarding who has
rights to assess:

From (3)

53	Mum:	Oh: lo:ve.
54		(0.4)
55	Mum:	That's a nuisance isn't it.
56	Les:	Ye[s.
57	Mum:	[They're getting terrible.
58		(0.3)
59	Les:	We:l [l I - I ↑said]
60	Mum:	[I-I mean ↑look what]
61		(0.2)
62	Les:→	I said to them. £↑This is British Telecom for you.(h)£=
63	Mum:	=Yes. .h An' ↑look what they cha:rge. They charge you
64		.h three pounds (just t'have) this blessed old thing
65		in your hou:se.
66		(0.5)
67	Les:	Yes.

Lesley has just told her mother that five people in her area have had
their phones cut off by the phone company. At line 53, Mum's
response is sympathetic, and then at line 55 she produces an assessment which, by means of the tag question, is epistemically downgraded. Lesley responds to this with a neutral token of agreement:
'yes'. As Pomerantz (1984a) has shown, 'yes' as a response to a first
assessment is not hearable as an agreement, agreements being
routinely performed by dint of upgrades of the first assessment.

Indeed, in this context, 'yes' as a weak agreement is hearable as an incipient *dis*agreement.[2] As such, it is met by a response which is a common one to less than robust agreements: an upgrade by the producer of the first assessment, in Schegloff's words, in order 'to draw the previously weak stance into a more vigorous alignment with the initial assessment' (1997: 177). Mum's upgrade undertakes to generalise from what had been an assessment of the single case, 'that's a nuisance' (line 55), to the wider pattern of an ongoing situation, 'they're getting terrible' (line 57). A negative assessment is thereby upgraded to something which is hearably a complaint. This upgraded negative assessment, like Jenny's 'all they need now is a little girl to complete it' in extract (1), follows on from a downgraded assessment by the same speaker, but is not itself downgraded. And, in a similar fashion to extract (1), there is a distinct lack of affiliation with the strong and untempered negative assessment. Mum's complaint is met by a pause of three-tenths (0.3) of a second: a clear marker of withholding. What ensues subsequently is a simultaneous start-up. As Lesley launches her response to Mum's upgraded assessment in the same way Jenny had done in (1) – with the counterpositional 'well' and the initiation of reported speech – Mum simultaneously resumes her own talk, apparently taking the pause after her complaint to indicate trouble that Lesley has with her assessment. Her resumption thus undertakes to clarify and elaborate. As in extract (2), the overlap results in both speakers temporarily dropping out, but it is Lesley who restarts her turn (an ordering which will be examined in due course, in the discussion of reported speech and overlap). When Lesley restarts, it is with recognisably the same words that she had used before, with only the 'well' – the marker of responsiveness to her prior turn – omitted, in recognition of the new sequential position of this current turn. The reported

---

[2] It might be argued that Lesley may have produced an agreement in upgrade had she not been overlapped by Mum's incoming turn. However, the terminal prosody with which the 'yes' is produced (and to which Lesley is surely committed before she gets overlapped) argues for Lesley not designing the beginning of her turn as preliminary to a subsequent upgrade.

speech stakes Lesley's prior claim to the complaint, in displaying her prior independent stance on the matter.

In this particular case, however, the recipient is not beaten back by the reported speech. Mum's response to Lesley shows that she is not deterred from continuing what she had started at line 60. In the first instance, she produces an acknowledgement: 'yes'. Like Tony's response to Marsha's reported speech in extract (2), 'Yeah', this does not treat the prior telling as informative, or mark it as information to be foregrounded or elaborated on. But unlike Tony, whose deflated 'Yeah' provided for Marsha to resume her attempt to answer his initial question, Mum subsequently simply continues, recycling what she had started at line 60, appending the restart to the acknowledgement by means of 'and', proposing what follows to be an addition to the ongoing jointly expressed grievance against British Telecom.

Mum's indomitability here contrasts strongly, as we have seen, with not only Tony in the face of Marsha's reported speech but also Jenny in the face of Vera's, in (1). At Vera's report of Bill's jocular response to her proposal to Jean, Jenny responds with laughter, thus clearly aligning with Vera in her presentation of the reported speech – indeed, in her own laughter even embodying Vera's own description of Bill's delivery ('laughingly'). Both Marsha and Vera, then, are able to use reported speech to assert – successfully – priority in rights to assess, and in each case the co-participant is thereby deterred from continuing with his or her own attempts to assess. What are we, then, to make of what happens in the wake of Lesley's reported speech in (3)? Clearly the reported speech here is insufficient to deter Mum. For the source of this we need to examine both the local sequential context and the interactional origins of her own complaint. In the first instance we recall that sequentially Mum had 'lost out', so to speak, to Lesley in the overlap at lines 59–60. As we have seen, after the pause at line 61, Lesley gets to recycle the beginning of her turn, and subsequently to complete it. The first possible completion of her turn provides an opportunity for Mum to recycle what *she* had launched in the overlap, but by this point she has other business – *Lesley*'s turn – to attend to first. So, conforming to the preference for contiguity in conversation (Sacks, 1987: 60), she firstly responds to Lesley's turn and only then attends to the recycling of her own aborted turn from line 60. Thus we have a sequential motivation for Mum's pursuit of her complaint at 63, but there are, in addition, strong interactional ones, which, it could be argued, themselves mobilise the sequential one: after all, a speaker who finds herself speaking in overlap and drops out is not thereby *impelled* to recycle her turn. To identify those interactional motivations, it is necessary to examine the very beginning of the call:

(8) [The beginning of (3); Holt:X-1-1-6]

```
 1   Les:      …o
 2             (0.3)
 3   Mum:      H' llo::::[(it's)
 4   Les:               [Oh hello [Mum
 5   Mum:                         [(me.)
 6             (0.2)
 7   Mum:      ↑H[ello,
 8   Les:        [How're you:
 9             (0.5)
10   Mum:→     ↑Oh: ↑thank goodn'ss the li:ne's ↑clear toni:ght,
11             (0.5)
12   Les:      Oh:. wasn't it [°clear°
13   Mum:→                    [↑It's been ↑awful this wee:k
14             (0.4)
15   Les:      Oh uh has ↑i:[t?
16   Mum:→                  [It seemed like a lot of pebbles in the
17            → wire all the time.
18   Les:      .hhh ↑Oh: dea:r.
19   Mum:      Mm:.
20             (0.3)
21   Les:      .hhh Uh:m (0.2) .k Well ↑we got cut off on Thursda:y,
22   Mum:      ↑Oh: dea:r. Thursday.
```

(20 lines omitted, during which Lesley explains that
they forgot to open the final demand for the bill)

```
43   Mum:      Oh: they make you pay f'r putting it on again too:.
44   Les:      Yes well we sent the money straight awa:y
45             (0.4)
46   Les:      .p
47             (0.2)
48   Les:      And we had it uh:m: back on on Fridee afternoon
```

```
49  Mum:   .hmhh:
50  Les:   But apparently they cut w- ↑fi:ve ↑people off in
51         Galhampto[n: on[: Thursday-
52  Mum:           [( ) ! [(      )
53  Mum:   Oh: lo:ve.
54         (0.4)
55  Mum:   That's a nuisance isn't it.
56  Les:   Ye[s.
```

The opening shows Mum's complaint to be so precipitate – launched
at line 10 with her response to hearing Lesley's voice, and line 13 –
that she disattends and sequentially deletes Lesley's opening inquiry
at line 8. She registers her concern with the phone company, then,
from the outset – indeed before Lesley – and it is in response to
Mum's complaint at line 13 and then at lines 16–17 that Lesley first
sympathises at line 18 and then, at line 21, launches a 'my side'
telling (Pomerantz, 1980) which formulates her own grounds for
complaint against the phone company. It is thus in these independent
grounds for complaint, alongside the local sequential motivations
for recycling and completing an aborted turn, that the origins of
Mum's hearable determination to press on with her complaint in the
wake of Lesley's reported speech may be found.

The initial observation that the turns in reported speech all
followed assessments has now been given more extended consideration. The three fragments suggest that the use of reported speech
may be a powerful (but not, as we have seen, invincible) device for
asserting one's own prior rights to assess.

5.4.2 Reported speech in the environment of overlap

Of the three common features of the exemplars initially noted, the
observation that the turns in reported speech are launched in
the environment of overlap is perhaps the least clear-cut. Only (3)
clearly shows the launch of the reported speech to be in overlap to
the extent that both speakers momentarily drop out, with the reported speech being subsequently relaunched. It is at this point – the
overlap – that the competitiveness which marks this sequence becomes overt. In contrast, both (1) and (2) in different ways are less
straightforwardly cases of competitive overlap. So, in (1), Vera
launches her reported speech in overlap with something which has

been observed to be designed specifically for overlap (Jefferson, 1979): laughter. And, as we noted earlier, the transcript of (2) suggests that the reported speech is launched just *after* an overlap (of Tony's 'Poor Joey'). Yet our earlier analysis of both has suggested that, in their different ways, the conjunction of reported speech and overlap is not happenstance but rather a function of the competitive nature of the reported speech in these contexts. So in (1) we note again that, although Vera launches her reported speech in overlap with something built for overlap, she resists both the invitation to laugh along and any overt affiliation with Jenny's prior assessment. The positioning of Vera's launch of her reported speech, then, only serves to underline the competitiveness of what she is launching.

In similar vein, what appeared initially (and on the transcript) to be a contrast case turns out – if the earlier proposal is sustained – to be an archetypal case of reported speech launched to be a competitive upgrade. For what was proposed earlier – that the reported speech is launched, not as the transcript in (2) suggests, with 'I- I, I told my kids' at line 43, and thus in the clear, but at 'ez a matter of fact' at line 41 – locates Marsha's introduction of the reported speech just after the beginning of Tony's overlap. It clearly belongs, then, alongside the other cases of competitive overlap.

Now, of course, three cases where reported speech is launched in overlap is not necessarily predictive; it is surely not a constitutive feature of reported speech that it be lauched in a particular position in the course of another's turn. That there *are* three such cases, however, is suggestive, and does underwrite the use of reported speech as a resource in competitive claims to assess in the following respect. Schegloff (2000b) notes that in three particular cases of overlapping talk he examines, it is the talk which embodies a new departure that gets taken up, rather than that which continues what was ongoing in the prior talk. He remarks:

if sustained as the preferred practice in further research, the upshot of these ways of proceeding would be to indicate a *general tilt to promote a forward movement of the interaction to new topical and action developments.*

(2000b: 41, my italics)

In a case such as (3), where Mum and Lesley find themselves in overlap, with Mum elaborating on her prior talk ('I mean', line 60) and Lesley initiating her turn in reported speech, Lesley's 'Well

I said' (line 59), in its apparent disjunction, is hearably not continuative of prior talk. It is Mum who drops out of the overlap. Here, then, is another element of support for Schegloff's observation regarding the 'forward movement of the interaction' – and also another possible source of the adversarial power of this form of reported speech. Its sequential disjunction proposes 'new topical and action developments' and, under Schegloff's proposal, thereby renders it more robust in, and more likely to emerge from, overlap.

Such, then, are some initial observations on the interactionally salient features of reported speech with regard to its position and composition. The general characterisation which emerges from our data is of a forceful interactional resource for making evidential claims. But this itself is in need of some contextualisation in the way of external evidence, and in this regard it may be instructive to offer a comparison of the exemplars discussed with a possible alternative. The following represent one such and, as we shall see, are not randomly chosen. In due course we shall see how a speaker hearably makes a choice between the two.

5.5 A comparative case

In the cases we have seen the sense of competition in the doing of assessments is scarcely veiled, with the overlaps, the lack of agreement markers before the launching of the reported speech, and the apparent lack of attention to the co-participants' prior turn. In the following cases, the speakers at the arrowed turns do, by contrast, show some overt attention to what has just been said:

(9) [Holt:5:88:2-4:25]
(Deena and Mark have been discussing the substantial cost of Deena's daughter's upcoming wedding.)

```
 1   Deena:   So anyway (0.2) everything seems to be [going alright]=
 2   Mark:                                           [ (-----------) ]=
 3   Mark:    = [.h h h h h h h h h ((fidgeting------------------) ) ]
 4   Deena:   = [Mark (if you sit down)'n take it'n day to da]:y,
 5            (.)
 6   Mark:    Ye:s
 7            (0.2)
 8   Mark:    .hhhh We:ll (.) I dunno I we view the f::::::::act that
 9            your kids're your assets really an' we'd rather spend
10            our money on our kids than [waste it]=
```

```
11   Deena:→                          [That is ]=
12   Deena:→ = [ex<u>a</u>ctly h o w  <u>I</u>   ]
13   Mark:     = [on ours<u>e</u>lves or an] ything else [.hhh      hhhh
14   Deena:→                          [That is ex<u>a</u>ctly what w<u>e</u>
15       →    said I s<u>a</u>id to Dwayne as <u>lo</u>ng as we've got a bit a'
16            [money to- (.) yo<u>u</u> [know as long as we've got=
17   Mark:    [hhmh             [hhmhhhhh
18   Deena:   =a- (.) no<u>u</u>gh money that if we <u>want</u> anythin::g at our
19            time a'life (0.4) we [c'n buy it.
20                                 [((clonk))
21   Mark:    .tY<u>e</u>:s.
```

(10) [Rahman B:1:JMA(13):3]M
(Jenny and Ann are talking about trailer tents, which can be towed behind
cars.)

```
1    Jenny:                      [.h Has ↑<u>N</u>ancy McC<u>a</u>rthy still <u>got</u>
2             hers. Cuz <u>she</u> yoo-↓<u>she</u> always <u>s</u>wore by [it when she=
3    Ann:                                          [Y<u>e</u>:s.
4    Jenny:   =<u>h</u>a [d it.
5    Ann:         [<u>I</u> don't ↑<u>k</u>now. I haven't <u>s</u>een (      ).
6    Jenny:   I haven't <u>n</u>oticed yeh .h bu- cz I kno- I <u>t</u>hink she's got a-
7             uh-m: one a'those: uh per<u>m</u>anent caravans. up in:
8             <u>G</u>rozeda:[le.
9    Ann:            [<u>A</u>:oh.
10   Ann:     Well tha's prob- yes [that (           )
11   Jenny:                        [An' she musta got rid'<u>v</u> the trailer
12            cuz I <u>k</u>now <u>s</u>he use to ih- yihknow ex<u>t</u>ol its <u>v</u>irtues but
13            that- then that's <u>N</u>ancy isn'it when y- hih hih hnhh
14            [.hunhh
15   Ann:     [I'm <u>s</u>ure it's m [uch <u>e</u>asier f 'to<u>w</u>ing.
16   Jenny:                     [.hhh
17   Jenny:→ <u>M</u>m- well that's w't she sai:d ih-it's bet<u>t</u>er th'n a
18            caravan because you c'n se<u>e</u> :: (0.2) <u>y</u>ihknow you c'n
19            you've got all yer <u>v</u>ision=
20   Ann:     [Y<u>e</u>:s.
21   Jenny:   [sort o:f.
22   Ann:     Y<u>e</u>:s.
23   Jenny:   .tch [an:d
24   Ann:          [Specially fer h<u>e</u>:r (t) (0.2) if <u>s</u>he wz towing.
25            (.)
26   Jenny:   <u>T</u>h[at's right.
```

(11) [Holt:1:1:6]
```
 1   Mum:   [Miriam's going next week,
 2   Les:   Ye:s: yes:.
 3          (0.4)
 4   Mum:   She ['s been in hot water with'er mum t'day,
 5   Les:        [M-
 6   Les:   Why: :?
 7   Mum:   .hh We:ll. (0.2) Uh you know (.) there's a cra:ze with the
 8          girls now to have (.) a secon:d. (1.1) ring ih- a secon:d
 9          uh earring in on[e ear.]
10   Les:                   [Oh: i]t's very chea:p isn't it.
11   Mum:→ It's very cheap yes'n this is u- this is what Ann said. An'
12          Ann said (0.3) she- she'll haf (.) tuh have another. (0.5)
13          .hh (.) hole in 'er ear.
14   Les:   Ye:s:.
15          (0.9)
16   Mum:   Lo'n beho:ld (0.3) Ann- (0.2) i-ih-hu took her tuh the
17          (1.4) to'er horse this morning.... ((story about Ann
18          discovering the second earring))
```

The attention to prior turn in the cases above is marked grammatically by being built into the very construction of the turn, with the proform 'this' or 'that' and a claim that what the co-participant said is what the speaker or another has already said.[3] In marked contrast to extracts (1)–(3), these examples would appear to be highly affirmative in claiming identity with what they have just heard in either something they themselves have just said or have heard someone else say. None show the markers of disaffiliation that we see in extracts (1) and (3); no turn-initial 'well' or, as in (2), upgraded assessment. However, on further examination, it is possible to see how the competitiveness that marks (1)–(3) is also present in extracts (9)–(11).

---

[3] There would seem to be no discernible interactional difference in the cases so far examined between 'this' and 'that', or indeed a difference between the quoting of oneself and the quoting of another. One possible distinction apparent from the extracts cited, which would need to be supported with more data, is that 'this' seems directly to follow a repetition of what was said, as in extract (11), line 11: 'It's very cheap yes'n this is u- this is what Ann said'.

In extract (9) Deena is moving to close down the topic at line 1 by means of an upbeat summary assessment in the form of an idiomatic expression (Drew and Holt, 1998): 'everything seems to be going alright Mark if you sit down 'n take it'n day to day (lines 1–4). After a somewhat delayed and neutral 'yes' and a pause – a far from enthusiastic receipt – Mark, however, resists the potential invitation to close proffered by this formulation and counters with another proverbial-sounding, formulaic piece of wisdom-giving. Deena's response is launched at the point where Mark's stance is projectable. The form of that response, eschewing a simple acknowledgement or token of agreement such as 'exactly', launching a more extended turn, is hearably moving to embrace Mark's position ('That is ex<u>a</u>ctly how I', lines 11–12) before she drops out in the face of Mark's persistence to the end of his turn. At line 14 Deena recycles the beginning of her turn, but this time modifies the claim: 'That is exactly what we said'. This, of course, claims to be a highly affiliative agreement. It is, as in (10), followed directly by a report of what was purportedly said, such that prosodically the claim and the evidence to support it are of a piece – 'That is exactly what we said I said to Dwayne' in (9) and 'that's what she said ih- it's better' in (10). In both cases the reported speech secures an extended turn at talk in what in both cases are hearably competitive environments. So in (9), Mark meets Deena's upbeat summary assessment in lines 1–4 with, as we have seen, only the most tepid of responses, with his own extended turn prefaced by the familiar markers of dispreference: pausing, 'well' and the prefatory epistemic disclaimer (Schegloff, 1996c: 62) 'I dunno'. It is in this environment of hearable resistance to her own assessment that Deena launches her claim – interruptively. Mark, in turn, does not take the first opportunity to drop out (at the end of 'waste it', line 10), nor indeed the next, at the end of 'on ourselves', line 13; his persistence, to the end of 'anything else', is hearably competitive. Deena's recycling of her prior turn in line 14 thus comes in the context of some considerable jostling for the floor.[4] Extract (10)

---

[4] There is some evidence to suggest that the switch from 'That is exactly how I' in lines 11–12 to 'that is exactly what we said' is also motivated by this competitiveness. One projectable continuation of line 11 is 'that is exactly how I feel', which is consonant, as an agreement, with Mark's

shows a similar case, again in the environment of assessment. After surmising that their mutual acquaintance Nancy must have disposed of her trailer, Jenny glosses what Nancy used to do: 'I know she used to... extol its virtues' (line 12). This contrasts with her earlier formulation, 'she always swore by it' (line 2), which had received a fast acknowledgement from Ann. Here, however, the comparatively elevated stylised formulation and the subsequent dismissive assessment, 'that's Nancy, isn't it' (line 13), receives no acknowledgement at the first opportunity, after 'isn't it'; Jenny's subsequent abandonment of her speaking turn to infiltrating laughter may be hearable as a more concerted attempt to elicit affiliation by means of inviting reciprocal laughter. Ann's subsequent response, focusing on the convenience of the trailer, is utterly disattentive to Jenny's critique of Nancy, and as such is hearable as highly disaffiliative. Jenny's response, a cut-off and prosodically level 'mm', stops short of a full acknowledgement, much less an agreement. With 'well that's what she said', Jenny reformulates what Ann has just said as what Nancy herself said earlier. Having been somewhat stranded by Ann's refusal to align with her in line 15, Jenny's claim and her subsequent quoting of what Nancy apparently said is deft in its identification with Nancy. For this formulation is another means by which a speaker can assert her prior rights to the stance displayed. Both Deena in (9) and Jenny here are asserting that chronology is on their side, and on this basis claiming epistemic priority. In both cases these get agreements, with the co-participants falling in with these claims. However, in (10) it is a measure of the competitiveness of the interaction that Ann's subsequent assertion at line 24, which syntactically builds off Jenny's report, nevertheless reiterates her earlier stance, expressed at line 15, and in so doing very strongly aligns with Nancy. Jenny's 'that's right' (line 26) in response takes up a far more overtly epistemically authoritative stance (see Heritage and Raymond, 2005; Clift, 2005).

stance as expressed in lines 8–10. A switch from a report about how she feels to one about what she and Dwayne said to each other – with supporting evidence – is stronger evidentially and thus constitutes an upgrade in this competitive environment.

Extract (11) shows a similar case of a speaker claiming prior rights to assess by virtue of chronology, although in this instance the co-participant hearably concedes priority; the format of the claim is modified accordingly. Lesley's response to Mum's account of someone in 'hot water' with her mother downgrades her claimed rights to assess the referent with a tag question, 'it's very cheap, isn't it', possibly in deference to Mum as story-teller. Just as in extract (3), this downgrading in first position is responded to with first a confirmation with a repeat, and then an agreement, just as Vera had responded to Jenny in line 2 of extract (1). Again, by confirming the assertion before responding to the question, as Heritage and Raymond (2005) put it, Mum can treat the fact that she held this position prior to, and independently of, Lesley's intervention. The priority matter, as indexed by the ordering of 'confirmation + agreement' is asserting her epistemic rights through repetition of the assessment. Even so, the format of the partial repetition, which itself is then proposed as formulating what Ann said, is, in being an endorsement of Lesley's assessment, hearably less competitive than the direct claims which launch their turns in extracts (9) and (10).[5] Extract (11), then, displays the same claim to epistemic priority as those in extracts (9) and (10), albeit in a comparatively less competitive format.

Furthermore, as a group, extracts (9)–(11) show claims which are comparatively weaker than those in (1)–(3). In the first instance they <u>are</u> simply claims, lacking the evidential immediacy of direct reported speech, and furthermore they are claims which build off the prior turns in ways which the direct reported speech in (1)–(3) studiously does not. Herein may lie the grounds for the claims in (9) and (10) 'that's what x said' being, as noted earlier, directly followed by a formulation of what was purportedly said: the formulation provides supporting evidence for the claim.[6] Or, at

---

[5] See Schegloff, 1996a on repetition as (among other things) agreement.

[6] Indeed, it is notable in this connection that in the one case where the formulation of what is claimed to have been said comes before the claim itself – 'this is what Ann said', line 11 in (11) – the speaker goes on to add another increment to her story in the form of reported speech, 'An Ann said she- she'll haf tuh have another' (lines 11–12). It is this increment, in direct reported speech, which ultimately provides the evidential basis for the speaker's claim as a source for what Ann said.

least, it appears to – because, of course, what is subsequently reported as having been said is *not* – contrary to the claim that prefaces it – what has been said in prior turn. So, in (9), Deena follows her claim 'That is exactly what we said' (lines 14–15) with a report of an exchange which is hearably different from what Mark had just said. The basis for the claim cannot, then, be in its formulation or its detail, but rather in its upshot: the *gist* of what Deena said to Dwayne is proposed as 'the same' as that extractable from what Mark had said in lines 8–13. In this respect, Sacks's observations on the 'achieved similarity' (1992b: 4) of second stories with reference to their first stories are pertinent here: speakers display their understandings of stories by producing second stories, in which their own relationship to the story events is the same as that in the first story (Lerner, 1993: 232). In similar vein, the claims in extracts (9)–(11) are made on behalf of a particular stance or position. To be evidentially compelling, the reported speech adduced to support that position must thus necessarily not be a literal replica of what has just been said – although, of course, it must resemble it sufficiently. So Mark's views on spending money, Ann's assessment of the trailer tent and Lesley's attitude to second earrings are all designed to be supported, and indeed trumped, by evidence that others had prior claims on them.

It would seem, then, that the examples of direct reported speech as shown in extracts (1)–(3) are relatively stronger evidentially than those shown in examples (9)–(11). One final example, which shows a speaker apparently repairing from one format to the other, would seem to support the relative strength of the first format over the second. In the following datum, the speaker at the arrowed turn, Jenny, first does an agreement with the assessment in prior turn and then launches what is recognisably about to be 'that's what', and conceivably, given the self-repair which follows, 'that's what Fazil said'. However, she pulls up short after 'that's', with 'uh yihknow' (line 29) marking the initiation of the self-repair. The product of the self-repair is, of course, 'Fazil said':

(12) [Rahman:B:1:JMA(13):7]
    (Jenny and Vera are talking about a neighbour ('she', line 1) who has just taken delivery of some new furniture ('it', line 2).)

```
 1    Jenny:                        [She w'z very upset actually cuz i- she's
 2                         £waited such a£ long [ti:me for it en I mean=
 3    Ann:                                [(              )
 4    Ann:       = [Ye:s.
 5    Jenny:     = [it's such en expe:nsive [set      isn't     it.]
 6    Ann:                                  [Where did she bu]:y th'm
 7                throu:gh. Barker en[Stone(°house°).
 8    Jenny:                        [Barker'n Stonehouse. Mm, .hh Fazil
 9                never liked the manager in there though, [Faz'l [w'd nevuh=
10    Ann:                                                 [No:, [well he-=
11    Jenny:     = [go in there,]
12    Ann:       = [h e ' s  a- ]
13    Jenny:     =M-[hm,
14    Ann:           [No you see I tau:ght the little bo:y.
15    Jenny:     Ye:s, =
16    Ann:       =En:: e-his (.) this: (.) the manager marrie:d, .hh this
17                mother who already had a little bo:y.=
18    Jenny:     =Oh :: ah[hm?
19    Ann:                 [En I: had this little boy en he use to come tsu
20                open night . . hh En I had heard thet'e wz very stroppy. Eez
21                ↑only y'know'e looks a kid imse:lf.
22    Jenny:     eYe:s.
23    Ann:       Anyway um (.) e-he 'e sort'v settled do:wn. .hh An' I (w)
24                met th'm about a fortnight ago they've gotta little
25                girl'v their own no[w.
26    Jenny:                          [Aoh::::.h
27    Ann:       Uh b't e-he's very offputting. Ra:ther (0.4) 't.hhh a
28                cocky little devil.=
29    Jenny:→    =i-Ye:s. Well that's uh yihknow Fazil said [(well I well=
30    Ann:                                                  [Mm.
31    Jenny:     =I I(h)h Ih(h)'m payin money I'll n(h)ot (sort'ev) heh
32                he[h .hehhhhhhhh
33    Ann:         [Yeh exactly.
```

There is internal evidence here to suggest that what Jenny is doing by means of the self-repair is upgrading her claim to epistemic priority by exchanging a 'that's what x said' format for the evidentially stronger 'x said' one.

Ann's query and candidate answer regarding where a mutual friend has bought her furniture (lines 6–7) is confirmed by Jenny, who then produces a negative assessment about the shop by means of citing her late husband's attitude to it. At the first possible opportunity – and, it turns out, in overlap, because Jenny continues – Ann does an agreement and launches what is recognisably shaping up to be an assessment, 'he's a-' (line 12), pulling back just before she produces the descriptor. Upon Jenny's back-down to a recipient stance at line 13, Ann does not proceed to complete her abandoned prior turn, but instead produces what is hearably the first element in an extended telling designed to provide evidence for her stance: first-hand experience of the manager. Ann's telling has thus been launched in the sort of competitive environment of assessment that is characteristic in our cases of reported speech. During its course, Jenny maintains, somewhat tepidly, the stance of recipient. At its end – Ann's assessment of the manager at lines 27–28 – Jenny, having declined to endorse Ann at the first opportunity (after 'offputting'), then pounces with a latched agreement, 'Yes'. This, however, lacks the upgrade which routinely marks agreements: a less than wholehearted ratification of Ann's position.

Both this, and her construction of what comes next, is of course entirely consistent with her own position as the *originator* of the negative assessment of the manager, at line 9. To fall in with Ann's assessment – 'cocky little devil' – would be to concede priority to Ann in rights to assess. So the subsequent 'Well that's uh yihknow Fazil said' (line 29) seems designed to reclaim first position. However, it would seem that 'that's what Fazil said' would still amount to a concession, given that the negative assessment she produced at line 9 was itself couched in terms of the manager's character, who 'Fazil never liked' (lines 8–9). 'That's what Fazil said' would thus simply be a reiteration of her original position. The switch from this format, mid-course, to the direct report, 'Fazil said', then, serves as an epistemic upgrade of what was beginning to be produced because it delivers evidence on its own terms. But it also accomplishes something else: what Jenny reports represents a return to what had been overlapped in Ann's competitive startup at line 10 – her observation that 'Fazil would never go there'. So the direct reported speech allows Jenny to reiterate the stance which she held prior to Ann's intervention, by reporting Fazil's position by means of what he said: 'I'm payin' money I'll not...'. What she constructs as his words at lines 29–31, then, ultimately provides the evidence for her report at lines 8–9.

Like the examples of direct reported speech in extracts (1)–(3), what Fazil is represented as saying is rendered as a recognisably formulaic phrase which is sufficiently identifiable from its beginning, so that, although it ebbs into laugh tokens, it is clear that Fazil is doing a complaint. While it resists direct endorsement of Ann's assessment, it nevertheless attends to it in reporting the grounds for Fazil's reluctance to patronise the shop. And, indeed, the evidential force of the direct reported speech here is suggested by the emphatic agreement it elicits: 'Yeh exactly' (line 33). In what has been a somewhat competitive jostling to assess, it is Jenny who reaffirms her priority in the matter.

We have seen, then, that although the format 'that's what x said' may be used adversarially in staking claims to epistemic priority, it is the direct reports of speech – 'x said' – which are evidentially stronger.

5.6 Conclusion

This collection of exemplars has suggested that reported speech is constructed to be distinctly recognisable as launching specific actions, while also being profoundly shaped by the interactional context in which it is placed. The reporting itself is the enactment of a position to which the other has just laid claim, the enactment itself serving to override its own status as produced after a first assessment. These fleeting uses of reported speech have provided a sequential basis for Holt's claim (1996: 241) that reported speech provides evidence. Alongside Heritage and Raymond's (2005) observations on the grammatical resources speakers draw upon in pursuit of a claim of epistemic priority, reported speech has been revealed as another such resource – and one that, in many cases, proves the trump card. The reported speech detaches the formulated position from the interactionally occasioned, in situ addressing of the matter: at moments when participants' primary rights to assess are being challenged, it is perhaps one of the most powerful evidential displays of having got there first.

6

Reported thought in complaint stories

Markku Haakana

6.1 Introduction

Research has been conducted on interactional reported speech, i.e. presentations of what interactants have said in an interaction (see e.g. Holt, 1996, 2000; Tannen, 1989; and other chapters in this volume), but the use of reported thought has attracted much less attention in interactional studies, and in studies of reported speech in general. In this chapter, I focus on the construction and design and use of reported thoughts – especially on *I thought that*-constructions – in one specific activity environment, complaint stories about the actions of other people. Previous research has already shown that there are some interactional environments in which speakers frequently make use of reported speech, especially of direct reported speech: story-telling seems to be the major (but not the only) environment for reported speech (see, for example, Labov, 1972; Holt, 1996, 2000), and there might be some types of stories that especially favour the use of (direct) reported speech. Holt (2000) analyses two such story types, complaints and amusing stories. In analysing a database of Finnish complaint stories,[1] I found that reported thought is also a recurrent device in complaint stories, and one of the devices that is used to construct complaint

---

[1] The current corpus consists of forty complaint stories, most of which are from everyday conversations; a couple of instances are from institutional interactions. The study of complaint stories is an ongoing research project of mine and the study of reported thought/speech is only one line of analysis.

stories *as* complaint stories. This chapter demonstrates that reported thought is a well-fitted device for constructing complaints.

The chapter also argues that reported thought deserves attention on its own – most often it has just been seen as part of reported speech, but its specific functions in interaction have not been analysed. Within linguistics, the construction and use of reported thought has been studied especially in literary texts, in narration of fictional texts (see, for example, Leech and Short, 1981: Chapter 10). Several grammatically oriented studies of reported speech include reported thought; thus, when discussing 'reported speech' most scholars subsume reported speech and thought (see, for example, McGregor, 1994; in Finnish, Kuiri, 1984; *Iso Suomen Kielioppi*, 2004: 1399–1428). This is understandable, since reported speech and thought can be grammatically constructed in the same way (*Iso Suomen Kielioppi*, 2004: 1490). As a conversation analyst interested in the design and sequential features of linguistic devices in interaction, what I find missing is analysis of how reported thought is constructed and used in interaction, and especially analysis of the interactional differences between reported speech and thought. There have been some studies that have dealt with the use of reported thought in interaction: for instance, Jefferson (1986) has studied the '*At first I thought*'-construction as a normalising device for extraordinary events. (Some observations are also in Labov, 1972; Holt, 1996: 233–236; see also Myers, 1999 on hypothetical reported discourse.) Nevertheless, reported thought deserves a more thorough interactional study which focuses on both its construction, the activities it is used to perform and its sequential environments.[2]

In the corpus of Finnish complaint stories, reported thought is recurrently found in a specific sequential environment: the narrator of the complaint story presents the reported thought as a silent reaction to a co-conversationalist's reported turn-at-talk. Extracts (1) and (2) provide typical examples:[3]

---

[2] Here I only deal with some aspects of reported thought in a very specific activity environment. Reported thought, however, can obviously be constructed and used differently in different kinds of activities and different kinds of interactions. This is an area for further research.

[3] The transcripts are presented as two versions: the first version includes the original Finnish utterance and a lexical and grammatical gloss

(1) [That bloody cat/telephone; extract of example (5)]

1   J :   vaikka   kyllä se vakuutti   et   joo   @mɪnä voin   vielä ajaa   joo@
          although PRT it assure-PST that PRT   I   can-1 still drive-INF PRT
2   £minä aattelin   et   joo   joo£ eh heh
          I   think-PST-1 that PRT PRT

1   J :   although she dɪd assure that yes @ I can still drive yeah@
2   £I thought that yeah yeah£ eh heh

(2) [Secretaries/telephone]
(Two secretaries of theatrical agencies talk about their bosses and how
they do not always understand the practicalities of the work. Here A is
reporting her boss assuming that something will now happen without a
problem and her subsequent thought presents a more practical orientation.)

1   E :   sitte (.)   Teroki   meil   oli   ohjelmistopalaveri   että no<
          then   1st name-CLI we-ADE   had   programme meeting   that PRT
2   (0.4) et   tää   toteutuu   nyt   sitte   ja
                 that this   be realized now   then   and
3   (aina) ele tää   sen   mukaa]   ni
          always live-PAS it-GEN   according to PRT
4   A :   [he he he he he he he he]
5   E :   mä aatteli   et   ↑niin ni   mitenhän   tää   nyt
          I   think-PST-1 that   PRT PRT   how-CLI   this now
6   toteutuu   et   siis   hetkinen et
          be realised that PRT   moment   that
7   A :   [eh eh eh eh eh eh eh eh eh   ]

1   E :   then (.) Tero also, we had a programme meeting
          ((he said)) that well<
2   (0.4) that this wɪll now then be realised and
3   [we'll go on with that   ] so
4   A :   [he he he he he he he he]
5   E :   I thought that ↑yeah so how will this now
6   [be realised that I mean waɪt a minute that]
7   A :   [eh eh eh eh eh eh eh eh eh   ]

(glossing symbols are listed at the end of the chapter). The second version
is an idiomatic translation into English. The line numbers in the English
translation match the numbers of the Finnish version. On most occasions, I have not translated the response particles such as *joo* and *nii(n)*,
following the example of Sorjonen (2001). If the meaning of the particle
is important for the analysed phenomenon, I take it up in the analysis.

Both instances include a report of somebody else's talk (extract (1) on line 1, extract (2) on lines 1–3), and the narrator's subsequent response, which is not portrayed as an utterance that was said in the interaction but as a thought (with the reporting utterance *minä/ mä aattelin et...* 'I thought that') the narrator presents herself as having during the narrated interaction. Through the use of reported thought, the narrator creates a multi-layered picture of the inter-action: on the one hand portraying what was said in the interaction, and on the other hand giving the current recipient access to what went on in the narrator's mind at the specific point of the narrated interaction. I shall argue that these kinds of reported thoughts are a device with which the narrator evaluates the narrated events – and especially the (verbal) actions – of the other, the antagonist, and thereby also guides the recipient in evaluating the story-in-progress. What separates reported thought from reported speech is that reported thoughts are *silent* reactions and, here more specifically, silent criticisms of the antagonist, i.e. they are something that was not brought to the interactional surface. Reported thought, then, deserves specific attention as something that was *not* said in the reported conversations and raises questions about why narrators report some-thing that was 'only' in their mind. This can have several uses in the interaction: for instance, through the use of reported thought the narrator can show that he or she indeed had a criticism in his or her mind but was sensible enough not to voice it to the co-interactant.

In this chapter, I analyse these sequences of reported speech and thought in detail. Towards the end of the chapter, I also discuss some forms of reporting that leave the distinction between speech and thought more or less open. There are ways of presenting con-structed dialogue in a way that does not make explicit whether the reported utterances were actually said or 'just' thought; for instance, reporting utterances of the type of *mä olin et* ('I was like'; see, e.g. Romaine and Lange, 1991). I shall present one of these more am-biguous cases and argue that, within complaint stories, these kinds of 'fuzzy' reportings can have their own interactional use.

6.2 Complaint stories, reported speech – and thought

The previous two extracts already showed that in complaint stories reported thoughts are closely associated with reported speech.

Thus, I shall start by explaining what I mean by the term 'complaint story' and by bringing together some observations about the use of reported speech in complaints. This section situates reported thought as *one* of the devices used in constructing complaint stories and in relation to reported speech.

With the term 'complaint story' I do not refer to just any kind of complaints. There are different kinds of complaints, and, as Dersley and Wootton (2000: 377–380) suggest, one has to be careful not to overgeneralise findings about a certain type of complaint to other kinds. In this chapter, I analyse stories which are complaints about a third party, i.e. about the 'transgressions or misconduct' (Drew, 1998a) of absent parties. I have borrowed the term 'complaint story' from Günthner (1997a), who analyses similar stories in German data. Günthner defines complaint stories as having the following features (1997a: 183): i) the narrator-cum-complainant appears as the protagonist in the narrative – this protagonist is the victim of some wrongdoing in the story-world; ii) the recipients of the complaint story are not part of the story-world and thus were not witnesses of the reconstructed events; iii) the antagonist and the wrongdoer who harmed, inadequately attacked, or wronged the protagonist is not present in the narrating situation. In effect, complaint stories are negatively loaded narratives about somebody who is not present in the current interaction, and the recipient has not been present in the situation now narrated.[4]

Günthner's study of complaint stories in German data (1997a, (but see also Günthner, 1999) and several studies of complaints in British and American conversations have shown that direct reported speech – with its accompanying prosody – is one central means of constructing complaints. It is one way of showing to the recipient(s) how the narrated situation and the conduct of the reported interactant really was worth complaining about. Naturally, reported speech is not the only means of constructing complaints as complaints. The speakers also make use of various kinds of assessments, displays of emotion, etc. (on constructing complaints, see Günthner, 1997a;

---

[4] Of course, actualisations of the activity type are not always clear-cut; the stories can resemble gossip (on differences, see Günthner, 1997a; Haakana, 2005) and also troubles-tellings (cf. Jefferson, 1986; Haakana, 2005).

Drew, 1998a; Haakana, 2005). But reported speech seems, nevertheless, to be a central device in complaint stories.

In the following, I shall show that not only reported speech but also reported thought is a recurrent and a delicate device for constructing complaints – at least in Finnish interactions. This can be seen in the following example, through which I shall present some previous findings about the uses of reported speech in complaints and raise questions about the role of reported thought within the story. In extract (3) Leena (L) is calling her fiancé Jari (J) from work and telling him about how she went to a professor's office hour at the university to get the grade of her final exam. It turns out that the grade is quite good, but Leena nevertheless finds the professor's conduct worth complaining about. She portrays the professor as unprofessional in certain aspects.

(3) [Professor/telephone]

```
1   L:  .h[h £no m]ä oon sitä    mieltä      että     mulle
            PRT I    be-1 it-PAR mind-PAR  that     I-ALL
2   J:  [£nii:.£]
         PRT
3   L:  kuuluki£        se    mutta  sitte   täs   on kyl  se   että    ne
         belong-PST-CLI it   but    then    here  is PRT  it   that    they/the
4       kysymysethän    ei    ollu mun       mielest   mitenkää  hirveen
         question-PL-CLI NEG   be-PPC I-GEN  mind-ELA  'in any way'  terrible-GEN
5       hyviä.
         good-PL-PAR
6   J:  [°°mm,°°      ]
7   L:  [.hh >ja ↑sit Kanto]la    kysy      multa  että .nhhh
            and then last name    ask-PST I-ABL  that
8   L:  että että< (0.5) <@niin. nämä (.) kysymykset  taisivat
         that that        PRT   these    question-PL  be likely-PL3-PST
9       olla, h aika helppoja.@>
         be-INF quite easy-PL-PAR
10      (.)
11  J:  [°°*mm:.*°°          ]
12  L:  [mut mä  en    sit]  siihen   sanonu  mitää     ja   sit
         but I   NEG-1 then  it-ILL   say-PPC anything  and  then
13      [vähä     ] (.) mä valitin       siitä    mitä  oli: *e*
         a bit         I   complain-PST-1 it-ELA   what  be-PST
14  J:  [°°eh heh°°  ]
15  L:  kysytiin      siit     Raijan          kirjasta  sitä   Ra:nskaa  ja
         ask-PST-PAS  it-ELA   first name-GEN  book-ELA  it-PAR  France-PAR and
16      Saksaa .hh        että    mä olin   odottanu  että   tulis  jotai
```

```
            Germany-PAR    that   I  be-PST-1 wait-PPC  that come-CON  some-PAR
17          laajempii          kysymyksii      et    ois        jonkinnäköinen synteesi
            large-COM-PL-PAR question-PL-PAR that be-CON some kind        synthesis
18          .mhh >sit se sano      mulle      @Niin, (0.6)    sellaisia
               then it  say-PST  I-ALL      PRT             such-PL-PAR
19          kysymyksiä        on  niin  vaikea   tehdä,h@
            question-PL-PAR is   so    difficult do-INF
20    J:    M(h)m[: m(h)h        ]
21    L:    [.mt mä aatteli    et ]    @<ki:va     ki:va>.@=
               I  think-PST-1 that     fine        fine
22    J:    =mh [h
23    L:         [vois   se   vähä  har£jotella       niitten      tekemistä£.
                  could  he   a bit practise-INF     they-GEN     make-INF-PAR
24    J:    .hhh niin  ku o:  on >tota< (.)   pohjakoulutustaki
                 PRT   as    is  that-PAR  basic-training-PAR-CLI
25          aika   hyvi.£ [hih hih heh heh heh ]
            quite  well
```

```
 1    L:    .h [h £well I] think that I did deserve£
 2    J:       [£nii : . £] ((yeah/yes))
 3    L:    it (=the grade) but then there is that issue that those
 4          questions y'know were not to my mind very
 5          good.
 6    J:    [°°mm,°°              ]
 7    L:    [.hh >and -then Kanto] la asked me that .nhhh
 8          that that< (0.5) <@well. these (.) questions were
 9          pretty easy I guess.@>
10          (.)
11    J:    [°°*mm:.*°°]
12    L:    [but I didn't] then say anything to that and then
13          [a bit        ] (.) I complained about what had: °e°
14    J:    [ °°eh heh°° ]
15    L:    was asked from that book by Raija that France and
16          Germany .hh I had been expecting that there would be some
17          larger questions that there'd be some kind of synthesis
18          .mhhh >then he said to me @Well, (0.6) such
19          questions are so difficult to make,h@
20    J:    M(h)m [: m(h)h         ]
21    L:          [.mt I thought that @<fi:ne fi:ne>.@
22    J:    =mh [h
23    L:        [he could prac£tise making them a bit.£
24    J:    .hhh Yeah as he has also quite a good basic
25          education£. [hih hih heh heh heh ]
```

In the extract, the narrator uses both reported speech and thought in constructing her complaint against the professor. Reported speech is used on several occasions but reported thought only on one occasion (line 21), which is a typical pattern in the corpus. I shall first focus on the instances of reported speech and discuss the functions of them, and then move on to analyse the use of reported thought.

At lines 1 and 3 Leena says that she thinks she deserves the grade she has received and then constructs a complaint about the professor: the questions in the exam were not good (lines 3–5). At lines 7–9 is the first occurrence of reported speech: the professor is reported asking about the simplicity of the questions. This utterance is presented as direct reported speech; it is presented as the professor said it in the situation (note the dialogue particle *niin* and the deictics of *nämä* 'these'). It has been pointed out in several studies (see e.g. *Iso Suomen Kielioppi*, 2004: 1459; Holt, 2000: 427) that at least in spoken language the distinction between direct and indirect reported speech is often hard to draw. In Finnish, one feature that makes this distinction even fuzzier is the use of the particle *et(tä)* ('that') before the direct reported utterance. In colloquial Finnish this is quite customary: although *et(tä)* has been considered often as a marker of indirect reporting, in spoken language it is quite commonly used with direct reported speech as well (Kuiri, 1984; *Iso Suomen Kielioppi*, 2004: 1465). (I have kept the *et(tä)* in the English translation, lines 7–8, as *that*.)[5] In this example, Leena does not use direct reported speech to present her own utterances, even though this often is the case in complaint stories. Instead, she offers a more gloss-like and indirect version of her activities (lines 12–17): she says that she 'a bit I complained' and details what that complaining consisted of. The professor's

---

[5] In colloquial Finnish, there are various ways of introducing reported utterances. The reporting 'clause' (or utterance) can be of the traditional type *he said/she thought*, but it can also consist of just a pronoun or a name and a particle: at least particles *et* and *niinku* can be used for this (*se et... se niinku.../he (that), he like*). (On reporting clauses/utterances in spoken Finnish, see, for example, Kuiri, 1984; Routarinne, 2003; *Iso Suomen Kielioppi*, 2004: 1485–1492; Haakana, 2005). Thus, the linguistic term 'reporting clause' does not always capture how reported speech is framed in interaction; in this chapter, I use the term 'reporting utterance' to refer to the clauses, particles, etc. that are used to frame (see McGregor, 1994) an utterance as reported speech.

response at lines 18–19 is again constructed as direct reported speech.

The previously mentioned findings about the uses of direct reported speech in complaints can easily be fitted to this example, too. Several explanations for the frequent use of direct reported speech have been suggested. One obvious reason is that complaints are very often about what other people have said – and also about how they said it (see, for example, Holt, 2000: 453). In (3), the complaint is not only about the questions not being good, but also about what the professor said during the encounter (for instance, the reported utterance at lines 8–9 could be heard implying that Leena got a good grade because the questions were 'too easy') and how he responded to Leena's criticisms. For this purpose – just presenting what was said as a target for criticism – indirect reported speech could probably be used as well. Why is direct reported speech chosen over indirect and other forms? The use of direct reported speech has been said to dramatise the narration and create involvement (see, for example, Labov, 1972; Li, 1986; Tannen, 1989; Holt, 1996, 2000) – it makes the telling more vivid and invites the recipient(s) to participate in the story-world and, thereby, also to align with the current narrator and his or her point of view towards the depicted events. Holt (1996, 2000) shows that direct reported speech is also used as an effective and economical way of providing evidence: by presenting what was said and how *it* was said as 'in the actual interaction' the narrator gives the recipient(s) the possibility of judging the antagonist's actions himself or themselves. As Drew (1998a: 321) puts it, 'the transgressor's words are left to speak for themselves'. Thus, the direct reported speech is a form of implicit evaluation: the speaker does not (at least not always) assess the antagonist's actions herself but 'simply' presents what the antagonist said and leaves the assessing to the recipient (Holt, 2000). In extract (3), we can see that the recipient of the story, Jari, responds to the reported speech at line 20 with a response token ('mm mh') and laughter. Direct reported speech is often used at crucial points of the story and is often the action the recipients respond to, with laughter, assessments, etc.

One important feature of direct reported speech is its prosody: it is often accompanied by prosodic and paralinguistic cues that can have several different functions (see, for example, Holt, 1996,

2000; Drew, 1998a; Günthner, 1997a, 1999; Klewitz and Couper-Kuhlen, 1999; Haakana, 2005). The prosodic marking of reported speech can be 'just' a quotation marker; a contextualisation cue that indicates that the strip of talk is to be interpreted as reported speech (see, for example, Gumperz, 1982). But the prosody has also been said to be a part of the dramatisation and evidence-building character of the reported utterances: the speaker can claim to present the reported utterances as accurate in several ways, not only in what was said but also in how it was said. For instance, in (3) Leena presents the professor's utterances with an animated voice (marked with @) – she makes her voice lower and also adopts a slower pace of talking while reporting the professor's talk; note also the pause at line 18 within the reported utterance, which further serves to give the impression of slowness). However, these kinds of prosodic and paralinguistic cues can also be seen as the speaker's evaluation of the reported speaker: with different kinds of animated voices speakers can portray someone's verbal behaviour as impolite, aggressive, stupid, etc. (see also Holt, 2000: 435).[6]

In spite of the observations that direct reported speech presents the reported utterances as they 'really were' and can be thus used as evidence, it is important to remember that the dialogues in these stories are best seen as 'constructed dialogues' (Tannen, 1989). There is no guarantee that the speakers in the narrated situation said anything like what is presented in the reported utterances (on this paradox, see Tannen, 1989; Holt, 2000). The use of direct reported speech is rather to be seen as a device that the narrator uses to do something in this interaction now: the teller chooses what he or she presents and the manner, and through these choices constructs a certain kind of picture of the situation and seeks a certain kind of response from the recipient.

---

[6] My impression is that the prosodic and paralinguistic features of reported speech can be quite conventionalised, i.e. that we have 'gram-maticalised' prosodic and paralinguistic resources for framing some reported utterance as 'mock innocent', 'rude', etc. (see Haakana, 2005). This aspect of conversational prosody has not been studied systematically yet.

Many of the previous observations on reported speech can also be fitted to the occurrence of reported thought. For instance, syntactically and prosodically reported speech and thought can be constructed in the same way: Leena's utterance at line 21 is built with a reporting utterance (*mä aattelin et* 'I thought that') and a reported utterance (*@kiva kiva@* 'fine fine'). The reporting is produced with an animated voice, in the same way as a lot of reported speech is. Furthermore, the reported thought is best seen as a part of 'constructed dialogue' in the same way as reported speech: there is, of course, no guarantee that Leena thought anything like that in the actual situation she is narrating, but here she chooses to construct a reported thought as a response to the professor's previous utterance. As in reported speech, reported thought can also be seen as a device for evaluating the narrated events. However, whereas with reported speech the narrator can leave the transgressor's words to 'speak for themselves', with reported thought the narrator can more clearly show how he or she evaluated the (verbal) actions in the situation depicted. In effect, reported thought offers more explicit evaluation than reported speech but nevertheless situates the evaluation in the story-world, not in the present interaction. The following section focuses on the construction and interactional uses of reported speech.

6.3 Reported thought: reportings with the verb 'think'

As already pointed out, in the corpus reported thought occurs much more seldom than reported speech. What one usually finds is that the teller uses a reported thought once within a story, as was the case in extract (3). Reported thought, understandably, does not construct dialogues as reported speech does (i.e. we do not get, *I thought... he thought... I thought...*, etc.). In the data, all the reported thoughts are constructed with the past tense (*I thought...*). Even though speakers can report the thoughts of others (based on making inferences, etc.), in my data, all the reportings are of the narrator's own thoughts, which are, through tense selection, depicted as thoughts that occurred within the narrated situation. The clearest cases of reported thought in my data are ones that are constructed with the reporting verb 'think' (in Finnish *ajatella*, which in the data mostly occurs in the colloquial form *aatella*). This verb clearly marks the reported utterance as a reported thought. However, there are also other ways of framing the reported utterance as 'thought' rather than speech and, in addition, there are some framings that leave this distinction open, as shown in the next section.

I shall start by analysing some cases where the reported utterance is framed with the construction *mä aattelin et* ('I thought that'). In the following, I shall discuss the use of reported thought from several angles: how they are constructed; their function as a device for evaluation (of the persons, their utterances and actions); and their function as *silent* criticisms, as something that was *not* said in the interaction currently narrated. As Labov (1972) stated in his analysis of narrative structure, both reported speech and reported thought can be used as devices for embedded evaluation of the story. In the complaint stories, the narrators can use the reported thought to show that there was indeed something to criticise in the talk and the actions of the antagonist. By showing what they themselves thought at the time of the interaction, they can give the recipient some guidance in assessing the story and in producing an evaluation that matches their own. A shorter extract of example (3) is analysed here, showing this in operation:

(4) [Extract of (3) reproduced]

```
13          [vähä   ] (.) mä valitin          siitä    mitä   oli: °e°
             a bit        I   complain-PST-1 it-ELA what   be-PST
14   J :   [°°eh heh°°]
15   L :   kysytiin       siit    Raijan            kirjasta      sitä      Ra:nskaa    ja
             ask-PST-PAS it-ELA first name-GEN book-ELA  it-PAR    France-PAR  and
16          Saksaa .hh          että    mä olin  odottanu että tulis    jotai
             Germany-PAR    that    I   be-PST-1 wait-PPC   that   come-CON  some-PAR
17          laajempii            kysymyksii       et      ois           jonkinnäköinen synteesi
             large-COM-PL-PAR question-PL-PAR that be-CON   some kind        synthesis
18          .mhh >sit  se sano        mulle      @Niin, (0.6)    sellaisia
                  then it  say-PST I-ALL     PRT                such-PL-PAR
19          kysymyksiä          on    niin    vaikea    tehdä,h@
             question-PL-PAR is    so      difficult  do-INF
20   J :   M(h)m[: m(h)h           ]
21   L :           [.mt mä aatteli   et]  @<ki:va ki:va>.@=
                      I    think-PST-1 that  fine      fine
22   J:    =mh[h
```

```
23  L:  [vois   se    vähä  har£jotella  niitten    tekemistä£.
        could  he   a bit  practise-INF  they-GEN  make-INF-PAR
24  J:  .hhh niin  ku   o:   on  >tota< (.)  pohjakoulutustaki
              PRT  as        is   that-PAR   basic-training-PAR-CLI
25      aika   hyvi.£ [hih hih heh heh heh ]
        quite  well
```

```
13          [a bit      ]  (.) I complained about what had: °e°
14  J:  [ °°eh heh°° ]
15  L:  was asked from that book by Raija that France and
16      Germany .hh I had been expecting that there would be some
17      larger questions that there'd be some kind of synthesis
18      .mhh  >then he said to me @Well, (0.6) such
19      questions are so difficult to make,h@
20  J:  M(h)m[: m (h)h          ]
21  L:          [.mt I thought that @<fi:ne fi:ne>.@
22  J:  =mh [h
23  L:          [he could prac£tise making them a bit.£
24  J:  .hhh Yeah as he has also quite a good basic
25      education£. [hih hih heh heh heh ]
```

At lines 18–19 Leena uses direct reported speech to present the
professor's answer to her complaint. At line 21 she presents her
silent response to the professor's turn-at-talk. Her turn is constructed as a reported thought with the reporting utterance *mä
aatteli et* ('I thought that') and the reported thought is the utterance
kiva kiva ('fine fine'), which is produced with an animated voice.
The utterance itself can be heard as an ironic one: the adjective *kiva*
is reduplicated, and the prosody of the utterance – and the overall
complaining context – lead to interpreting the lexical contents of
the utterance in an opposite way; that is, the professor's answer is
anything but fine.

With this utterance Leena shows how she herself interprets the
professor's talk; that his answer is worth complaining about.
In effect, reported thought is one of the ways to show that the activity at hand is a complaint and to guide the recipient to the same
interpretation. Here, Jari has already responded to the direct
reported speech at line 20 with laughter (produced through the
response particle 'mm mh'), thus showing that the answer the

professor gave was something to laugh at. Leena's reported thought further directs the talk into assessing the professor's behaviour in terms of its professionalism: at line 23, Leena then produces an utterance which constructs a kind of directive to the professor ('he could practise'). With this utterance she moves from the narrated situation to the present one: the utterance at line 23 does not report her thoughts in the narrated situation but rather transforms the professor as a target of assessment here-and-now (note the third person reference *se* 'he'). Jari goes on to give grounds for why the professor should know better. In this extract, the interactants assess the narrated events together with the same type of evaluation, and reported thought is used as a device for arriving at this assessment.

Extract (4) showed that, in conversational story-telling, thoughts are presented in the same way as spoken utterances. Leena's direct reported thought is prosodically marked and also ironic in nature. In effect, the reported utterance is something that could have been said in the situation, but through the reported thought construction is now presented as something that was *not* said.[7] With reported thoughts the speakers can give a multi-layered picture of what happened in the narrated situation: on the one hand, the speaker details what was taking place on the conversational surface; and on the other, they can indicate what was happening beyond the actual interaction, what they did not say – and how they perceived and evaluated the situation as it was developing turn by turn. Reported thought, then, is used as a silent, critical response to the co-interactant's turn-at-talk and functions as an evaluation device through which the narrator presents his or her own evaluation of the depicted events.

Extract (5) shows another instance of this pattern. In this conversation between two brothers, Juha (J) is telling his brother (Ari) about what happened the previous night. He starts his story by

---

[7] Note that in extract (4), besides reported thought, Leena also uses other ways to indicate what was *not* said in the narrated interaction: although she says that she 'complained a bit' (line 13), she also says that she did not say anything in response to the professor's question see extract (3), line 12 – after this extract, she also says, 'I didn't start arguing with that'.

saying that he is 'bitter' (not shown in the extract) and goes on to explain why. This is a complaint about a cat but also about the actions of Juha's wife. She has prepared a wonderful dinner with wine and Juha is ready to enjoy his life. Then she remembers that her cat (which is in a different apartment) is outside and somebody has to go and let it in. She herself is already drunk and cannot drive, and Juha has to leave to take care of what he himself calls 'that bloody cat'. The reported thought occurs at line 13 in response to the wife's utterance, in which she is trying to assure Juha that she is still capable of driving:[8]

(5) [That bloody cat/telephone]

```
 1  J:  £mjnä aattelin    et    nyt   minä£  tässä s-  niinku  kunnolla  syön
         I     think-PST-1 that  now   I      here      PRT     properly  eat-1
 2      ja    juon    vähän  tuota    vjjniä   ja   sitten  minä  siirryn   kahtomaan
         and   drink-1 a bit  that-PAR wine-PAR and  then    I     move-1    watch-INF-ILL
 3      televisiosta    hh manitpoissia hh      ja   na_:utin elämästä  ni   e_:ikö  ä
         television-ELA     name of TV show-PAR  and  enjoy-1 life-ELA   PRT  NEG-Q   s
 4      tämä   yks   saa   piähäsä     että .hh  @herranjestas  se   on  se< hh
         this   one   get   head-ILL-POS that          'Good God'     it   is  it
 5      Mikki          ulukona@ (0.3)
         name(cat)      out
 6      .mt se  pittää piästä  sisälle .hhh  ja niinpä    se   oli    sitte   että
         it   must  get-INF inside         and so-CLI   it   be-PST then    that
 7      °en    minä voinu    juua     sitä    viiniä°.
         NEG-1  I    can-PPC  drink-INF it-PAR  wine-PAR
 8      (0.4)
 9  J:  itehän     se   oli    jhan  jo      kekkulissa  heh [heh
         herself-CLI it   be-PST quite already 'drunk'
10  ?A:                                                      [(°hnh hnh°)
11  J:  £ ei    se voinu    aj(h)aa he heh £
          NEG   it can-PPC  drive-INF
12  J:  vaikka    kyllä se  vakuutti  et   joo  @mjnä voin  vielä  ajaa     joo@
         although  PRT   it  assure-PST that PRT  I     can-1 still  drive-INF PRT
13      £mjnä aattelin    et   joo  joo£ eh heh
         I     think-PST-1 that PRT  PRT
14      (.)
15  J:  .hhh .hhh
16      (.)
17  J:  kyllä   minä sitten  kun  tulin        takasin sieltä   niin join
         PRT     I    then    when come-PST-1   back    there    PRT  drink-PST-1
18      viiniä
19      wine-PAR
```

[8] Note that at line 1 Jari starts telling what he was planning to do before his plans were destroyed, and employs here another kind of use of reported thought ('I thought that', line 1): telling of thoughts that are subsequently shown to be mistaken.

```
1    J:    £I thought that now I'll£ e- like eat properly
2          and have some of that wine and then I'll go an watch
3          Manitpois on television hh and enjoy life then doesn't
4          this one get it in her head that .hh @good god that< hh
5          Mikki is outside@ (0.3)
6          .mt it has to be let inside .hhh and so it was then that
7          °I couldn't drink that wine°.
8          (0.4)
9    J:    she herself y'know was quite tipsy already heh [heh
10   ?A:                                                  [(°hnh hnh°
11   J:    £she couldn't dr(h)ive he heh £
12         although she did assure that yes @I can still drive yeah@
13         £I thought that yeah yeah£ eh heh
14         (.)
15   J:    .hhh .hhh
16         (.)
17   J:    I did then when I came back from there I had some
18         wine
```

At line 12 Jari uses direct reported speech to depict his wife telling
him she could still drive; this utterance is produced with an animated voice that presents the speaker as drunk. Jari's response to
this utterance (line 13) is constructed as a reported thought with
the reporting utterance *minä aattelin et* ('I thought that') and the
reported utterance consists of the reduplicated response particle *joo*
('yeah'). He also laughs at this point (end of line 13), whereby he
could be heard inviting the recipient to laugh also (on laugh invitations, see Jefferson, 1979; on laughter in reported speech, see Holt, this
volume). His recipient does not join in with the laughter, however:
Ari participates quite minimally throughout the whole sequence.[9]

---

[9] Ari's laughter (line 10) is marked with a question mark; I am not sure
whether he participates in laughing at this point. Ari's minimal presence
in this story can be caused by many things: for instance, maybe he does
not want to take part in evaluating the actions of Juha's wife. Responding
to complaint stories has not yet been studied in any depth (see Günthner,
1997a; however, also Mandelbaum, 1991/1992). This is an area of study
that I intend to get into; I have already started to analyse recipient
responses in institutional interaction (Haakana, 1999, unpublished) but
a more thorough study on everyday talk is needed.

We have now seen two extracts of complaint stories in which the narrator employs reported thought. Through these examples, some more general issues about the use of reported thoughts in complaint stories can now be discussed.

Reported thought can be constructed in the same way as (direct) reported speech: the thoughts are presented as utterances that employ prosody in the same way as reported speech and that could have been said in the actual situation. Thus, reported thought is like reported speech in its design (see also *Iso Suomen Kielioppi*, 2004: 1490), but through the reporting utterance (*I thought that...*) the speakers present it as something that was not said in the interaction. In the light of the previous examples one could wonder whether reported thought tends to be more minimal as utterances; namely, Jari's reported thought utterance (extract (5), line 13) bears a striking resemblance to Leena's *kiva kiva* in (extract (4), line 21). In Jari's turn the reduplicated item is the particle *joo*, the use of which in the reduplicated form has not yet been studied thoroughly (on the particle *joo*, see Sorjonen, 2001). Here, *joo joo* displays the speaker's disbelief ('I do not believe you'), i.e. through this utterance Jari shows that his wife was not capable of driving even though she was claiming to be. Thus, in these extracts the reported utterances are quite minimal, consisting of just response particles (*joo joo*) or assessment terms (*kiva kiva*). This is often the case with reported thought, but not always. As further cases show, the 'thoughts' can also be longer and more complex syntactic structures (see extract (6), for example).[10]

In both cases – and in the corpus more generally – reported thought is used as a device for evaluation. In (4) Leena evaluates the professor's answer in critical terms, and in (5) Jari presents his wife's actions as complainable. The reported thought is used as one of the devices for evaluating the story and often is used, like reported speech, at a crucial point of the story, at its climax – which is the case with the previous examples. In (4) the recipient comes in to evaluate the depicted events quite strongly in accordance with the complainant, but in (5), even though the narrator

---

[10] In order to get to the – possible – structural differences between reported speech and thought, one would need a much bigger corpus, especially a large collection of reported thoughts.

invites the recipient to join in (with laughter, for instance) in this evaluation, the recipient does not join in the laughter, nor otherwise take up the criticism the narrator is constructing. Thus, the reported thought is a device for both presenting and inviting evaluation, but it does not necessarily manage to create recipient response (see fn. 9).

Another important feature of reported thought is that it presents silent criticisms. In (4) Leena indicates that she has criticised the professor's questions, but through the reported thought she shows that she did not – openly – criticise the professor's response to her complaint. In (5) the story does not show any signs of Jari openly criticising his wife's actions to her. Any critique he had is presented to have been 'just' in his thoughts. By portraying their criticisms as 'only thoughts' the narrators can also give a certain kind of a picture of the narrated situation: the antagonist behaved 'badly' (unprofessionally, stupidly, etc.) but the narrators did not start criticising the antagonist. Thereby they can also depict themselves in a certain light, for instance, as reasonable persons who did not want to get into an argument.

A further striking feature of the previous examples is that the narrator *only* portrays his or her 'mental' response to the antagonist's actions, i.e. the narrator does not present how they actually responded to the professor's answer or the wife's assurance of being capable of driving. Thus, only the response they had in their minds is shown to be relevant for this narrative here-and-now. However, sometimes the speakers report both their verbal response and their thoughts. This is nicely illustrated in the following extract, which also highlights the difference between surface and internal, 'mental' response. In (6) the narrator (M) details/discusses her experiences in a shoe shop, where she is trying to order some special shoes which are made and dyed for her. It turns out that she should pay an advance and she does not have enough money with her. The salesperson is depicted in a critical light from the beginning of the narrative: she is referred to as *eukko*, which is often used to refer to an older woman but can also be used as a pejorative description of a woman, as it is here. In response to the salesperson's actions, the narrator reports both her thoughts (lines 8–9) and her verbal response (lines 9–10):

(6) [Advance payment/telephone]

```
1   M:  ja   sit   se   eukko              halus      tota .mhh etukäteis
        and then  it   woman (pejorative) want-PST PRT      advance
2       mikä  se  nyt  etukäteismaksua.=
        what  it  now  advance payment-PAR
3   K:  =ai jaa.
        PRT
4   M:  no   eihä   mul   ollu   rahaa.   mul  oli  rahaa    yhdeksänkymment
        PRT  NEG-CLI I-ADE have-PPC money-PAR I-ADE had  money-PAR ninety
5       markkaa  sit   se  halus .hh        kakssataa, .mh   ↑ja  mä  oli    vaa  sit<
        mark-PAR then  it  want-PST         two hundred  and  I   be-PST just then
6       no   ei  mul  ei  kyl  ollu    nyt  sen   vertaa mukana, .hh  sit  se
        PRT  NEG I-ADE NEG PRT  have-PPC now  it-GEN much  with        then it
7       hi:rveesti  pohti       siinä   et  voikoha  se   nyt   sitte .hh  lähettää
        terribly    deliberate-PST there  that can-Q-CLI it   now   then       send-INF
8       niitä   sinne    värjättäväks    ku   mul  ei   oo  rahaa  ↑sit  mä °a-°
        they-PAR there    dye-PC-TRA      PRT  I-ADE NEG  have money-PAR then I
9       aatteli    et   mä  en   tässä   nyt  rupee  mitään  kerjäämään. =mä
        think-PST-1 that  I   NEG-1 here    now  start  anything beg-INF-ILL   I
10      sanoin   mä ↑voin tulla     sitten  tilaamaan    ne  joku  toinen kerta.
        say-PST-1 I   can-1 come-INF then    order-INF-ILL they some  other  time
11  K:  joo:.
        PRT
```

```
1   M:  and then that woman wanted uhmm .mhh advance
2       what is it now some advance payment.=
3   K:  =ai jaa. ((oh I see/oh really))
4   M:  well I didn't y'know have money. I had ninety
5       marks then she wanted .hh two hundred, .mh -and I was then just<
6       well I didn't really have that much with me, .hh then she
7       terribly deliberated about whether she can now then .hh send
8       them there to be dyed since I don't have money -then I °th-°
9       thought that I'm not going to start begging here for anything.
10      =I said I -can come then to order them some other time.
11  K:  joo:. ((yeah))
```

What is noteworthy about the two reported utterances is that the
reported thought is more critical and affective in nature than the reported speech. The reported verbal response ('I can come then to
order them some other time') portrays the narrator as giving up her
position and giving in to the salesperson's point of view. The reported
thought, on the other hand, displays a more affective stance: through
the utterance *mä en tässä nyt rupee mitään kerjäämään* ('I'm not
going to start begging here'), the salesperson is depicted as putting
the narrator in the position of 'begging' and expresses the narrator's
strong refusal of being in such a position. Thus, again the reported

thought serves to construct the narrated situation as complainable: through the use of reported thought the narrator not only shows what happened in the situation but also how she interpreted it and, again, gives the recipient access to the affective keying of the story.

The phenomenon described above – the constructed dialogue between reported speech and thought – seems to be a conventionalised device for portraying certain kinds of situations and constructing complaints. Further evidence for this pattern can be found in Hyvättinen's (1999) analysis of reader's columns in Finnish young people's magazines. The letters and stories sent by the readers often present dialogues, and within these dialogues Hyvättinen has found similar uses of reported thought.[11] Thus, at least in Finnish

---

[11] One of Hyvättinen's examples is presented here as a point of comparison (no gloss line is provided for this extract). The writer tells about a conversation with her mother. The utterances in italics are analysed as reported thoughts: only one of them has the reporting clause (*ajattelin* 'I thought') in it, but the other utterances with italics have a parallel syntactic structure and therefore are easily interpreted as reported thought also (extract from Hyvättinen, 1999: 32; youth magazine *Sinä and Minä* (*You and me*)).

Äsken äiti kertoi lähtevänsä taas matkalle. 'Ethän sä suutu?' se vielä kysyi. 'En tietenkään,' kuulin sanovani... *Vaikka sä menetkin toisen miehen luo.* Äiti kertoi, etten saakaan uusia kenkiä ja farkkuja. 'Ymmärräthän sinä, kun tämä lamakin on ja työttömäksi kohta joudun,' se selitti. 'Joo ymmärrän.' *Vaikka sä lupasitkin, ajattelin.* 'Muistathan huolehtia siskostas ja veljestäs ja laittaa ruokaa, kun ei se isä osaa,' se sanoi. 'Joo, joo,' kuulin taas vastaavani... *Vaikka sinähän se äiti olet.*
  Painan pääni tyynyyn ja kyynel vierähtää, mutta ensi kerralla kyllä sanon sille ajatukseni, ensi kerralla... (*Sinä and Minä*, October 1994)

Just now mother told me she was going on a trip again. 'You won't get upset?' she still asked. 'Of course not,' I heard myself saying... *Even though you are going to another man.* Mother told that I won't be getting new shoes and jeans after all. 'You do understand, there is this depression going on and soon I am going to be unemployed,' she explained. 'Yeah I understand.' *Even though you promised, I thought.* 'Remember to take care of your sister and brother and cook, since your father doesn't know how,' she said. 'Yeah, yeah,' I heard myself answering again... *Even though you are the mother.* I put my head on the pillow and shed a tear, but next time I will tell her what I think, next time...

(*Sinä and Minä*, Octover 1994)

Hyvättinen analyses the use of reported thoughts in these stories as a way of bringing up a second level to the interaction: on the surface,

conversations the pattern of reported speech/reported thought is recurrently used in presenting complaints about the actions of others. Although reported thought has not been the focus of other interactional studies of reported speech, some similar examples can be found, for instance, in Holt (2000).[12] In the following extract from a complaint story, Lesley is employing reported thought (lines 8, 10 and 11) as a silent crictical response to an antagonist's turn-at-talk. In extract (7) (from Holt, 2000: 433–434) Lesley is reporting a conversation with a woman who has asked her to help at a forthcoming event. The story portrays the woman's behaviour as complainable in several ways. For instance, she has said that Joyce has suggested Lesley as a next person to be called (lines 1–2), which Joyce denies (line 19). The reported thought, however, occurs as a response to the woman's turn, which takes up Lesley's account (teaching, in lines 4–6) for not being able to help:

(7) [Holt:O88:1:8:10]

```
 1   Lesley:   An' ↑then she rang me up 'n said that (.) Joyce
 2             suggested that I[(   help)] ↑huh [hah huuh↑
 3   Joyce:                  [Ahhh:::: ]      [Ohhh:::::::.
 4   Lesley:   hu-uh .hhhhh [↑So I said um .khhh W'I'm sorr[y I'm=
 5   Joyce:                [(     )                       [(   )
 6   Lesley:   =teaching she said .hh ↑↑Oh: (.) ↑oh my dear, well
 7             how lovely that you're involved in ↑↑tea↓ching.
 8             A[n' ↓I: thought .hhh
 9   Joyce:    [Ohh:.
10   Lesley:   ↑Well al↑right then p'haps I'd like to suggest
```

everything goes smoothly – in the extract the daughter responds to mother's turns-at-talk with affiliating turns ('of course I won't get upset', 'yeah I understand') – but in her thoughts she is very critical of the mother's actions. The situation and the mother's actions and talk are shown to be complaint-worthy but this is not brought to the conversational surface.

12 I would like to thank Elizabeth Holt for drawing my attention to extract (7) and helping me to analyse it.

```
11              you ↑↑f'the nex' supply pe(h)ers[(h)on
12   Joyce:                                      [UH::::h
13   Lesley:   h[eh-uh heh-uh heh-uh huh
14   Joyce:     [heh.
15              (0.5)
16   Joyce:    She said um::n e::m did I know if you were
17             tea:ching.
18              (0.2)
19   Joyce:    I didn:'t suggest you at all [she-  ]
20   Lesley:                              [No n]o: no:
```

In her analysis of the extract, Holt says that Lesley's report of the
woman's response (at lines 6–7) is 'used to convey the reported
speaker's inappropriately positive, and consequently condescend-
ing, reaction to the news that Lesley is currently supply teaching
(i.e. temporarily taking the place of an absent teacher)' (2000: 429).
The reaction is overdone and comes off as patronising. In her
subsequent reported thought, Lesley takes up on these aspects: in
her thoughts she is ready to suggest the woman as the next supply
teacher. With this thought Lesley seems to be commenting on the
other's (overdone) enthusiasm for teaching, which she perhaps does
not share herself. On the interactional surface, however, things are
presented as going smoothly. In the present interaction, Lesley's
reported thought manages to get affective responses from Joyce:
the interjection 'UH::::' at line 12 and laughter (line 14) which is,
however, quite minimal compared to Lesley's own laughter. This
extract suggests that the pattern analysed in this Chapter is not
specific to Finnish conversations alone.

6.4 Reported speech or thought?

Through reported thoughts the teller of a complaint story presents
a certain kind of picture of the situation: the antagonist was behav-
ing in a way that is worth complaining about, but the teller did not
bring his or her criticisms up in the interaction. On the surface, the
interaction went smoothly (more or less), but underneath it was
more stormy. The utterances that are reported as thoughts are
something that could have been said in the interaction but were
not. We shall now move on to look at a case in which the narrator

constructs such a depiction of the interaction that she – possibly – did say something back to the antagonist, demonstrating that the co-interactant's actions were complainable. In the following case it is not possible to distinguish whether something was said or 'just' thought. I shall analyse a case of reporting that leaves open the distinction between reported speech/thought and argue that this fuzziness can be quite functional within complaint stories. By presenting their actions as (possibly) 'saying something back' or 'criticising the antagonist' the speakers can portray themselves as more active participants in the situation, and thus perhaps even in a more 'heroic' light.

When constructing reported utterances, speakers can construct them as clearly reported speech by choosing a verb like *say* in the reporting utterance or they can use verbs that clearly construct the reported utterance as thought (*think*). However, speakers also have other choices that leave the distinction between speech and thought unclear. One of them is discussed here briefly: the reportings with the verb *be* (i.e. reportings of the type *I was like...*). This type of reporting has been studied at least in English (Romaine and Lange, 1991), and there are some observations on this type of reporting in Finnish conversations as well (see, for example, Routarinne, 2003; Haakana, 2005).[13] One feature, mentioned both in studies of English and Finnish, is that it does not specify whether the reported utterance has been said or thought. This construction has presumably many different functions but I shall discuss it here only with the distinction between speech and thought in mind. In the extract following,[14] two teenage girls (M and T) are talking about a girl they both know. They both have a complaint story about this girl (Nadja); T has just finished hers and here M starts to tell about a incident that took place in the school. Nadja once publicly

---

[13] In Finnish, this type of reporting often includes particles that are quite difficult to translate. Particles *niinku* ('like'), *sillee* ('in that way', 'like that'), *vaa(n)* ('just') and *et(tä)* ('that') can occur in combinations: *se oli et, se oli sillee et, se oli vaa et, se oli niinku vaa et...* My 'idiomatic' translations of these particles throughout the chapter are quite rough: it is very difficult to know what precise form in English would capture the subtle differences between different types of reporting utterances.

[14] I am grateful to Sara Routarinne for letting me use this extract from her data (Routarinne, 2003).

commented on M's bra, which was detectable through her shirt. Within this story M uses reportings of the type 'I was like' at least on two occasions, at lines 4 and 16 (and possibly at line 10 as well).

(9) [Bra/telephone]

```
 1  M:  no  mulle  se(h)  ain      t : aas  h:uus      niinku
        PRT I-ALL  it     always   again    shout-PST  PRT
 2      ain      keskel        käytävää     tai< (.)  kerran  et .h
        always   middle-ADE    corridor-PAR or        once    that
 3      ai  sull      on Minnu   noi     Seppälä       rintsikat=
        PRT you-ADE   is 1nameF  those   (trade mark)  bra-PL
 4      >mä oli       et< °ä°eh ei  et   a:i mh mi- h mist    sä
        I   be-PST-1  that  NEG that PRT     what-ELA  you
 5      sen      tiedät.   .hh@>no ku   mä    tiedän   ku     niiss
        it-ACC   know-2    PRT    'cause I     know-1   cause  those-INE
 6      on tos       toi    tommone   poikkil:eikkaus ni   se<
        is there-INE that   such      cross-section   PRT  it
 7      näkyy  >ku    on tommone<   raskas   paita?.h@
        show   when   is  such      heavy    shirt
 8      (.)
 9  T:  n: n:ii:=
        PRT
10  M:  =(mä - et) @↑hä hä. (.) ai    jaa.@
        I      that          PRT PRT
11      ku     mul[l  olji  se  mun  vihree   neulep:aita
        cause  I-ADE  had   it  my   green    pullover
12  T:  [joo,]
        PRT
13  M:  ni  ku      se  painuu       °sillee°.
        PRT 'cause  it  sink/drop    like that
14      (0.5)
15  T:  ((haukottelee:))  .h[hh
16  M:                      [>mä oli<    sillee   et    @↑joo 't
                            [I   be-PST-1 that way that  PRT   that
17      kyl  mä  ihan   tiedän@  ke(h)rtom(h)att(h)ak(h)i
        PRT  I   quite  know-1   tell-INF-ABE-CLI
18      va(h)rsink(h)i k(h)iv(h)a  k(h)u  oikeen (0.5)  @huudat@. hhmhhh
        particularly    nice        when   really        yell-2
19      (1.0)
20  ?M:  (mitää).
```

```
 1   M:   well to me she(h) always shouted like
 2        always in the middle of the corridor or< (.) once that .h
 3        oh you have that Seppälä bra Minnu=
 4        >I was like< °e°eh no (that) mh how- h how do you
 5        know that. .hh@>well I know because there's
 6        a kind of cross-section in it so that it<
 7        shows >when you have that kind of< a heavy shirt?.h@
 8        (.)
 9   T:   n:ii:= ((yeah))
10   M:   =(I - (that)) @↑ha ha. (.) oh I see.@
11        cause I [had ] that green pullover
12   T:          [joo, ] ((yeah))
13   M:   y'know because it drops °like that°.
14        (0.5)
15   T:   ((yawning))    .h[hh
16   M:                   [>I was< like (that) @↑yes
17        I happen to know really@ with(h)out y(h)ou tell(h)ing ((it))
18        e(h)special(h)ly n(h)ice th(h)at you really (0.5)= @shout@.hhmhhh
19        (1.0)
20   ?M:  (anything)
```

The first occurrence of *mä olin et* ('I was (that)') is at line 4, where M constructs a response to Nadja's utterance. Here the reporting can be seen to be a case of reported speech: M's reported utterance is a question which subsequently gets an answer from Nadja (starting from line 5). Thus, sometimes the context can reveal that the reported utterance is reported speech (not thought). At line 10 M reports again her response: here the reporting utterance is difficult to hear – it does not necessarily have any verb in it (see fn. 5). The reported utterance at this point is laughter and a response particle *ai jaa*, which is used as a response to new information. For the present argument, the most interesting occurrence of reporting is at lines 16–18, where M constructs a more substantial reply to Nadja's comments on her bra. Here the reporting can be seen as an ambiguous one – neither the reporting utterance (*mä olin sillee et* – 'I was like (that)') or the context make it clear whether this is something that M actually said to Nadja – Nadja's response is not presented here. M's reported utterance has elements of criticising Nadja: M conveys that the information she has been given is unnecessary (she knows it; line 17) and ironically comments on Nadja's shouting (lines 17–18). This appears to be a place where the speaker uses reporting in a way that deliberately leaves the distinction between reported speech and thought open: M can imply that she criticised the antagonist but does not say it in explicit terms. The semantics of the reporting verb can also imply that this was 'just' a thought. The recipient does not take up on this reporting in any way.

I have now presented one way in which the speakers can construct their reportings in a way that does not make it explicit whether the reported utterance was said or thought. There are several other ways of making the distinction between reported speech and thought unclear (see Haakana, 2005). For instance, a lot of the reportings in conversation are produced with no reporting utterance at all (see, for example, Klewitz and Couper-Kuhlen, 1999), as what can be called 'zero quotations' (Mathis and Yule, 1994; see Holt, this volume), and often the reporting utterances in colloquial Finnish are produced without any verb (see fn. 5). These ways of constructing reported speech make it possible for the speakers to convey ambivalent pictures of the reported situation. Within complaint stories, these kinds of ambiguous reportings can sometimes be used to the speaker's benefit: to give or imply a picture of the situation in which the speaker possibly resisted the antagonist by criticising him or her.

6.5 Conclusion

In this chapter I have analysed the use of reported thought – and its relation to reported speech – in complaint stories. I have shown that not only reported speech but also reported thoughts are recurrently present in constructing complaint stories. In this chapter I also argued that it is worth considering reported thought separately from reported speech: although the presentations of reported speech and thought have a lot in common, there are also distinguishing features. Reported thought deserves special attention as something that was *not* said in the depicted interaction.

I started with cases in which the reported utterance was clearly presented as a thought through the selection of the verb in the reporting utterance. I showed that reported thoughts are used as a reaction to reported speech: reported speech of the antagonist and reported thought of the narrator occur in a sequence in which reported thought is used as an evaluation device. They are used to present a silent criticism towards the person that is the target of the complaint. Through the use of reported thoughts the narrator creates a multi-layered picture of the narrated situation by showing what happened not only in the interaction but also 'underneath' the surface, i.e. in the narrator's mind. With these thoughts the narrator can show how he or she evaluated the other's words and actions in the narrated interaction and thereby also guide the current recipient in evaluating the story. Consequently, the use of reported thought is one of the ways the narrator can construct his or her story as a complaint story and guide the recipient to offer responses which match this kind of affective keying.

Narrators can also choose to use ways of reporting that leave the distinction between speech and thought open. Here I presented one such technique (reporting utterances with the verb *be*), but there are also others. I argued that this fuzziness can sometimes be quite functional: the narrator can imply that he or she actually criticised the antagonist or fought back in the situation but does not have to claim this in more explicit terms (such as with a reporting utterance, 'I said').

Undoubtedly, reported thought can have different functions in other types of interactional contexts, and it can also be constructed in different ways; the findings presented here cannot be generalised to all occurrences of reported thought. On a more general level, this analysis suggests that it is rewarding to pay close attention to the ways the reported utterances are framed as reported utterances. Narrators make choices in constructing the reporting utterance: they can select the verb ('speak', 'think', etc.) or, at least in Finnish, a construction without a verb (*se niinku* 'he like', *se että* 'he (that)'), or they can choose to construct the reported utterance without any reporting utterance. Through different types of reporting utterances speakers can portray the narrated situation differently; here we have considered cases of reporting something as clearly said or thought and cases where this distinction is not clear. In my data, there are also several other types of reporting utterances that have not been presented here. For instance, speakers can use the following kinds of constructions which can also be seen as cases of reported thought: *vähän mun ois tehny mieli mennä sanoo sil et* ('I really wanted to go and say to her that'), *mä meinasin sanoo et* ('I was about to say that', 'I almost said that'). These reporting utterances, however, portray the situation in yet a slightly different way: these are thoughts that were almost said. Thus, utterances can be presented as 'said', 'thought' and also as 'almost said' (see Haakana, 2005). More detailed study of the different types of reporting utterances and their functions is an area for future interactional research on reported speech.

Glossing symbols

The Finnish examples are provided with a lexical and grammatical gloss. In the examples, I have not separated the morphemes of the Finnish original lexemes. The principles of glossing are modified from Sorjonen (2001), which also provides a list of some structural features of colloquial Finnish.

The following forms have been treated as unmarked forms, not indicated in the glossing: i) nominative case, ii) singular, iii) third person singular, iii) active voice, iv) present tense. Different infinitives and participial forms have not been specified.

Abbreviations used in the glossing are

1, 2, 3:   first, second, third
        person ending

Case ending abbreviations

ABE   abessive
ABL   ablative
ACC   accusative
ADE   adessive
ALL   allative
ELA   elative
GEN   genitive
ILL   illative
INE   inessive
PAR   partitive
TRA   translative

Other abbreviations used:

CLI   clitic
COM   comparative
CON   conditional
INF   infinitive
NEG   negation
PAS   passive
PC   participle
PL   plural
POS   possessive suffix
PPC   past participle
PRT   particle
PST   past tense
Q   interrogative

7

Designing contexts for reporting tactical talk

John Rae and Joanne Kerby

This chapter concerns a feature of the use of DRS in stories in conversation.[1] Previous work on stories has concerned issues such as when and how stories are initiated; how recipients may co-participate in them – and how this may condition the delivery of a story; and how stories may be closed and responded to. However in this chapter we are concerned with a story-construction practice which occurs within stories and which is illustrated in extract (1).

(1) [JK][2]

```
1   Russ:  ... I'm sitting there and
2          they goes There he is
3          .hh ran off yeah an I knocked on this door right
4          didn't even kno(hoh)w: whose it was hih hih
5          (.)
6          I goes this is my ↑uncle's house and
7          they all went no agh ah hah an ran off and
```

[1] We want to thank the young people and staff at the centre where the data examined here were recorded. We've received helpful comments on various versions of the work presented here: particular thanks are due to Charles Antaki, Rebecca Clift, Paul Dickerson, Paul Drew, Derek Edwards, Liz Holt and Nithya Rae.

[2] The data used here come from a weekly group discussion slot held at a day centre in the South of England which is attended by young people who, among other reasons, have refused to go to school, have been disruptive at school or have been directed by the youth court. Further details are provided in Kerby and Rae (1998). Briefly, thirteen

This is a fragment of a story in which Russ is reporting how he evaded some people who were chasing him. Our analysis will focus on the context (which the speaker provides in line 4) for the DRS (which he reports in line 6). Notice that in line 6 Russ uses DRS to report something he had said: 'this is my ↑uncle's house'. He produces this report as an action in a series of actions and events, which are formulated in various ways.[3] Schegloff (2000a) has referred to the differences in detail that may be noticed between formulations which are glosses of actions (e.g. 'I knocked on this door') and ones which (purportedly) reproduce actual actions (e.g. 'they goes there he is') as differences in *granularity*. The practice that we aim to examine is that the immediate context for the DRS in line 6 is not a formulation of an action or event but is, rather a gloss: 'didn't even kno(hoh)w: whose it was hih hih'. This gloss enables us, and the audience of Russ's report (but not the original audience), to see that the DRS in line 6 is a form of tactical talk. In order to examine this practice we will focus on some of the ways in which contexts can be prepared for the delivery of DRS, then some of the linkages between reported actions in stories, and finally some of the properties of representing responsive actions through DRS.

7.1 Framing a quotation

The importance of the context which a speaker (or writer) provides for a quotation was emphasised by Bakhtin:

The context surrounding reported speech plays a major role in creating the image of a language. The framing context, like the sculptor's chisel, hews the rough outlines of someone else's speech, and carves the image of language out of the raw empirical data of speech life...

participants took part; all were male aged between 14 and 16. In order to preserve the participants' anonymity, their names, (and certain other details), have been changed. In most cases new pseudonyms have been assigned in each extract reported.

[3] We have followed D. Davidson (1980) in considering actions to be special cases of events; namely, ones which involve behaviour where agency is relevant.

The words of the author that represent and frame another's speech create a perspective for it; they separate light from shadow, create the situation and condition for it to sound.   (1981: 357–358)

Such creative opportunities are used dramatically by Fox in a story in which he reports how he defeated a drug search (see extract (2)). He uses a historical frame to describe how he had a cigarette paper in his possession; the paper is elaborately downgraded to constitute little more than a piece of litter. Against this backdrop one policeman's action on finding this 'scrumpled up' cigarette paper is reported using DRS, which is enunciated in a tone of exaggerated pride:

(2) [JK]

1   Fox :   → I had I'd <u>one</u> Rizla in my pocket (.) not even in a
2   → packet just a scrumpled up (little) (0.7)
3   Fox :   → one goes Ahhh (.) you could get nicked for that,
4   Greg: hugh huh [ugh
5   Fox :   [hih hih
6   Fox :   → get nicked shut up

In extract (2) the context for the production of DRS is a description of a situation to which the reported talk is responsive. However, in our data a frequently occurring context for the presentation of DRS is the representation of an *action* to which the repeated talk is responsive; moreover, such actions are often represented by a high-granularity formulation – namely DRS.

(3) [JK]

1   Ben: =An Edward Smith goes (0.4) weren't the little one?
2   (0.3) it was 'im in the green ja:cket (.)
3   → the Ol' Bill grabbed me goes right, you're nicked (.)
4   → I went ↑Fuck off!

Here Ben uses direct reported speech (DRS) to report a reaction (line 4) to a police-related action (line 3). Here then, some police action (a) is reported using a direct quotation: 'the Ol' Bill grabbed me goes right, you're nicked' and it is followed by a response from the speaker, again reported using a direct quotation (r): 'I went ↑Fuck off!'. The sequence of actions being reported thus involves the components shown schematically in extract (4).

(4)

a→   ((formulation of police action involving DRS))

r→   ((formulation of speakers' action involving DRS))

Further examples are shown in extracts (5)–(9).

(5) [JK]

1 Ben: =An Edward Smith goes (0.4) weren't the little one?

2   (0.3) it was 'im in the green ja:cket (.)

3 a1→   the Ol' Bill grabbed me goes right, you're nicked (.)

4 r1→   I went ↑Fuck off!

5 a2→   he went you're nicked (.) get in the back of the van

6 r2→   I went n<u>o</u> I huh- hh

7   he grabbed me put my arms behind me back ((smiley
             voice))

(6) [JK]

1 Ben: a→ Goes t<u>a</u>ke your shoes and socks off

2   r→ Goes why

(7) [JK]

1   a→   an he goes you're being searched

2   r→   goes why

3   we <u>thi</u>nk we've got you in- (.) in possession of

4   dr<u>u</u>:gs

5   (.)

6   Alex: bad in it

(8) [JK]

1 a→ an they goes err (.) t<u>a</u>ke off your shoes (.) (yeh)

2 r→ (0.7) (I went) take off your shoes? (.)

3 r→ went no (.) why (.)

4   they went we 'ave to sw- we have to search your

5   shoes as well (.)

Thus, while extract (3) is particularly concerned with providing a context which aims to make the policeman's triumphant announcement of his discovery look ludicrous, extracts (4)–(8) are concerned with providing a context for the speaker to report what he or she said. This thus reverses one aspect of Bakhtin's account: rather than it being a matter of 'The words of the author that represent and frame another's speech' (1981: 357–358), instead speakers can be concerned with how the words of another can frame the author's speech.[4]

[4] It has been widely noted that, while speakers using DRS may claim to report what was said, this may not be the case at all. Couper-Kuhlen (this volume) and Haakana (this volume) consider reported thoughts. Furthermore the DRS format can be used for hypothetical or made-up speech. Thus Neil in extract (i), and Dan in extract (ii), consider hypothetical interactions with the police or a judge.

(i) [JK]

```
1  Neil:        Yeah just imagine fifty of us walking down the road
2               (0.4)
3               the Old Bill'll go past (0.3)
4        →      Oh (.) no!. [RIGHT lads!
5  (Pete):                  [ cos half of us are gonna be [in cars
6  Neil:                                                   [shht
7        →      (.) you're nicked (ghuh) (hugh)
```

(ii) [JK]

```
1  Dan:         You know if you turn round to a policeman (.) an
2               then ees (.) er arguing with you (.)
3        →      you turn round and y'say Well my opinion is that
4               your fucking dirty cunt (.) fuck off (.)
5               you can't get nicked for it 'cos you're entitled to
6               your own opinion according to the Law (1.3)
7               everyone's entitled to their own opinion
8  Fred:    So
9  Dan:  →  Even if you stood up in court and went
10             my opinion is that you're a fat cunt to the (.)
11             Judge (0.6) he can't do nothing to you cos
```

In such cases, because no claim has been made that anyone actually produced such words, they cannot be being used as evidence in quite the sense that Wooffitt (1992) and Holt (1996) discuss. Rather than being built as a display of evidence concerning something which has happened, these are demonstrations concerning how certain situations work, the only means by which a subsequent action may be heard as responsive to an earlier action; and indeed an action may be heard as responsive to another action without it being reported with DRS or the prior event being reported with DRS.

7.2 DRS and practical demonstration

In extracts (3)–(8), speakers are presenting themselves as having been defiant, and they are doing this through reproducing the talk which they claim to have produced in those situations and the talk which they were responsive to. In other words, they are purporting to demonstrate their defiance not by saying what they did or said something, but rather by showing what it was that they said. DRS can thereby be used to make implications about aspects of the reported speaker's cognitive state and/or their stance (see Schegloff, 1984; Clift, this volume).

The distinction between description and demonstration was noted by Clark and Gerrig (1990) in their account of 'quotations as demonstrations'. They state that 'quotations depict their referents'. However, one thing which is missing from the Clark and Gerrig account of demonstration is consideration of how quoted actions may be responsive to other events.[5] This is explicitly considered by Holt, who, in considering the evidential value of DRS remarks that 'by reproducing the "original" utterance or utterances speakers can provide access to the interaction being discussed, enabling the recipient to assess it for himself or herself' (1996: 229). That is, speakers may report interactions rather than isolated single actions. What is crucial here is how a speaker may be concerned with what a reported action is responsive to. In the case of extracts (3)–(8) (as often appears to be the case), the circumstances to which a reported action is responsive are reported just prior to the report of the responsive action itself. Thus a report of the context in which the responsive action occurred is the context for the report of the responsive action. Furthermore, as was stressed previously, in extracts (3)–(8) the report of the context in which the responsive action occurred, and the report of the responsive action itself, are both implemented using DRS.

While even a decontextualised quotation may be used to demonstrate something of the quoted speaker's character, presenting a

---

[5] This suggests a distinction between 'direct reported speech' and 'quotation'. DRS generally involves, or is concerned with, the context in which the reported action occurs. In quotation, on the other hand, the importance of this context recedes.

report of the action to which that speaker is responding has deeper implications about that speaker. Conversation analytic work has drawn attention to how the way a speaker conducts themselves can make details available to their hearers which may be used to make judgements about them. That is, the way a speaker chooses to conduct themselves can be highly consequential for the way they are subsequently treated. For example, a party's failure to respond to a question may suggest problems with their state of readiness, or whether they heard or understood the question. Thus a speaker's conduct can have consequences for how an interaction unfolds in that what happens next may be geared to addressing the absence of a reply. However, such a delay may not be just an interactional matter. Rather, it may lead the party who asked the question to show concerns about the capacity of their recipient. In this way a speaker's conduct may reveal, or claim, features concerning what might be glossed as the speaker's character or identity. Of course, these two facets – interaction and identity – may be inter-linked. Indeed, in some circumstances what might seem to be a narrowly interactional matter, such as the time it takes someone to respond to an invitation, can lead the party who made the invitation to show concern with the invitee's interest in, or availability for, the invitation (Drew, 1984; J. Davidson, 1984). Sacks (1992a, 1992b) discusses how certain forms of question may be used as everyday personality tests, precisely because of what the recipient's response reveals about themselves. Finally, clinical testing is highly reliant on making connections between patients' responses and purported constructs (see, for example, Bergmann, 1992, on psychiatric assessment; Maynard and Marlaire, 1999, on educational assessment).

7.3 Constraints on reports of actions as context for DRS

So far we have been concerned with showing that, in conversational story-telling, DRS may occur in the reporting of sequences of actions. Reporting an action – for example, with DRS – provides a way of showing the reported speaker's stance and/or their cognitive state, which may have implications for their character or identity. However, it is evident that there are circumstances reported by a speaker where there are constraints on the extent to which

DRS – even though it is a high granularity formulation – can be used to demonstrate what a party is up to. Reconsider extract (1), reproduced and extended as extract (9), where, as noted previously (and for reasons which we will examine in more detail later), a report of an action in a series of actions does not immediately follow a report of an action.

(9) [JK]

1	Russ:		I'm sitting there and
2			they goes There he is
3			.hh ran off yeah an I knocked on this door right
4		→	didn't even kno(hoh)w: whose it was hih hih
5			(.)
6			I goes this is my ↑uncle's house and
7			they all went no agh ah hah an ran off and
8		→	I didn't even know whose it was and
9			this big gee:zer come to the door
10			(0.8)
11			goes ↓Who a you (.) went hhh! .hhh
12	Steve:		huh huh huh huh
13	Russ:		an jus ran off

In this extract, a sequence of reported actions contains interpolated talk which does not report an action. Extract (9') reproduces extract (9) schematically, action by action, with the actions numbered. The lines which do not report actions are arrowed. There are eight actions; three are descriptions (A2, A3, A6), while the remaining five use DRS (A1, A4, A5, A7, A8).

(9') [JK]

A1   they goes There he is (line 02)
A2   .hh ran off yeah (line 03)
A3   an I knocked on this door right (line 03)
      → didn't even kno(hoh)w: whose it was hih hih (line 04)
A4   I goes this is my ↑uncle's house (line 06)
A5   they all went no agh ah hah an ran off and (line 07)
      → I didn't even know whose it was (line 08) and
A6   this big gee:zer come to the door (line 09)
A7   goes ↓Who a you (line 11)
A8   went hhh! .hhh (line 11)

Thus the reported action A4, 'I goes this is my ↓uncle's house', does not immediately follow reported action A3, 'I knocked on this door right'. Rather, what it follows is a comment: '[I] didn't even kno(hoh)w: whose it was', which does not report an action but (amongst other things) provides information about the reported participant's cognitive state. There are two grounds on which this comment can be described as parenthetical, or as interpolated. First, it appears that the sequence of actions could have been reported as knocking on the door, then saying that it's the uncle's house. Second, the comment provides information which is not apparent from the reports of these actions.[6]

This story concerns how Russ, through implementing a ruse, evaded some people who were pursuing him. A particularly elegant feature of this report is how the logic of the ruse is captured. Russ's report demonstrates to Steve, his audience, how the ruse was built out of talk-in-situation. Rather than explaining what he did, Russ assembles a report out of various actions and events. This account involves coordinating reports of talk and of actions, but also involves reports of cognitive states.

The ruse involves leading his pursuers to believe that he has reached a house which can provide some form of sanctuary. One issue involved in Russ's telling of his story occurs by virtue of it being a report of a deception. Through being a deception (told from the perspective of the perpetrator), two separate understandings are relevant within the story: Russ's beliefs on the one hand, and the beliefs of the party to be deceived on the other.

However, describing what happened, as seen by the deceived party, would not capture the deception. After all, if they had seen the deception it would not have been a deception. So Russ needs to find a way of telling the story in a way which makes sense of the actions of the deceived party and which informs his current audience that a deception was under way. Inserting the comment 'didn't even know whose it was' enables his recipient to appreciate something that the reported recipients were not in a position to see.

[6] One feature of the design of this stretch of talk is its incorporation of laughter. There is a laughter particle within the 'know' and it is followed by two laughter particles. This talk is thereby marked. Also, there is the intensifier 'even' before 'know'.

The importance of a party's grounds for action is examined in detail by Sacks in another early lecture, which concerns the 'inference making machine' used by parties to an interaction. Sacks examines some lines from a phone call (extract (10)) between a man who has had some kind of domestic troubles (B) and a social worker (A).

(10)

1	A:	Yeah, then what happened?
2	B:	Okay, in the meantime, she [wife of B] says,
3		Don't ask the child nothing.
4		Well, she stepped between me and the child,
5		and I got up to walk out the door.
6		When she stepped between me and the child,
7		I went to move her out of the way.
8		And then about that time her sister had called the
9		police. I don't know how she...what she
10		...
11	A:	Didn't you smack her one?
12	B:	No.
13	A:	You're not telling me the story, Mr B.
14	B:	Well, you see when you say smack you mean hit.
15	A:	Yeah, you shoved her. Is that it?
16	B:	Yeah, I shoved her.

Sacks is concerned with how the social worker, apparently on the grounds of what Mr B has said, is able to offer in line 11: 'Didn't you smack her one?' Furthermore, this isn't a tentative conjecture which is retracted in the face of B's denial, 'No' (line 12). Sacks identifies that B has produced a report of various events which contain a missing stage: why it was that the wife's sister called the police. Sacks proposes that the social worker has available to him social/cultural knowledge of why a person described as 'her sister' might call the police. Indeed, we might add that B's 'I don't know how she...what she' seems to orient to the sister having some reason as being an issue, but denies knowledge or understanding of what that reason might be.

In Extract (9) Russ's 'didn't even kno(hoh)w: whose it was hih hih' (line 4) reveals that his knocking on this door was not an instance of knocking on the door of someone who is known to

you. His 'didn't even' locates that something which should properly
have been present is missing.

Russ's story goes on to reveal that his ruse was successful: in
response to his announcement that 'This is my↓ uncle's house' (line
6), his pursuers 'ran off' (line 7). However, his story goes on to
concern itself with another consequence of his having knocked on
someone's door: the door being answered by that person. Russ
proceeds to reuse the same expression which occurred in lines 3–4
'didn't even kno(hoh)w: whose it was hih hih'. In line 8 he says,
'I didn't even know whose it was'.

By virtue of issuing a summons (knocking on someone's door),
the story now potentially involves two overlapping series of events:

1. the pursuit and its ending when he claims to be summoning
    his uncle – that is, the implications for his pursuers of the
    knocking on the door;
2. the summoning by knocking on the door of the occupant of
    the house.

Line 8 thus stitches together two sub-stories. First, it perhaps
looks back to the story just finished, underscoring that Russ
lost his pursuers, even though he didn't even know whose door
he was knocking on. Second, it introduces what happened with
respect to the occupant of the house. The relationship between
these two stories is rather intricate because, on the one hand,
'this big gee:zer come to the door' (C) is a consequence of this
knocking on the door, and claiming it is his uncle's house (A),
which also had as a consequence the pursuers running off (B).
However, the 'big gee:zer' coming to the door is not a consequence
of the pursuers running off. A causes B, and A causes C, but,
although C follows B (both historically and within the story),
B does not cause C.

Indeed, as a consequence of managing one tricky situation (es-
caping his pursuers), Russ is now faced with managing another
tricky situation (dealing with the occupant of the house). The
challenges of this second situation are worked up by the description
of the party who has responded to his summons, 'this big gee:zer',
the deep gruff tone of his voice, and the ways in which the legitimacy of Russ's having knocked on the door is challenged.

In extract (11), Alan also faces the problem of describing a piece of deception; in particular, preparing the context for a piece of DRS (in line 9), such that his current audience can appreciate its deceptive nature.

(11) [JK]

```
 1  Will :  nah 'ee got the bus [the bus=
 2  Alan:                        [Bob chucked the Bus Pass out
 3          didn' he (.) I forgot about that (.)
 4          and I [lent him my ] photo card one
 5  Chris:        [what did Will-]
 6  Alan:  an he got on the bus with that (.)
 7          he leaned out the window
 8       → pretended that he was shouting goodbye
 9          he goes See you later dropped my bus pass
10          it went Zzzzrm (.)
11          an I just picked it up of the floor (.) walked off (.)
```

Rather than reporting a series of actions (which might be glossed as 'he got on the bus with that, he leaned out of the window, he pretended that he was shouting goodbye, he goes "see you later"'), the talk prior to the action described using DRS – namely, '[he] pretended that he was shouting goodbye' – appears not to be a prior action but a gloss of the action subsequently reported with DRS. Thus 'this is my ↑uncle's house' (in (9)) and 'See you later' (in (11)) have been preceded by talk which provides recipients of these reports with resources to appreciate that the reported action involves deception. Both these cases involve using psychological concepts; however, there are other resources to bring out the nature of a piece of reported talk.

In extracts (9) and (11), speakers are faced with the problem of displaying the very falsehood which the talk, as produced in its original setting, was designed to accomplish. It is therefore unsurprising that using DRS to depict the allegedly successfully deceptive talk encounters the problem of making apparent *now* (to the present recipient) the very deception which those allegedly same words did not make apparent *then* (to the reported recipients). Extracts (9) and (11) show that one practice which can be used to provide recipients with resources to understand what is being reported is to produce, just prior to the DRS, details which show that the reported talk implemented a deception.

A different form of modification to DRS in a series of reported actions occurs in extract (12). Here, Dan reports a story in which he was replying with 'no comment' to police questions (line 1). He uses DRS to report the policy which he was following: ' I w's going no comment no comment'. In omitting police talk from this part of his report, he implies that he was saying 'no comment' without any consideration for what the police were saying. However, he then reports that the police tried to catch him out with an apparently innocuous question, which was preceded by an elaborate preface (lines 2–5).

```
(12) [JK]
 1   Dan:     I w's going no comment no comment
 2            and he goes if you (.) don't answer to the next
 3            question (0.5) we're gonna take your trainers and
 4            your jacket from your possession (0.5)
 5            he said what're you wearing (0.8)
 6            and I was about to say Yeh I'm wearing jacket and
 7            trainers (1.2) but (.) no comment (.)
 8            If I'd said Yeh I was wearing jacket and trainers (.)
 9            I would have looked like a dick-head in court 'cos I
10            was answering questions tha' I wanted to answer (.)
11             °and I would have been in shit  (0.8)
12            it's like an admittance of guilt
13   (   ):   huh
```

In line 7 Dan proceeds to report that he did reply to this with 'no comment', but his report of the police officer's question does not constitute the immediate context for his report of his answer. Rather, he interpolates a report of what he almost said, 'and I was about to say Yeh I'm wearing jacket and trainers'. This captures the apparent naturalness of this answer as responsive turn (note the turn-initial 'yeh') and provides a contrast in the emerging narrative for what he reports as his actual turn: 'no comment'. He observes how a prosecutor could make use of the transcript to show that he was being selective in his answers, and again uses DRS to develop this.

The particular feature we want to focus on is how Dan brings into prominence the response he gave. He sets up his response of 'no comment' as a kind of astute, tactical choice by contrasting it with a response which might have been given. In fact he contrasts it with a response which he not merely considered, but almost gave: 'he said what're you wearing (0.8) and I was about to say Yeh I'm wearing jacket and trainers'.[7]

7.4 Discussion

Our analysis identified a constraint on the capacity of DRS to represent what talk is doing in certain situations. Although DRS is a resource of formulating actions with high granularity, its capacity to represent just what a speaker said is at the same time a constraint on its capacity to represent what might be deceptive or tactical about what was said. However formulations in talk are situated in the sense that they are delivered in specific contexts to audiences for whom they are designed. As Bakhtin (1981) noted in his discussion of reported speech in writing, speakers can create a context for reported speech which thereby presents that talk from a particular perspective. We identified a situated practice – speakers' use of descriptive glosses to provide the immediate context for DRS – and we examine how it enables speakers to address the reported participants' understandings and alignments as well as present co-participants' understandings and alignments. In representing some reported action as clever or devious, speakers have the task of designing a report such that that action is intelligible to their audience without making it so obvious that its cleverness is lost. We analysed how reports can be designed such that DRS is coordinated with other forms of reporting to create contexts for each other.

---

[7] A further observation about this extract is that it topicalises the issue of skill and judgement in the application of a rule. Dan is following the policy of saying 'no comment'. But, as Sacks (1992a) remarks in the case of children being sanctioned for misapplying a rule, Dan has to work out whether or not there are limitations on this rule at the point where the test case was presented. This demonstrates that even 'just' following a rule requires judgement. In fact 'just following a rule' is a matter of interactional achievement.

We examined how this addresses the diversity of understandings and alignments among the present co-participants.

In addition to their bearing on the linguistic resources used in the design of contexts for DRS, these findings have implications for psychology, (particularly social psychology). Everyday reasoning about the causes of social action (or 'social behaviour', as it is more generally considered in social psychology) have been extensively considered under the rubric of 'attribution theory' stemming from the work of Fritz Heider (e.g. 1958).[8] The analytical benefits of respecifying the study of everyday explanations in terms of every-day talk have been elaborated by Edwards and Potter (1993) and Antaki (1994). The present analysis has identified a specific junc-ture where accounts can occur: prior to a piece of DRS to show (inter alia) what the talk to be reported constitutes. In the two cases identified where this occurs, the ascription of mental states is one of the resources which can be used in constructing such accounts. An alternative way to make a claim about the character of reported talk is to report what might have been said. It is interesting for attribution theory that the use of psychological accounts seems to be used in rather restricted cases – ones involving tactical talk, otherwise speakers can often provide detailed evidence about identity and character without using psychological concepts at all.

7.5 Conclusion

Speakers can produce intricate analyses of people's conduct through constructing representations of their actions. Speakers have resources for constructing the context for a representation of an action in order to show what action or event the target action is responsive to. Thus one resource for representing the action or event to which some action is responsive is to use DRS, which therefore means that DRS often occurs as a representation of an action in a string of actions. However, in this chapter we examined

---

[8] There are historical connections between this work and ethnomethod-ology (one of the influences on conversation analysis) with a common ancestry in phenomenology. These connections are somewhat obliterated by the different trajectories taken by ethnomethodology and attribution theory. See Maynard (1996) for a discussion.

cases in which the context for DRS was not an action, but rather a gloss of an agent's cognitive state. We showed that this gloss was an interpolation into a string of action representations and was engendered by the speaker's reporting of a deception which required showing the conduct as received by the parties to be deceived, and at the same time showing the recipient of the report that deception was under way and how precisely the very words which had been used constituted deception.

8

Active voicing in court

Renata Galatolo

8.1 Introduction

This chapter, an exploratory study of the functions of DRS in legal testimonies, investigates the use of DRS in witnesses' answers to questions posed during direct and cross-examination. The analysis will focus on the evidential and moral function that DRS has in this context. The evidential function of this discursive device is emphasised by the fact that witnesses often locate it in the expanded parts of their answers, after having given a general description or evaluation of discursive events. The moral function of DRS emerges when witnesses use it to accomplish actions which they are forbidden by court procedure from accomplishing overtly, such as expressing opinions or evaluations of events or situations they recount. This analysis focuses in particular on lay witnesses. Because they testify not as experts giving an informed opinion about elements of the case, but as individuals who are required to demonstrate that they have experienced the facts they recount directly, lay witnesses in particular must find strategies for conveying anything that goes beyond simple description.

8.2 Witness examination and cross-examination

The data used in this study are taken from an Italian criminal trial, a murder case, that attained a good deal of notoriety, in part

An earlier version of this work was presented at the Conference of the International Association Dialogue Analysis in Lugano, 29 June–July 4 2002. I am indebted to Paul Drew for his extensive comments on a previous draft of this chapter. I also want to thank Alessandra Fasulo and Luca Greco for their comments on a previous version.

because the victim seemed to have been selected according to random criteria and in part due to suspicions that the two defendants, two university researchers in the field of law, had been motivated by misplaced professional curiosity to attempt a sort of macabre academic exercise in committing the perfect crime. The data discussed in this chapter come from witness examination and cross-examination; that is, from the stage of the trial in which evidence is produced. During this stage, witnesses are interrogated by the prosecutor and by the defence lawyers so that they may orally produce evidence before the jury. In the examination, the prosecutor or defence lawyer interrogates his or her own witnesses in order to produce new information – that is, information which has not already been produced in the trial. During cross-examination, the prosecutor or the defence lawyer interrogates witnesses from the opposing side in order to submit the version of facts already reconstructed during the examination to a verification. Both during examination and cross-examination, talk is organised in question–answer sequences. Whatever actions participants accomplish must be accomplished through questions and answers (Atkinson and Drew, 1979). In trial interaction, as in most institutional contexts, turn types are pre-allocated (Drew and Heritage, 1992). During examination and cross-examination, the prosecutor and the lawyers must interact with the defendants and the witnesses, asking them questions, and witnesses must limit their participation to answering these questions. The pre-allocation of turn types guarantees the legal professional's control over witness contribution. By asking questions, in fact, they allocate the turn and predetermine the form and content of witness contribution.

According to Italian legal code, the alternation of questions and answers can be interrupted by the judge, who can ask a question to clarify aspects that emerge from interrogation,[1] or to denounce a violation of procedural rules. The opposite side may interrupt in order to make objections; that is, to denounce violations of interrogation rules.

---

[1] The judge is the only professional in court who – at the beginning and during the trial – doesn't know the prosecution's version of facts; that is, the results of the police inquiry that culminated in the trial.

During examination and cross-examination, the interaction is only apparently dyadic. All questions and answers are produced for an overhearing audience (Heritage, 1985), formed by all the ratified participants (Goffman, 1981), who are present in court. Among them, the jury is the main addressee. Everything produced during the trial will in fact be used by the jury in forming its opinion and supporting the final verdict.

The code of criminal procedure establishes which questions may be asked and when they may be asked and also what witnesses can do when answering. Constraints on the activity of asking questions mainly concern restrictions in terms of the topic and the form questions take.[2] Questions must be about facts and aspects of facts which have some relation to the crime. Different questions can be asked during examination and cross-examination. During examination, the interrogator is not allowed to ask leading questions – that is, questions which supply their own answers, thereby influencing the witness. This restriction is meant to counteract the relationship that exists between the interrogator and the person being interrogated. Because they represent the same side in the trial – that is, the prosecution or the defence – and support the same version of facts, the resulting testimony could be conditioned. If allowed to ask leading questions, the interrogator's influence over the witness would be strengthened to a dangerous degree, which could have an impact on the veracity of the testimony. During cross-examination, on the other hand, leading questions are allowed. Hence, during this stage, the interrogators have stronger means at their disposal than during examination. This is one of the reasons why this is the more adversarial stage of the trial.

The code also establishes what witnesses can do when answering. These rules are different for lay witnesses and expert witnesses. Lay witnesses are called to give testimony because of their direct experience and first-hand knowledge of some facts connected to the crime. Expert witnesses, such as ballistics experts or doctors, are called because of their special competence in

---

[2] For an analysis of the types of questions and their coercion degree, see Adelsward et al. (1987) and Danet (1980).

domains useful for evaluating evidence. The main difference between these two categories regards what they can or can't do when giving testimony. Expert witnesses are called to evaluate evidence; that is, to give their opinion on evidence, primarily material in nature, that has already been presented during the trial. Lay witnesses describe what they saw or what they heard and are prevented from expressing their opinions and evaluations.

Whatever a witness decides to say, his or her first duty is to demonstrate that he or she is answering the questions. In court, constraints as to what constitutes a response to a question are in fact very strict (Penman, 1987)[3] and behaviour such as reluctance or evasiveness is considered particularly serious. In all likelihood, a reluctant witness will be suspected of acting in bad faith, by trying to hide something.[4] Witnesses' credibility is linked to their ability to demonstrate willingness to collaborate by providing fitting answers, and to demonstrate that they have had direct experience of the facts presupposed by their witness status, by giving evidence of having heard or seen what they claim.[5]

Witnesses can avoid answering a question by claiming difficulties in remembering. This can be a useful strategy, because it permits them to answer without answering. By saying that they don't remember, witnesses neither admit nor deny what has been revealed in the previous turn, while retaining the possibility to change their mind at a later moment (Drew, 1992).

When answering questions, an important resource witnesses can use to partially control the information given is to expand upon their answers. The expansion of an answer is the part of the answer

---

[3] Upon observation of trial interaction, which focused on cases in which violations were denounced, Penman (1987: 211) concludes that in court there is a strong demand that the maxim of quantity be respected, meaning that the information provided correspond precisely to what has been requested, that nothing more be added and that unsolicited information not be given.

[4] See Komter (1988) with regards to the dilemma that arises when a witness feels compelled to answer in order not to arouse suspicion that they are hiding the truth but does not wish to say things that might be incriminating, which is experienced in particular by defendants.

[5] For an analysis of interactional practices that witnesses can use for fitting these two contextual requests, see Galatolo (2003).

that follows the minimal answer projected by the form of the question.[6] After having produced the requested answer, they can expand upon it, and in so doing gain an initiative interactional space in which they can produce alternative descriptions of facts (Drew, 1992), contextualise the information by giving further details, or produce accounts and justifications (Drew, 1979).[7] During examination, expanded answers are often solicited. During cross-examination, if produced after the requested answer, an expanded answer may or may not be tolerated. The degree of tolerance of expanded answers seems, then, to depend on the degree to which the expansion is solicited by the question and also on whether or not this occurs during examination or cross-examination.[8] During cross-examination, the interrogators are generally more coercive and less inclined to allow the witness initiative.

8.3 The trial

The trial cited in this chapter was held to determine who was responsible for a murder committed in 1997 at the University La Sapienza in Rome. The 22-year-old victim, Marta Russo, a university student, was killed by gunshot as she walked through the campus.

The trial began in 1998. The first verdict confirmed the public prosecutor's reconstruction of the events, which established that the shot was fired from the window of classroom number six of the Department of Philosophy of Law, and that it was fired by two researchers from that department, the defendants Scattone and Ferraro. Professor Bruno Romano, the director of the department, was acquitted of charges of aiding and abetting the murderers. During the trial, Maria Chiara Lipari and her father, Niccolò Lipari, two prosecution witnesses, played an important role in supporting the

[6] For a more extensive analysis of expanded answers, see section 8.4.
[7] In his analysis of justifications and excuses given by witnesses, Drew (1979) sustains that they have the main function of anticipating subsequent questions in order to prevent and control the allocation of blame.
[8] Previous quantitative analyses of the answering behaviour of defendants and witnesses (Adelsward et al. 1987; Luchjenbroers, 1997) have shown that expanded answers are generally less frequent than minimal answers and that they are more frequent (even if not significantly), during direct examination than during cross-examination.

charges against Romano. The 1998 verdict was confirmed in an appeal to the Court of Cessation on November 2002.

Most of the participants in the trial have a hybrid identity, being experts in law in their professional life and lay witnesses or defendants in the trial. Most of the data I analyse in this chapter come from the examination and cross-examination of two lay witnesses, Maria Chiara Lipari, a researcher in the Department of Philosophy of Law, and her father, Niccolò Lipari, professor at the same University. Maria Chiara Lipari, probably the more important witness for the prosecution, claimed that she entered room number six immediately after the fatal shot was fired from one of its windows, and saw Scattone and Ferraro, the defendants, near a window. Scattone was holding a pistol and Ferraro was standing near him. During the trial, Maria Chiara Lipari is questioned about this circumstance and about whether or not Professor Romano put pressure on her, in order to convince her not to collaborate with the investigators. Professor Lipari is interrogated mainly for verifying his daughter's testimony on Romano's behaviour.

8.4 The sequential location of direct reported speech

Analysis has shown that the representation of past discursive events through the use of DRS – along with descriptions, accounts and justifications[9] – is often located in the expansion of witness answers. The expansion of the answer is the part that follows the minimal answer, in which the speaker provides information that was not strictly, nor explicitly, requested by the question.[10] In the

---

[9] For an analysis of the use of accounts and justifications in witness responses, see Drew (1979).

[10] Stivers and Heritage (2001: 151) define the expansion of an answer in a similar manner: 'ways in which a patient expands her answers – volunteering more information than was asked for'. Clayman and Heritage (2002: 245) propose a similar analysis of interviewers' answers, articulated in minimal answers plus elaboration. Adelsward et al. (1987: 328) define the *expanded responses* in courtroom interaction as follows: 'conversational contributions clearly responding to the interlocutor's previous turn but expanding beyond what is minimally required by the latter'. For an analysis of the functions of expanded answers in medical interaction, see Drew (1998b).

case of a 'yes/no' question, the possible minimal answer will be the 'yes/no' answer,[11] and in the case of a <u>wh</u>- question it will be any part of the answer that addresses information explicitly requested in the question.

In the following example, the prosecutor interrogates one of his witnesses, Maria Chiara Lipari, about the comments Mrs Alletto, another witness for the prosecution, made to her about the morning when the murder was committed.[12] In her answer, the witness produces a minimal positive answer, followed by an expansion, in which she reports Alletto's words.

(1) [Maria Chiara Lipari Examination: Tape 3 – 0.42.06 – 538]
PM: Public Prosecutor, L: Witness

1	PM:	*la Alletto e:h le ha*
		did Mrs. Alletto e:h did she
2	L:	*hm*
		hm
3	PM:	*avuto modo↑ (.) di dirle (.) di farle*
		have the opportunity↑(.) to speak with you (.) to make
4		*qualche commento su quel <u>giorno</u> cioè <u>su</u>*
		any comments about that day or rather about
5		*[quella=*
		[that=
6	L:	*[s:ì*
		[y:es
7	PM:	*=mattina di venerdì↑*
		=Friday morning↑
8	L: →	*sì*
		yes
9	→	(1.0)
10	L: →	*disse: (.) .hh che poi si ricorda dottoressa Lipari eh↑*
		she sa:id (.).hh you remember don't you Doctor Lipari eh↑

---

[11] On the syntactical constraints of 'yes/no' questions and the subsequent evaluation of conforming and non-conforming answers independently from the evaluation of preferred and dispreferred actions, see Raymond (2000).

[12] Mrs Alletto was the secretary of the Department of Philosophy of Law. Her testimony had a central role for the prosecution's thesis, but it was

In extract (1), at line 6, the witness produces a first answer 'yes' in overlap with the prosecutor's question. At line 8 she then repeats the 'yes', providing the minimal answer requested by the 'yes/no' form of the question. Then, the form 'she said' (line 10), which immediately follows the pause at line 9, begins the expansion of the answer introducing Mrs Alletto's words (line 10). The pause following the 'yes' (line 9), can be interpreted as evidence of the witness's orientation towards seeing the 'yes' as a possibly complete answer. After the 'yes', the prosecutor could have taken the turn, asking a subsequent question, but he doesn't, and the witness continues her turn. The initial 'yes' corresponds to a complete turn constructional unit (TCU), and the expansion beginning with 'she said' is a new TCU.[13] What follows is then co-constructed as an expansion of the first part, in which the witness animates Romano's voice (line 10).

In extract (2), taken from Professor Lipari's cross-examination, a defence lawyer asks the witness if, as he was leaving at the end of the encounter he had with his daughter, Maria Chiara Lipari, and Professor Romano at the University, he heard Professor Romano ask his daughter to inform him about the eventual developments of the investigation. The question is important in verifying whether or not Professor Romano had tried to exercise control over Maria Chiara Lipari's collaboration with the investigators. The witness answers by giving a minimal positive answer, and then expands the answer by reporting Romano's words.

(2) [Niccolò Lipari cross-examination: Tape 5 – 1.24.28 – 1262]
DF: Defence Lawyer, NL: Witness

```
1    DF:    quando: ehm: (.) vi siete congedati(0.7) eh il professor
            when: ehm (.)you left (0.7) ehdid professor
2           Romano ha- invitato- sua figlia (0.5) a- metterla-
            Romano invite- your daughter (0.5) to- inform-
```

particularly weak because she decided to testify only after Ms Lipari told the prosecutor that she had seen Mrs Alletto with the two defendants, Scattone and Ferraro, when she entered room number six.

[13] 'By *turn constructional unit*, it may be recalled, we meant to register that these units *can* constitute possibly complete turns; on their possible completion, transition to a next speaker becomes *relevant* (although not necessarily accomplished)' (Schegloff, 1996c: 55).

3		*a metterlo-al corrente (.) e:h di quelli che avessero potuto*
		to inform him- (.) e:h about what could
4		*essere se vi fossero stati(.) eh nuovi interrogatori nuovi=*
		be if they took place (.) eh the new interrogations new=
5	NL:	*s[ì*
		y [es
6	DF:	*= [coinvolgimenti: di sua figlia:=*
		= [involvement: of your daughter=
7	NL:	*sì*
		yes
8	DF:	*=nelle indagini↑*
		=in the investigation↑
9	NL: →	*sì=disse: (.) disse mi raccomando:: tienimi informato*
		yes=he said: (.)he said mind you inform me
10		*di qualunque novità altrimenti mi offendo*
		about any news otherwise I will take offence

In extract (2), the witness produces the minimal answers 'yes' three times, at lines 5, 7 and 9. The first two 'yes' responses are not treated as definitive answers to the question, and in both cases the lawyer continues to specify the question, specifying the content of Romano's hypothetical requests to his daughter (lines 6 and 8). At line 9, immediately after the third 'yes', the witness speeds up the speech. In the transcript, the equal symbol (=) at line 9 indicates the particular contiguity between the word 'yes' and the word 'he'. In speeding up the speech, the witness doesn't shape the prosody so that it comes at a temporary closure corresponding to the end of the first TCU of the answer. The speaker thereby avoids the possibility that his interlocutor takes the turn after the 'yes'. This use by the speaker of the *rush-through* device (Schegloff, 1982) can be interpreted as evidence of the speaker's recognition of the first 'yes' as a possible complete answer to the question. What follows is then constructed as an expansion upon the first part of the answer, 'yes'. As in extract (1), the witness introduces the quotation with the introductory past form of the verb 'to say', followed by the animation of Romano's voice ('mind you inform me about any news otherwise I will take offence').

Extract (3) contains a brief elaboration of the minimal 'yes/no' answer which precedes the expansion of the answer:

(3) [Maria Chiara Lipari examination: Tape 5 – 0.05.52 – 82]
PM: Prosecutor, L: witness

1   PM: *mi scusi ma le capitava spesso che il professor Romano*
             excuse me but did it happen often that Professor Romano

2   *di sera la chiamasse a casa per sapere*   [*come stava*↑
             in the evening called you at home to ask [how you were↑

3   L: [*n:on era mai -*
                                                         [it had never -

4   →   (.) *non era mai capitato .hhh e:: hm disse (2.0)*
             (.) it had never happened .hhh e:: hm he said (2.0)

5   *pt .h lei ha visto niente (0.5) ha sentito niente*↑
             pt .h did you see anything (0.5) or hear anything ↑

In extract (3), the minimal negative answer 'no' is substituted
by the negative sentence 'it had never happened' (lines 3–4), which
partially repeats some elements of the question 'did it happen
often' (line 1).[14] Even if minimally expanded, this first part is a
direct answer to the question. The expansion of the answer is introduced by a series of elements, an in-breath, a prolonged hesitation
followed by another hesitation (line 4), all of which have a pre-
beginning function signalling an incoming new TCU (Schegloff,
1996c: 93). The production of such elements, in correspondence
with the transition-relevance place (Sacks et al., 1974), prevent the
interlocutor from taking the turn, signalling a further incoming
production, serve as evidence that the speaker sees the first part of
the answer as a possible complete answer. At line 4, following the
pre-beginning elements, the witness introduces the quotation using
the introductory verb 'said' followed by DRS ('did you see anything
(0.5) or hear anything', line 5).

    Despite the fact that the expansions in extracts (1)–(3) are ac-
complished using different devices, they all have the same structure;
that is, a minimal or direct answer to the question, which corresponds to the first part of the answer, and a subsequent expansion
which is introduced by the verb 'to say' followed by the animation
of someone else's words. An important difference among extracts

[14] About the function of partially repeating the question in answering, see
    Clayman and Heritage (2002: 247).

(1)–(3) regards the degree to which the expansion can be judged to have been solicited or not by the question. In extract (1), the question explicitly seeks the incidental comments Mrs Alletto could have produced about Friday morning, and in so doing it seems both to anticipate and request more information than a simple 'yes/no' answer. The explicit reference in the question to Alletto's eventual comments seems to be an implicit request that Maria Chiara Lipari report those comments. Furthermore, the exchange occurs during a witness examination – that is, during an interrogative stage in which the prosecutor and his witness collaborate in providing all the information and elements potentially useful in supporting their version of the facts. In this regard, it is reasonable to suppose that, in asking questions, the prosecutor tries to guide his witness in establishing his expectations about her answer; that is, in making it clear which elements she should mention in order to produce a good answer. In this same regard, it is reasonable to suppose that the witness will tend to treat all the elements of the question as implicitly useful suggestions she should consider when producing the expected answer. Then, in extract (1), both the form of the question and the context in which it is produced contribute to legitimating the interpretation that it is an indirect request for the witness to report any comments that might have been made by Alletto, that Friday morning. The witness's answer is then constructed as an expanded answer, but the expansion is partly solicited by the question.

In extract (2), as well, the form of the question – that is, the fact that it makes explicit reference to the content of the conversation ('did professor Romano invite- your daughter (0.5) to-inform- to inform him-(.) e:h about what could be if they took place (.) eh the new interrogations new= involvement: of your daughter=in the investigation↑') – seems to function as an implicit solicitation that the witness report the past dialogue being referred to.

The degree of solicitation of the expansion is very different in extract (3). In this case, the expansion, which is made through the use of DRS, is not suggested by the question. The question doesn't contain any elements suggesting the witness give detailed information about what Professor Romano said when he called the witness, nor does it elicit a report of what Professor Romano said. The answer goes beyond the question's frame.

Hence, despite the constructional similarity of expanded answers, the degree of the expansion (which is related to the content
and structure of the question[15]) becomes another element requiring
consideration.

In the data, the indirect solicitation of reporting past dialogue
is more frequent in examination than in cross-examination. In
cross-examination, it is more common for DRS to be solicited
explicitly by questions in which the witness is asked to confirm,
or not, quotations produced in previous testimonies or dialogues
resulting from interceptions. This difference can be explained by
the professional's necessity, while examining their own witnesses,
of not being coercive. At this stage, the lawyer or the prosecutor
wants to create before the jury the impression that the information
is being given spontaneously. The more a witness seems to speak
spontaneously, the more the jury will have the impression that the
testimony is truthful, unsolicited and unprepared. The indirect
solicitation of reporting dialogues, as showed in extracts (1) and
(2), obtains this effect.

The more important interactional consequence of the different
degree to which the expansion is requested by the question resides
in the fact that unsolicited expanded answers can be sanctioned
more easily by the interrogator, especially during cross-examination.

Despite the frequency of expanded answers and despite what
witnesses do in the expansions, previous studies (Atkinson and
Drew, 1979; Danet, 1980; Adelsward et al., 1987; Luchjenbroers,
1997) all agree in considering expansions as a resource for witnesses when giving partially solicited or unsolicited information
that can influence the jury's evaluation of the testimony. The phenomenon of expanded answers is then treated as a positive signal of
witness participation in the interaction, which counterbalances the
strong interactional asymmetry in favour of professionals that
characterises trial interaction.

---

[15] In their analysis of defendants' expanded answers in court, Adelsward
et al. (1987) introduce the evaluation of the degree to which the answer
goes beyond the question, defining it as the initiative-response degree.
They analyse the defendant's expanded answer as weakly or strongly
initiative depending on the extent to which it was solicited by the
previous turn.

8.5 The use of direct reported speech as evidence

In the context of direct and cross-examination, witnesses mostly use DRS as an evidential[16] – that is, as a discursive device for encoding the sources of the information they provide (Philips, 1992; Stygall, 1994). The evidential function of DRS is linked to the fact that the ability to recall the exact proffered words is generally interpreted as being evidence of having directly and effectively heard those words. The ability to give details about events is commonly associated with having had a direct experience of those events.[17] Ordinarily, people use evidence when the state of affairs being evidenced is uncertain or problematic (Pomerantz, 1984b). In testimonies, witnesses use DRS as an evidential because of the defensive character (Sacks, 1970, 1971) of their stories. In a trial, stories are elicited and told to uphold competing versions of facts and, especially during cross-examination, their credibility is continually subject to verification. Consequently, the job of the witness is not only to relate an experience, but also to relate it in a credible manner, giving evidence in support of what they say in order to limit and to prevent doubts from the opposing side. This is why stories in court are constructed not simply by claiming that events took place but by supplying evidence that they took place.[18]

In using DRS as evidence, witnesses display their orientation to the specific request of the context of saying how they know what they say.[19] This rule reflects the general orientation of exercising the control over evidence through the control of its sources typical of this context (Philips, 1992).

---

[16] The evidence definition I assume is that provided by Pomerantz (1984b: 608): 'The concept of evidence provides for a scene, an event, an artefact, etc. that *qua evidence* is thought of as being relevant in determining the nature of some other scene, event, artefact, etc.'

[17] On the characteristic features of a credible narrative in court, see Conley and O'Barr (1990); and O'Barr (1982).

[18] The phenomenon of the use of DRS as evidence is observed in other contexts where stories are defensively designed, as shown by Wooffitt (1992, 2001, this volume) in his analysis of medium–sitter interaction.

[19] This constraint is valid only for lay witnesses; that is, for witnesses who give their testimony because of their first-hand knowledge (direct experience) of facts.

Among witnesses, lay witnesses are asked to give evidence for what they say in order to prove the single aspects of the story they support, but also in order to legitimate their status as lay witnesses. In addition to demonstrating the truthfulness of their story, lay witnesses are required to demonstrate that they have first-hand knowledge of the facts. The use of the evidentials, including DRS, is then strictly related to the lay-witness status. Giving evidence is a means of activating lay-witness identity.

In the data, the evidential function of DRS is often highlighted by the fact that DRS serves to provide details of information previously given.[20] In the following example, the prosecutor asks the witness if she had any conversations about the murder with anybody from the department where she worked. The witness gives an implicitly positive answer, directly giving the name of the person who asked her for information about what she saw or heard in relation to the murder ('Fiorini', line 4), and then she partially reproduces the conversation, reporting the words of that person.

(4) [Maria Chiara Lipari Examination: Tape 3 – 0.40.54]
PM: Public Prosecutor, L: witness

1	PM:	*in istituto quindi da lunedì (0.7) in poi (0.7) avete*
		so in the Institute from Monday (0.7) on (0.7) did any of you
2		*scambiato o lei personalmente ha scambiato (0.5) impressioni*
		exchange or did you personally exchange (0.5)impressions
3		*commenti con- con qualcuno↑ con [chi↑*
		comments with- with anyone with [whom↑
4	L:	[*Fiorini Fiorini mi tirava::*
		[Fiorini Fiorini brou:ght
5		*spessissimo fuori l'argomento (.) spesso insomma parlando:*
		the topic up frequently with me (.)often just talki:ng
6	→	*(.).hh mi chiedeva: ma tu c'eri↑ allora:: hai visto qualcosa*
		(.).hh he asked me but were you there↑ so:: did you see anything
7	→	*hai sentito qualcosa:*
		did you hear anything

---

[20] Vincent and Perrin (1999) describe this same phenomenon as the *support function* of DRS and counter-oppose it to its *narrative function* on the basis that the latter makes the narration go on, while the former doesn't contribute to the narrative progress.

After having said that Fiorini, a colleague at the university, often brought the subject of the murder up with her (lines 4–5), at line 6 the witness introduces Fiorini's words using the verb 'ask'. The use of this introductory verb and the animation of Fiorini's voice producing three consecutive questions ('but were you there ↑ so:: did you see anything did you hear anything', lines 6–7) permits her to show that she spoke with him about the fact, leaving all the responsibility of that speaking to her interlocutor. By using the verb 'ask', the witness conveys the idea that if the conversation took place, it's because Fiorini asked her for some information. The animation and the fact that she introduces it with the verb 'ask' both support what the witness has already described as 'Fiorini brou:ght the topic up frequently with me' (lines 4–5).

In extract (5), the prosecutor's question is about the encounter at the university between the witness, Professor Lipari, his daughter, Maria Chiara Lipari, and Professor Romano. The encounter and the conversation that took place on that occasion are often mentioned during the trial. The most disputed aspects of this part of the story concern the hypothesis that the encounter was energetically sought out by Romano and that during it Romano tried to influence Maria Chiara's decision to testify.

(5) [Professor Lipari examination: Tape 5 – 1.03.16 – 85]
PM: Public prosecutor, NL: witness

1	PM:	*ci può in qualche modo e:h riferire (0.7) >di<cosa*
		can you in somehow e:h tell us (0.7)
2		*si parlò ↑(0.7)in quell'inco↑ntro=*
		>what< you spoke about (0.7) during that encounter=
3	NL:	*=l:'incontro si articolò in questo modo (.) nella prima*
		=th:e encounter went like this (.) in the first
4		*parte del colloquio Romano e:h ci: hm disse alcune battute*
		part of the conversation Romano e:h made hm a few remarks
5		*.h sullo svolgimento delle indagini .h i:- in tono*
		.h about the course of the investigation .h i:- using a tone
6		*h:::m direi: .hh così sostanzialmente negativo*
		h:::m I would sa:y .hh basically doubtful
7		*sulla loro incidenza=*
		in regard to its effectiveness=
8	→	*=non hanno niente in mano non ci sono elementi*

9   →   =they have nothing in their hands there are no elements
        .h e::h *nemmeno la traiettoria può essere attendibile perché il*
        .h e::h even the trajectory isn't reliable because the

10 →   *movimento della testa.h e:h della: povera ragazza può avere*
        movement of the poor.h e:h girl's head may have been

11 →   *inciso in maniera .h determinante e simili*
        a determining factor and so on

In the first part of the answer (lines 3–7), Professor Lipari briefly describes the first part of the conversation he had with Romano and his daughter, focusing on Romano's conversational contribution, which is described as 'a few remarks .h about the course of the investigation .h i-using a tone ... basically doubtful in regard to its effectiveness' (lines 4–7). Subsequently, at lines 8–12, the witness animates Romano's voice, reproducing the remarks he has just characterised as doubtful. The remarks are effectively all critical towards the results of the investigation and they are produced with a droning intonation.[21] The quotation is produced without any introductory verb and it is located in the expansion of the answer by using the *rush through device* – that is, by speeding up the speech at the end of line 7. In the subsequent part of the answer, the witness animates Romano's voice in order to detail and support what has been briefly described in the first part.

In extract (6), the question is part of a larger line of questioning about the telephone calls Professor Romano made to Chiara and her family. The number of telephone calls and the content and the tone used by Professor Romano are important elements for establishing whether or not he actually tried to influence Chiara's testimony.

(6) [Niccolò Lipari examination: Tape 5 – 1.02.23 – 70]
PM: public prosecutor, NL: witness

1   PM: *e:h le sembrò in qualche modo eh: un: tono eh: diverso*
           e:h did it seem to you somehow eh: a: different eh: tone

2   *dalle altre volte↑(.) quello della sera*
           compared to the other times↑ (.) the tone used on the evening

3   *del ventidue mag-maggio↑*
           of Ma- May twenty second↑

---

[21] For a further analysis of the intonation in this example, see pages 217–219.

4	NL:	*era for:temente interessato a parlare con Chiara=*
		he was <u>really</u> determined to speak with Chiara=
5		*=usò quest' impre- quest'espressione*
		=he used this impre- this expression
6	→	*io <u>debbo</u> assolutamente parlarle*
		<u>I</u> absolutely have to speak with her

In the first part of his answer, Professor Lipari describes the attitude Professor Romano had when he expressed his desire to speak with Lipari's daughter, Chiara ('he was <u>really</u> determined to speak with Chiara', line 4). He doesn't produce a description of Romano's tone, as requested by the questioner, but a description of his attitude. The implication is that he is giving a positive answer to the question about the strangeness of Professor Romano's tone. At this point, the witness expands upon the answer by introducing a direct quotation of Romano's words ('he used this expre-this expression <u>I</u> absolutely have to speak with her') at lines 5–6. The witness avoids describing Romano's tone and chooses to animate it, providing the audience with the opportunity to directly witness it. The effect of the quotation, through the emphasis on 'I' (line 6), followed by the adverb 'absolutely' – which both have the effect of showing Romano's determination – is that of transforming the impression of the witness into a matter of fact. What is a subjective evaluation in the public prosecutor's question ('did his tone seem') becomes a certified state of affairs in the answer, 'he was <u>really</u> determined to speak with Chiara' plus quotation. Showing Romano's attitude through the activation of his voice, the quotation serves to certify Romano's attitude of strong motivation.

In extracts (4)–(6), DRS is located in expanded parts of the answers.[22] Both the sequential location and the content of DRS orient interpreters towards seeing it as a development upon a particular earlier affirmation, thus as evidence in support of previous statements. In all the examples, the second part of the answer, containing the animation of voices, is offered to the audience as an

---

[22] The use of the term 'expansion' doesn't necessarily refer to the first expansion of the answer – that is, to the expansion immediately following the initial minimal answer.

opportunity to have direct access to the same experience the witness had – that is, as an opportunity to directly verify what the witnesses have previously said.

A distinguishing factor between extracts (4)–(6) concerns the descriptive or evaluative character of the first part of the answer. In extract (4), the witness reports that Fiorini frequently spoke with her about the murder without expressing any evaluation of his words and the subsequent animation shows Fiorini's conversational initiative. In (5), the initial brief report of Romano's conversational behaviour is partly evaluative. Romano's tone is described as doubtful and it is so represented through the content and intonation of his remarks. In (6), on the other hand, the initial report is strongly evaluative. It concerns Romano's attitude, which is defined as really determined to speak with Chiara. The following voice activation supports the witness's evaluation through the representation of Romano's directive turn, both through its syntactic structure and its intonation.

As showed in the previous examples, witnesses mostly describe or evaluate the speech discursive event before reproducing it. In so doing, they give the audience instructions as to which aspects of the past discursive event the voice animation is intended as evidence.

In this respect, those examples are different from cases in which DRS is directly produced as answering to the question, without any introduction, as in the subsequent example (in the omitted lines, the lawyer says to the judge that he was just asking the question the judge asks at lines 1–2):

(7) [Niccolò Lipari: Tape 5 – 1.15.42 – 754]
P: The President, NL: Niccolò Lipari, prosecution witness

1   P: *questo è il punto (.) la reazione del professore Romano*
         this is the point (.)what was Romano's reaction
2   *(.)quando si parla di Alletto quale è stata*↑
         (.) when you spoke of Alletto↑

    [14 lines omitted]

3 NL: → *ADE:SS:O (.) la:scia:mo cadere queste cose car- Chiara (.)*
        now let's just drop these things de- Chiara (.)
4   → *qui si tratta di riprendere a lavorare nell'istituto (.)*
        it's time to start work again in the institute (.)
5   → *per: raccogliere i frutti di ciò che tu hai seminato (.)*
        to reap the benefits of what you have sown (.)
6   *non si fece nessuna ulteriore insistenza rispetto (.)*
        there was no further insistence regarding (.)
7   *al contenuto della testimonianza*
        the content of the testimony

In extract (7), the witness answers the question by directly reporting Professor Romano's words (lines 3–5), without any previous description or evaluation and without any introductory verb. In this case, the DRS has the function of answering the question and not of supporting previous answering components. It maintains its evidential function, which is linked to the effect it creates of directly showing the events, but the witness doesn't previously suggest which element or aspect of the discursive event the voice animation should be interpreted as evidence for. In this case, evidence is offered for the audience's evaluation, apparently without framing.

Hence, the location of DRS in expanded parts of the answer – which is the more frequent location in our data – permits the witnesses to highlight the evidential function of DRS, orienting interpreters towards seeing it as a development of an earlier affirmation and to determine for which elements and aspects DRS will be interpreted as evidence.

8.6 The moral function of direct reported speech[23]

In the previous section I showed that in locating DRS after an evaluation the witness has the possibility of objectifying that evaluation, making it seem factual. This possibility, offered by DRS, of creating an effect of factuality regarding subjective aspects of the testimony, can be exploited by witnesses also for covertly conveying

---

[23] The *moral function* refers to what Drew calls *doing moral work*, which he defines as 'providing a basis for evaluating the "rightness" or "wrongness" of whatever is being reported' (Drew, 1998a: 295).

their attitude about persons and events. Witnesses can communicate subjective evaluations directly through the animation of voices; that is, even when ostensibly simply representing past discursive events.[24]

In the context of testimony by lay witnesses, this use of DRS can be a useful tool for bypassing the rule which prevents witnesses from expressing opinions about, and evaluations of, the facts they report. Those restrictions force the witnesses to exclude both affects and attitudes from their discourse in producing an objective report of facts.[25] This is why, in this context, witness use of an apparently objective representation of speech can be a powerful device for accomplishing strongly evaluative actions, such as the allocation of blame and responsibility. In the context of the trial, these are very sensitive actions because they can have an important role in affecting the jury's deliberation.[26]

In the following example, I will examine this possibility through the analysis of a case in which the witness uses DRS to convey an implicit negative evaluation of the morality of Professor Romano, one of the defendants. The immediate context of the example is a stage of Professor Lipari's examination at which the prosecutor is asking questions about Romano's behaviour during the period immediately following the murder, (that is, during the investigation). In this part of the interrogation, the general goal of both the prosecutor and the witness is to give a version of the story which

---

[24] On this point, see also Besnier (1993), Buttny (1997), Günthner (1998), Holt (2000) and Galatolo and Mizzau (2003).

[25] In his analysis of the Nukulaelae population use of DRS, Besnier (1993: 161) outlines a very similar situation. That population uses DRS for communicating affect because of local norms which prevent them from overtly communicating it.

[26] If compared with what Drew (1998a) says about the types of actions which in ordinary conversation normally engender implicit and unstated moral purposes, in court this use seems to be different. In ordinary conversation defensive actions are mostly associated with implicit moral work, while condemnatory behaviours are mostly accomplished through explicit moral work. This contrasts with what happens in witness testimonies. As witnesses can't make open accusations, they tend primarily to do so using implicit and covert devices.

can demonstrate Romano's guilt – that is, to demonstrate that Romano tried to bias the investigations.

(8) [Niccolò Lipari examination]
PM: public prosecutor, NL: witness

1	PM:	*e::h quando poi lei successivamente la mattina dopo: (.)*
		e::h later when you the next morni:ng (.)
2		*eh si recò insieme con sua figlia a parlare con il professor*
		went with your daughter to speak with Professor
3		*Romano(.) questa decisione di anda- di accompagnare-(.)*
		Romano (.) was this decision to go- to accompany- (.)
4		*sua figlia- fu presa da >lei< da lei*
		your daughter-was it your decision
5		*o fu sua figlia che [:*
		or was it your daughter tha: [t
6	NL:	[NO NO *mia fi:glia eh*
		[NO NO my daughter eh
7		*mi disse che non intendeva an<u>d</u>arci u::so*
		told me that she didn't want to go she u::sed
8	→	*quest'espressione perché non mi <u>fi</u>do*
		this expression because I don't trust him

In extract (8), the prosecutor's question is about who decided – the witness or his daughter, Maria Chiara – that she should have been accompanied by her father to the encounter at the University with Romano ('was this decision to go to accompany- (.) your daughter-was it your decision or was it your daughter tha:t', lines 3–5). The question is not complete, probably because of the witness's overlapping at line 6, when Niccolò Lipari produces a double and loud 'NO NO'. It is not clear to which part of the question the double 'no' is a response, and the following account (lines 6–8) doesn't help to make it less ambiguous. The account, in fact, evokes a third possible version – which is an alternative to both the possibilities proposed by the question – of the manner in which Lipari made the decision to accompany his daughter Maria Chiara to the encounter. This third alternative becomes clear in other parts of Niccolò Lipari's interrogation, where the witness says that when Maria Chiara expressed her decision not to go he told her that he didn't agree with that decision and Chiara called Professor Romano to fix an appointment with him ('I responded that it seemed extremely ill-advised for her to go so she called him and we set up an appoint- they set up an appointment').

In the account (lines 6–8), the witness initially reports what Maria Chiara told him ('my daughter eh told me that she didn't want to go') and then he introduces Maria Chiara's words ('she u::sed this expression'), using a form which is rarely used in ordinary conversation. Comparing it with the more frequent introductory verbs such as 'say' or 'tell', this seems to be a more technical form which emphasises the claim of just reproducing what was said, limiting itself to the level of the linguistic (re)production, without any claim about what was meant. The witness then animates the voice of his daughter, saying, 'because I don't trust him' (line 8). In this case, DRS introduces a new element to the answer – namely, the reason Maria Chiara didn't want to go to the encounter. Unlike the examples analysed in section 5, here DRS does not serve to support previous elements of the answer, but rather to furnish an account of his daughter's refusal to meet Professor Romano. By introducing, at line 8, the idea that his daughter didn't want to go to the encounter with Professor Romano because she didn't trust him, Niccolò Lipari introduces another person's past moral evaluation of Professor Romano, which seems to have the function of casting a general shadow over Romano's morality. Romano's potential blameworthiness emerges indirectly from the witness's reporting of his daughter's past description of her feeling towards him, particularly the fact that she didn't trust him. Depicting his daughter's negative reaction to Romano's request to have an encounter with her, and saying that it was because she didn't trust him, the witness encourages the listeners, then the jury, to treat those elements as indirectly proving that Romano's behaviour was effectively blameworthy.[27]

---

[27] This seems to be similar to those instances described by Drew (1998a: 309) as being reports of reactions to offences and transgressions which serve to support the threatening character of the behaviour to which they react.

A witness may accomplish moral work by using DRS to represent someone else's reaction to a fact or a person that the witness wants to depict as morally condemnable. The same effect can be obtained by directly illustrating the behaviour of the person to blame.

In the following excerpt, in which Professor Lipari describes the conversation he had with his daughter and Romano at the University on 22 May, it's the representation of Romano's conversational contribution that accomplishes an implicit moral work, depicting Romano as a cynical man.

(9)[28] [Niccolò Lipari examination]
PM: Public prosecutor, NL: witness

```
1    NL:    =l: 'incontro si articolò in questo modo (.) nella prima
            =th:e encounter went like this (.) in the first
2           parte del colloquio Romano e:h ci: hm disse alcune battute
            part of the conversation Romano e:h made hm a few remarks
3           .h sullo svolgimento delle indagini .h i:- in tono
            .h about the course of the investigation .h i:- using a tone
4           h:::m direi: .hh così sostanzialmente negativo
            h:::m I would sa:y .hh basically doubtful
5           sulla loro incidenza=
            in regard to its effectiveness=
6     →     =non hanno niente in mano non ci sono elementi
            =they have nothing in their hands there are no elements
7     →     .h e::h nemmeno la traiettoria può essere attendibile perché il
            .h e::h even the trajectory isn't reliable because the
8     →     movimento della testa.h e:h della: povera ragazza può avere
            movement of the poor.h e:h girl's head may have been
9     →     nciso in maniera .h determinante e simili
            a determining factor and so on
```

Professor Lipari begins his answer by summarising the overall gist of Romano's words (lines 1–5). He then quotes Romano developing what has already been described as 'a few remarks .h about the course of the investigation .h i:-using a tone h:::m

---

[28] A more extended transcript of this excerpt has already been presented at pages 209–210.

I would say .hh basically doubtful'. In the first part of the answer, the witness's use of the term 'remarks' (*'battute'* in Italian), makes it sound as if Romano's comments were made lightly, as if he was speaking of something of little importance. The quotation (lines 6–9) has the form and the prosody of a list. The first three items of the list have the same intonation contour (*non hanno niente in m*ano non ci sono elem*e*nti .h e::h nemm*e*no la traiettoria puo-essere attend*i*bile 'they have nothing in their hands there are no elements .h e::h even the trajectory isn't reliable,' lines 6–7).[29] After the third item ('even the trajectory isn't reliable'), the speaker constructs a subordinate sentence beginning with 'because'. The list seems to be interrupted, but at line 9, in correspondence with the word 'determin*a*nte', the speaker begins the list again by re-introducing its prosody – that is, by putting the accent on the word 'determin*a*nte', he incorporates the previous subordinated sentence in the list, completing the incorporation by using the concluding generalised list completer 'and so on' (line 9), which is a typical last item of a list. In so doing, the speaker seems to accomplish a retroactive list assimilation (Jefferson 1990). The structure of the list highlights an apparent contrast between the serious content of some of the remarks and their location in the list. The use of the list form and prosody suspends any effect of foreground or back-ground, so that all the elements contained therein seem to be of equal importance. The droning intonation used by the witness, which results from his repetition of the same intonation contour in producing the first three items ('they have nothing in their h*a*nds there are no elements .h e::h *e*ven the trajectory isn't reliable') and is then reproduced, even if downgraded, on the word *determin*a*nte* ('determining factor', line 9), contributes to this suspension of any effect of foreground or background. The list form also presupposes a semantic compatibility between the items that compose it (Selting, 2003: 58), a sort of 'sameness' of all the items (Jefferson,

---

[29] In her analysis of list prosody, Selting (2003: 9) affirms that 'it is not so much the particular intonation contour that is constitutive of lists, but a variety of similar contours *plus* the repetition of the chosen contour for at least some or even all of the list items'. The author affirms that the prosody can be used to present some items as a list even if the syntax and the wording alone might allow other interpretations (Selting, 2003: 51).

1990) which, in this circumstance, has the effect of assimilating some general evaluations about the investigation (the first three items on the list) and the mention of the movement of the poor girl's head, which is a much more tragically human aspect of the event. The witness's use of a list to report Romano's words might help to convey a negative moral evaluation of Romano because of his seemingly unmotivated scepticism regarding the investigations, and because he is depicted as having treated as similar such different aspects of the event. The use of the list structure, with its semantic and intonation cues, is thus an attempt to carry out the special moral work of depicting Romano as someone who, by treating dramatic and less dramatic events as equal tools for convincing his interlocutors that the investigation was irrelevant, demonstrated his own cynicism.

The analysis has shown that even an apparently straightforward representation of events through DRS can accomplish implicit moral work, particularly the allocation of blame. This is done by activating the voice of a person reacting to the person to blame, as in example (8), or by directly activating the voice of the person to blame, as in extract (9). And this is done mainly through the sense of the words being reproduced (extract (8)) or through other aspects of the speech, such as the structure and intonation of the quotation (extract (9)). In all cases, through the apparent objective representation of past discursive events, witnesses covertly depict someone's behaviour as blameworthy and in so doing they can affect the jury's opinion without violating the rule which requires them simply to report what they heard and saw. Furthermore, using DRS witnesses can express moral evaluations while avoiding being questioned as to the significance conveyed. The interrogators can't react to what has been covertly conveyed and must limit themselves to treat DRS as what it claims to be: an objective representation of past discursive events.

8.7 Conclusion

The analysis of witness use of DRS during examination and cross-examination confirms some of the functions already recognised for this form in other contexts – mainly the function of providing evidence, already recognised by Wooffitt (2001, this volume) in his study of medium–sitter interaction and by Holt (1996) in ordinary conversation. The analysis has shown that, in legal testimony, that function is highlighted by the frequent sequential location of DRS in the expansions of the answers. In witness responses, DRS often provides detail and context for information already introduced in the first part of the answer. The specificity of the witnesses' use of DRS as an evidential resides in its being not only a useful device for objectifying and proving assertions, but also an important device for the activation of the lay witnesses' status. Lay witnesses are requested to prove that they have a first-hand knowledge of facts, and the ability to reproduce past conversation by quoting the exact words – in court, as in ordinary conversation – is treated as proof that the speaker heard directly that conversation.

Another important function of DRS in legal testimonies is that of accomplishing moral work. This function refers to the possibility of using what is apparently the most objective form of representation of past dialogues; that is, the activation of voices, to convey evaluations of those dialogues and of the people who participated in them. Different aspects of speech, including content, structure and prosody, can contribute to conveying a moral evaluation of people and events that serve to support or counter a special version of the events. In the trial context, this function is particularly important because it permits witnesses to express their opinions and impressions without explicitly violating the rule that prevents them from doing so. By using DRS, witnesses can objectify personal opinions and evaluations. They can, furthermore, avoid being questioned and challenged as to the significance thus conveyed. Interrogators cannot, in fact, question or dispute what has only been alluded to, but not stated.

9

Speaking on behalf of the public in broadcast news interviews

Steven Clayman

9.1 Introduction

When interviewing their prominent guests, broadcast journalists will sometimes present themselves as asking questions on behalf of the public. Such questions are framed as being raised not – or not only – for the journalist's own benefit, nor for the benefit of some elite individual, but on behalf of a larger collectivity such as the broadcast audience, the citizenry, or the populace more broadly conceived.

This basic phenomenon can take a variety of distinct forms. One way of 'speaking on behalf of the public' involves the use of direct reported speech attributed to the public in some formulation (arrowed below). This example is from an interview with a basketball player who had physically attacked his own coach ('PJ'). Note that 'IR' and 'IE' below denote interviewer and interviewee, respectively.

(1) [CBS *60 Minutes* 8 March 1998: Spreewell]
```
1  IE:       ...You don:'t talk to people the way .hh PJ: talked to me
2  IR:  →    People might be saying Hey kid. .hh You ear:n (0.2)
3       →    millions and millions of dollars, .hh Live with it.
4            (0.2)
5  IR:       Forget the respect, take your money,
6  IE:       When you're dealing with respect: uh: money is not
7            a issue.
```

After the IE (at line 1) defends and justifies his violent conduct by reference to his coach's disrespectful remarks, the IR counters (lines 2–3, arrowed) by pointing out that, given the 'millions and millions of dollars' earned by the IE, he should be able to 'Live with it.' This counter is framed as something that 'people might be saying'. Correspondingly, the ensuing talk is designed specifically as direct reported speech, the onset of which is marked by the use of a turn-initial particle and summons in mid-turn position ('H<u>e</u>y kid'), and by the shift to a more idiomatic register and a heightened level of animation in the delivery of the subsequent remark (Holt, 1996).

A similar footing can be achieved without the use of direct reported speech per se, as when questions are framed as an expression of the public's *views*, *attitudes*, or *concerns*. For instance, when an official investigator of Americans missing in action (MIA) in Vietnam is asked whether he thinks remains might be found, this issue is cast as a primary concern both to the families of MIAs as well as to ' <u>a</u>ll Americans' (arrowed).

(2) [PBS *MacNeil/Lehrer* 23 October 1992: Missing in Action]

```
 1   IR:      General obviously as you know there are two mm
 2    →       basic con<u>ce</u>rns here: that the <u>fami</u>lies have, and- and
 3    →       all Americans have, the 'c-course the re<u>mains</u> of
 4            people who are <u>dead</u> and where they .hh >do you think
 5            there may be remains foun:d? They've been bur:ied,
 6            in various places and (thuh/their) records may
 7            reflect where they are, is th[at co[rrect?]
 8   JV:                                    [tch  [.h h h] h Well.
 9            In a- in ad<u>dit</u>ionly: (.) uh:: (0.5) thuh photographs
10           that- f'r example the photographs that we have <u>now</u>:...
```

Here the public is portrayed as responsible – not for the actual words that the IR is saying, but for the underlying agenda being pursued in and through them.

In yet another variant of this phenomenon, a question can be portrayed as being *produced for the public* without necessarily expressing either their words or their underlying concerns. Consider this question from an interview with US Senator Bob Dole. Before asking Dole whether he would support a tax reform bill (lines 4–5), the interviewer (IR) offers a prefatory comment on the purpose of the question. He first suggests that he is seeking clarification for himself (lines 1–2), but he subsequently modulates that footing by noting that it's also for the benefit of 'those people who're watching the programme' (arrowed).

(3) [NBC *Meet the Press* 8 December 1985: Bob Dole]

```
1  IR:    ...Senator? .hhh (.) u::mI wanna get- (.)
2         cl<u>ea</u>r:: in my <u>ow</u>n mind and h<u>o</u>pefully
3    →    for those people who=watching the programme,
4         <u>Do</u> y<u>o</u>u supp<u>or</u>t (0.5) the:: b<u>i</u>ll that came outta
5         the House Ways 'n Means Committee on tax reform.
6         (1.4)
7  BD:    Well I'm a=little like th' pr<u>e</u>siden'.=I support the
8         process, 'n I think uh:: .hh thuh b<u>i</u>ll its<u>e</u>lf...
```

This question is framed as motivated by the goal of informing the public, here formulated as the broadcast audience who will be enlightened by what will follow.

In general, then, 'speaking on behalf of the public' encompasses a family of allied practices of the sort analysed by Erving Goffman (1981) under the rubric of 'footing'. These practices, although distinct in their particulars, nonetheless share a common property – they enable journalists to distance themselves from, and deflect responsibility for, the substance of their remarks, and they do so in a very particular way. Such practices cast the journalist, in effect, as a 'tribune of the people' who is acting primarily for the benefit of some broader populace. That questions are framed in this way may at first seem quite natural and unremarkable, a straightforward reflection of the journalist-interviewer's actual professional role. The ideal of public service is deeply ingrained in the culture of journalism as a profession (Schudson, 1978), and it is commonly understood that the interviewer's job is to serve the public by functioning as its surrogate when confronting elected officials and other elites. Indeed, when broadcast journalists reflect on the craft of interviewing, they frequently portray themselves as striving to ask questions on behalf of the public – or at least the segment that is tuning in. In a recent book about the prominent *Nightline* programme, Ted Koppel characterised his role this way:

My assumption is always that the audience is listening closely. When I ask a question, it's something I think the viewers want asked. I'm their representative.   (Koppel and Gibson 1996: 157)

A similar view was expressed by Mike Wallace, of *60 Minutes* fame, in a documentary on classic television interviews.

Television interviewers, folks like me, are a kind of surrogate for you...
None of us could keep our jobs for a day if we didn't ask the questions that
you out there wish that somebody had the common sense or the nerve or
the foolishness to ask.

However, the relationship between the professional culture of
journalism and actual journalistic practice is complex and by no
means straightforward. A line of thinking running from Mills
(1940) through Garfinkel (1967) to studies of contemporary journalism (e.g. Tuchman, 1972) demonstrates that lofty ideals get
invoked and implemented in thoroughly practical ways that enable
actors to manage various contingencies and problems that arise in
everyday life. Correspondingly, when journalists formulate themselves as public servants, they are not simply playing out a preor-
dained cultural script. This is plainly apparent in the selectivity with
which this practice is deployed. Interviewers overtly frame their
questions on behalf of the public only occasionally and in a limited
range of interactional environments. Thus, far from being a straightforward reflection of unadulterated professionalism, this practice is
best understood as a mode of self-presentation – a style of questioning employed methodically to manage specific contingencies and
problems that arise in the course of the interviewer's work.

This chapter examines the journalistic practice of overtly 'speaking on behalf of the public' in broadcast news interviews. Data are
drawn from a wide range of news interview material, most of
which was broadcast in the United States over the past twenty
years. The analysis focuses on the main questioning environments
in which this practice is deployed, and what it accomplishes
therein. As we'll see, this practice draws on generic properties of
direct reported speech and related phenomena (Goffman, 1981;
Li, 1986; Clark and Gerrig, 1990; Holt, 1996, 2000), but in a
way that furthers a set of specialised tasks intrinsic to the institutional context of broadcast journalism. Moreover, an adequate
understanding of this practice and its functions requires attention
to both the position of the public-framed question within the
overall structure of the interview, and the substance of the question
itself in relation to its immediate sequential context.

9.2 Opening and resumptive questions

Interviewers explicitly frame their questions on behalf of the public
in an occasional and non-random manner, so that the practice tends

to 'cluster' in certain interactional environments. One such environment involves the launching of an interview or a major section of it.
Some public-framed questions appear as the very first question that
opens the interview, as in the following:

(4) [ABC *Nightline* 5 June 1985: Corporate Mergers]

```
 1  IR:      Joining us now li:ve in our New York studios, Malcolm
 2            Forbes. Chairman and editor in chief of Forbes magazine,
 3            one of thuh nation's best known business journals. (.)
 4            .hh And from our affiliate WXYZ in Detroit.
 5            Professor Walter Adams, professor of economics, and
 6            former president of Michigan State University.
 7     →      .hhhh Professor Ada:ms to: those millions of people out
 8     →      there who=uh never hope to control a billion dollar
 9     →      corporation, an' frankly don't care one way or another,
10     →      why should they.
11            (1.5)
12  WA:       .hhh Well thee: uh- problem with these megamergers...
```

Others appear midway through an interview, when new IEs are
brought in to join the discussion in progress. For example:

(5) [ABC *Nightline* 6 June 1985: Nuclear Power/Waste]

```
 1   IR:     With us now live in our San Francisco bureau is
 2            Doctor Jacob Fabricant. (.) Professor of Radiology at
 3            the University of California Medical School, .hh and a
 4            medical advisor to the: cleanup committee:, for the
 5            Three Mile Island nuclear plant. .hh And in our
 6            Washington bureau Robert Pollard. a nuclear safety
 7            engdance:r? who resigned from the Nuclear Regulatory
 8            Commission .hh in nineteen seventy six .h because he
 9            felt the agency was not adequately protecting .h the
10            public's health an' safety.
11            .hh Mister Pollard uh:: that's (.) kind of a
12            fascinating .hhh background because I'm sure
13     →      people are er- particularly concerned what would
14            cause someone to resign. Whaddayou mean: .hh when
15            you say you felt the agency was not adequately
16            protecting thuh public's health 'n safety.
17            (0.2)
18   RP:      .hhh ((clears throat)) Well I certainly believe
```

Finally, on commercial broadcasts, public-framed questions also follow commercial breaks that occur midway through the interview, where they are used to resume the interview in progress. The first excerpt, involving Senator Bob Dole, followed just such a hiatus.

(6) [NBC *Meet the Press* 8 December 1985: Bob Dole]
```
 1 IR:    We are back on Meet the Press, with the:
 2        Senate majority leader, Bob Dole of Kansas.=
 3        =Senator? .hhh (.) u::m I wanna get- (.)
 4        clear:: in my own mind and hopefully
 5    →   for those people who=watching the programme,
 6        Do you support (0.5) the:: bill that came outta
 7        the House Ways 'n Means Committee on tax reform.
 8        (1.4)
 9 BD:    Well I'm a=little like th' presiden'.=I support the
10        process, 'n I think uh:: .hh thuh bill itself
```

These public-framed opening/resumptive questions share several common features. First, such questions tend to be both open-ended and relatively innocuous. They are open-ended in that they solicit responses at a rather coarse level of granularity (Schegloff, 2000a). Excerpts (4) and (5) both invite the interviewee to comment on a broadly focused issue (problems with corporate mergers, problems with the Nuclear Regulatory Commission). Only the resumptive question in excerpt (6) – a 'yes/no' question asking whether the IE supports a specific piece of legislation – is more tightly focused. Correspondingly, such questions are also comparatively benign in that they do not express or imply anything critical of or hostile toward the IE.

Second, across these questions 'the public' takes on a consistent sense and reference. It is not the population in general that the IR is referring to, nor the citizenry or voters, but rather the *broadcast audience* that is presently tuned in. This is most explicit in excerpts (4) ('to: those millions of people out there', lines 7–8) and (6) ('for those people who're=watching the programme,' line 5), but it is also the case (albeit less explicitly) in excerpt (5). Here the IR, after introducing the IE as a nuclear safety engineer 'who resigned from the Nuclear Regulatory Commission', comments that this is a 'fascinating .hhh background' (line 12) because 'people are er-par<u>tic</u>ularly concerned what would cause someone to resign' (lines 13–14). Since this particular IE is not at all well-known, reference to 'people' here is to be understood as the immediate broadcast audience who has just been informed of the IE's resignation.

Third, the questions do not express or imply any specific attitude or stance on the part of the public toward the issue, only puzzlement or an information gap that the subsequent discussion is projected to resolve.

Why is it that these particular questions are affiliated with the public in this particular way? A clue may be gleaned from the talk that immediately precedes each question. This prior talk is occupied with the task of introducing – or, in the case of excerpt (6), reintroducing – the IEs to the audience. Introductory talk appears in excerpt (4) on lines 1–6, excerpt (5) on lines 1–10, and excerpt (6) on lines 1–2. A hallmark of such preliminary talk is that it is addressed directly to the audience, and indeed this is the only juncture in a news interview that is formally audience-directed (Clayman and Heritage, 2002: Chapter 3). This audience-directed pattern of address embodies a distinctive participation framework that contrasts sharply with the bulk of news interview talk. Most of the time, IRs and IEs address their remarks to each other, while treating the audience as a party of 'overhearers' who are indirect recipients of the talk in progress (Heritage 1985; Clayman and Heritage, 2002: Chapters 3, 4, and 8). Thus, while the audience momentarily becomes a more central player in the participation framework during the interview's introductory phase, they recede into the background during subsequent talk.

The introductory talk is constituted as audience-directed through both non-vocal and vocal means. At the non-vocal level, IRs face the camera and talk into it during most of the introductory talk. Even when the guests are co-present within the studio, IRs do not gaze toward them during this phase of talk. Correspondingly, they refer to their guests in the third person when introducing them, deploying their full names (often with titles) for this purpose.

Excerpt (4), line 5: 'Professor Walter <u>A</u>dams'
Excerpt (5), line 6: 'Robert <u>Pol</u>lard'
Excerpt (6), line 2: 'S<u>e</u>nate majority leader, B<u>o</u>b Dole'

By virtue of such practices, IRs are plainly addressing the audience in a direct way.

By contrast, when IRs proceed from the audience-directed introductions to the interviewee-directed questions (or question prefaces), they mark the transition by redirecting their gaze away from the camera and toward the IE, and by using a reduced person-reference form.

Excerpt (4), line 7: 'Professor Ada:ms'
Excerpt (5), line 11: 'Mister Pollard'
Excerpt (6), line 3: 'Senator'

In conjunction with the IE-directed gaze, the reduced form is analysable as an address term which treats the IE as the second person target of the talk. This shift in address is subsequently maintained and reinforced when the IR begins speaking on behalf of, rather than to, the audience.

Accordingly, the tendency for opening/resumptive questions to be framed on behalf of the audience can be understood in relation to this reconfiguring of participation frameworks. On the one hand, this practice is a lingering remnant or trace of a prior direction of address and the participation framework that it embodies. That is, the IR's heightened orientation toward the audience appears to 'bleed into' opening/resumptive questions, where it takes a new form consistent with the new participation framework at hand. What previously involved directing remarks toward the audience becomes, within the question, a matter of speaking on the audience's behalf.

But this practice is not merely a residue of what came before; it is also a constitutive feature of the current framework. It furthers the reconfiguration whereby the audience is relegated to the role of 'overhearer' of an interaction taking place primarily between IR and IE.[1]

---

[1] This gaze shift is not always visible on camera. In some cases, just as the IR winds down the introduction and launches into the question or question preface, the camera cuts to a close-up of the IE. In such cases, the new participation framework is evident to the audience mainly through changing person-reference forms within the talk itself.

9.3 Sensitive and aggressive questions

Other usages of the practice seem tied not to the position of a given question within the overall structure of the interview, but rather to the substantive particulars of the question itself in its immediate sequential context. IRs often invoke the public when raising questions that are in some way sensitive or aggressive.

The following instance occurred in an interview with ousted Philippine President Ferdinand Marcos, when Marcos was asked about his wife Imelda's enormous shoe collection. Prior to this interview, Imelda's shoe collection had been widely reported in the news media, and was treated as emblematic of the extravagance and excess of the recently ousted Marcos regime. Consequently, what might otherwise be regarded as an extraneous personal matter had become, by the time of the interview, a well-known and deeply symbolic political issue. The infamous character of this issue is apparent in the brief and elliptical way it is introduced (line 5) – the shoe collection is merely referred to without elaboration – and the way in which Marcos anticipates the thrust of the question before it is completed (lines 6 and 8).

(7a) [ABC *Nightline* 4 April 1986: Ferdinand Marcos]
```
1  IR  : →  Whe:n people heard I was coming out (.) to do an interview
2         →  with you (1.0) you know what most people are interested in?
3  FM :     Mm mm.
4            (0.4)
5  IR  :     Your wife's:: three thousand pairs of shoes.
6  FM :     How many shoes
7  IR  :     How many sh[oes
8  FM :                  [can you wear: (0.2) in (.) twenty years.
9  IR  :     Exactly (.) how many can you?
```

Notice that, as the IR first begins to raise this sensitive issue (lines 1–2), he makes a special point of indicating that it is 'what most people are interested in'.

None of the previous questions to Marcos were framed in this way. The IR began with comparatively open-ended and sympathetic questions regarding Marcos's own experiences, opinions and plans for the future.

These questions are offered straightforwardly, without any overt reference to the public. It is only with the distinctly unflattering matter of the shoe collection that the IR makes a point of emphasizing that this is a matter of broad public concern.

(7b) [ABC *Nightline* 4 April 1986: Ferdinand Marcos]

    IR: President Marcos, you're a very proud man. I think even your
          enemies recognise that. Tell me a little bit about what it has been
          like for you these past few weeks...
    IR: Where can you go? I mean, it must be a terribly humiliating
          experience. At one point you were thinking of going to Spain...
    IR: So what you're really saying is that in some fashion the American
          government was helping the rebel forces against you...

This practice is not limited to political interviews. The next example is from an interview with a gay couple, one of whom was then dying of AIDS. At one point the IR asks them to explain why they love each other (see line 17).

(8) [ABC *Nightline* 19 September 1986: AIDS]

     1   IR: You know (.) in <u>one</u> sense (0.4) this story: your story has
     2   been a story of w:atching (0.3) a dise:ase take its toll:.
     3   But in another sense, (.) it has been (0.8) very much a:
     4   chronicle of a love story. (0.4) You two love each other
     5   very mu:ch don't you.
     6   (0.3)
     7   KM: Yes indeed.
     8   JS :   .hhh .hhh ((sniffling, possibly tearful))
     9   KM: .hhh ha ha.
    10   IR: →   That's: somethin:[g <u>a</u>lso: that (.) a lot of people in the=
    11   KM: [come on
    12   IR: →   =straight community, (0.3) have a great deal of trouble
    13   →   understanding, I'd I don't know whether it's I (.) you know
    14   if someone said to me explain why you love your w<u>i</u>fe (0.3)
    15   I'm not sure uh I could d- (.) could do that to their
    16   satisfaction e<u>i</u>ther but let me .hhh ask <u>you</u> both (0.6)
    17   w:hy (1.6) why do you love each other. (0.3) Jack?
    18   (2.4)
    19   JS: This is the most special human being I've ever met in my life...

The delicacy of this question stems not only from its deeply personal character, but also because it asks the IEs to explain something that ordinarily requires no explanation. As a general principle, explanatory accounts are called for when behaviour is unanticipated or out of the ordinary (Scott and Lyman, 1968; Heritage, 1988). Accordingly, by asking them to account for their loving relationship, the IR could be taken to imply that the relationship is abnormal or deviant.

Much of the lead-up to this delicate question (lines 10–16) is an effort to soften or mitigate what is to come. The IR observes (lines 13–16) that the question would be difficult for a 'straight' person such as himself to answer – this not only exhibits a modicum of empathy, but it also normalises the question by casting it as one that could in principle be asked of anyone. More importantly for our purposes, the IR frames the question as having been motivated by the puzzlement of 'a lot of people in the straight community' (lines 10–12, arrowed). He thus presents himself as speaking on behalf of the majority. By way of contrast, a prior question (lines 1–5) asking them to confirm what had been implicit in the discussion thus far (that they love each other) is comparatively innocuous and contains no overt reference to the public.

In the context of sensitive/aggressive questions like those in excerpts (7) and (8), speaking on behalf of the public has, from the IR's standpoint, certain practical advantages. Consider first the issue of professional neutrality. By invoking a responsible third party – whether elite or public – IRs distance themselves from the line of questioning and the views being expressed within it, thus taking up a formally neutral or 'neutralistic' posture (Clayman, 1992; Clayman and Heritage, 2002: Chapter 5). IRs present themselves, not as pursuing a purely personal agenda, but as impartially relaying the concerns of others.

Invoking the public has the additional benefit of legitimising a line of inquiry. By claiming that the public wants or needs to know about some matter, IRs imply that it is appropriate and justifiable to ask about it. In this connection, notice that the IR is not referring to the viewing audience per se in these examples, but rather some broader populace. With the public offered as the primary rationale for the question, the reason why it is being raised of a given IE at a given moment, the question is thus presented as legitimate.

Finally, this practice increases the pressure on IEs to be forthcoming in response. It is more difficult for an IE to sidestep or evade a question that has been legitimated in this way, because that could be taken as an offence not merely to the IR but to the broader public that he or she claims to represent.

To further illustrate these points, let's consider a range of cases involving transparently adversarial questions. We begin with questions that counter or disagree with something an IE has just said. A comparatively mild example of this sort took place during an interview with Larry Spreewell, the basketball player who had physically attacked his own coach. We already touched on this case in example (1) above; an expanded excerpt appears below (excerpt (9)). Here Spreewell seeks to defend his action by portraying it as a justifiable response to the harsh and offensive style of his coach 'PJ' (lines 1–13). As he put it, 'It was about <u>PJ</u> disrespecting me as a ma:n' (lines 6–7), and he concludes by invoking a general moral rule ('You d<u>o</u>n:'t talk to people the way .hh PJ: talked to <u>me</u>' in lines 12–13) that casts the coach's conduct as improper.

(9) [CBS *60 Minutes* 8 March 1998: Spreewell]

```
 1  IE:      It was all about .hh- (0.2) the: the resp<u>e</u>ct
 2           factor with me. I mean I (don'-) I think with
 3           P̲J his- .hh his coaching style is (such) that
 4           (0.5) ya know he likes to get- he likes to
 5           discipline you=('n) get on guy:s. And I'm
 6           saying we're men. .hh It was about my: It was
 7           about P̲J disrespecting me as a ma:n.
 8           (.) (A[n' it-)
 9  IR:           [P̲erson to person.
10  IE:      P̲erson to p̲erson.
11           (0.2)
12  IE:      Person to person you (don:') .hh you d̲on:'t talk
13           to people the way .hh PJ: talked to m̲e.
14  IR: →    People might be saying H̲ey kid. .hh You ear:n (0.2)
15           m̲illions and millions of dollars, .hh L̲ive with it.
16           (0.2)
17  IR:      Forg̲et the respect, take your m̲oney,
18  IE:      When you're dealing with resp̲ect: uh: m̲oney is not
19           a i̲ssue.
```

In response to this exculpatory account, the IR (lines 14–17) proposes that, given the 'm<u>i</u>llions and millions of dollars' Spreewell earns, he should be able to 'Live with it.' This response directly undermines Spreewell's account, and thereby casts his violent actions as unjustified. Significantly, the IR delivers this pointed riposte, not on his own behalf, but as something that 'People might be saying' (arrowed).[2]

IRs do not invoke the public merely to dispute something an IE has said; ordinarily, something more than a simple disagreement is involved. Oppositional responses containing this practice also tend to embody a hostile commentary on the IE's moral character – in the vast majority of cases they are derogatory or incriminating. This element is present, albeit somewhat indirectly, in the preceding example, and it is even more apparent in the next one. This is excerpted from an interview with a convicted child molester who has served out his sentence but remains in confinement because he has been judged a continuing threat to society. The IE, arguing for his release, makes an impassioned claim to have been cured of his propensity to molest (lines 1–5), and he begins to cry at this point (lines 5–6).

(10) [CBS *60 Minutes* 12 January 1998: Stephanie's Law]
```
 1  IE:   Well the law was the one that brought me here. (0.5)
 2         But it was me that decided that I wanted to stop ( )
 3         .hh I want to stop the molesting, I want to stop the
 4         offending, I want to stop the hurting? (0.2)
 5         ((sniff)) I want to heal myself. ((crying))
 6         (2.5) ((sniff:::))
 7         (2.5)
 8  IR: → Do you know that there're people watching (0.7) who
 9         will say: that that's: part of the deal he's doing=
10         ya know.
11  IE:   Oh I know. But I was an em[osh-
12  IR:                            [That's part of the act.
13  IE:   ((sniff))=Well- (0.5) .h I wish they'da known me before...
```

At this emotionally charged moment, just when the IE appears to be highly vulnerable, the IR counters by proposing, in effect, that he

---

[2] The IR's reference to 'people' echoes the IE's parallel usage in the prior turn (line 13). This may explain the IR's choice of this specific term over other broadly-synonymous terms such as 'the public', 'viewers', etc.

is merely faking it (lines 8–10), presumably as a ploy to win release from prison. And when the IE attempts to respond (line 11), the IR cuts him off to reiterate this point (cf. Jefferson, 1973), characterising the IE's emotional plea as 'part of the act' (line 12). Once again, this disparaging retort is framed as something that 'people watching... will say' (arrowed).[3]

In a more extreme variant of this practice, the IR steps back from the specifics of what has just been said by the IE to mount a broader attack on the IE and his or her profession. A global denunciation of this sort occurred in an interview with a 'dog psychiatrist' who uses psychiatric principles to treat canine behavioural and emotional problems. At the opening of this segment, the IE is praising a dog at his side (line 1).

(11) [NBC *Dateline* 16 December 1997: Dog Psychiatry]

```
 1  IE:      Goo:d boy:.
 2  IR:  →   A lotta people would hear: (.) about your profession.
 3  IE:      Ye:s.=
 4  IR:      =and say that's a bunch o'poppycock.
 5  IE:      Ye:s,
 6           (0.2)
 7  IR:      And you say:?
 8           (.)
 9  IE:      I say they're entitled to their opinion. .hh And I would
10           also say to those people that they'll believe that (0.9)
11           .h right up until their very favourite dog growls at them.
12           (0.2) .hh And then you'd be surprised at how quickly .hh
13           people can suddenly become a convert.
```

The IR asserts that the IE's profession is 'a bunch o' poppycock' (line 4). Obviously this denunciation is neither responsive to nor targeted at the previous turn at talk; it is aimed at the entire profession as it has been represented by the IE over the course of the encounter. And once again, this remark is cast as something that 'A lotta people' would say (arrowed).

---

[3] The IR's reiteration in line 12 syntactically parallels the original formulation in line 9, and this makes it hearable as a reiteration and thus still an expression of what the 'people watching' will say.

In all three of the preceding cases, just as the IR launches into a question that is both oppositional and derogatory, he adopts a tribune-of-the-people stance that both neutralises and legitimates what is to come. Moreover, it is notable that in these more aggressive cases the footing shift is achieved specifically through the vehicle of direct reported speech. This is not coincidental; the use of direct reported speech enables the IR to employ idiomatically colourful and affect-laden expressions ('He̲y kid... Li̲ve with it', 'part of the a̲ct' and 'bunch o'po̲ppycock') that would otherwise be a jarring departure from the formal register normally employed by broadcast journalists. When responsibility for such expressions is deflected onto the public, IRs can use them to heighten the oppositional character of the action while at the same time retaining a posture of professionalism.

Finally, it should be noted that the neutralising/legitimating import of 'speaking on behalf of the public' is exploited not only within interviews as they unfold; it can also be exploited after the fact, as the interview is being replayed, analysed and discussed. In Ted Koppel's book about the *Nightline* programme (Koppel and Gibson, 1996), there are extensive transcripts depicting noteworthy interview moments. In the midst of one such excerpt from a highly adversarial interview, just before a particularly hostile question is delivered, Koppel-the-narrator interrupts Koppel-the-interviewer to point out that 'When I ask a question, it's something that I think the viewers want asked. I'm their representative' (1996: 157). This isolated quotation was featured at the beginning of this chapter – now re-embedded in its textual context, its immediate practical import becomes transparent. It invites readers of the book to analyse the upcoming antagonistic question as having been properly motivated.

9.4 Defending and pursuing

If IRs invoke the public when taking the offensive, they also do so when the initiative is reversed and they are defending themselves against an IE's criticism or attack. Here the neutralising and legitimating character of the practice has a defensive import, and it enables the IR to continue to pursue a line of questioning in the face of objections.

For example, when Pat Buchanan was interviewed after he
became President Reagan's Director of Communications, he was
questioned about his influence on the increasingly ideological tone
of the President's speeches. Buchanan strongly objects to the idea,
and he accuses the IR of having 'demeaned the President' (line 1) by
suggesting that Buchanan was 'running down there at night <u>sneak</u>-
ing <u>phr</u>ases or (<u>l</u>ine:s) .hhh into sp<u>ee</u>ches an' the pr<u>e</u>sident doesn't
know what he's s<u>a</u>ying' (lines 2–5).

(12) [ABC *Nightline* 3 June 1985: Pat Buchanan]

```
 1  PB :    ... It dem<u>ea</u>:ns the Pr<u>e</u>sident to sugg<u>e</u>st that someone
 2           say Pat Buchanan or <u>anyone el</u>:se .hh is running down
 3           there at night <u>sneak</u>ing <u>phr</u>ases or (<u>l</u>ine:s) .hhh into
 4           sp<u>ee</u>ches an' the pr<u>e</u>sident doesn't know what he's
 5           s<u>a</u>yi[ng. .hhh]
 6  IR: →    [No Pat ] <u>I</u> don't think anyone's sug[ g<u>e</u>st ]ing=
 7  PB:                                          [(sure)]
 8  IR: →    =that, I think what people <u>are</u> suggesting is that the
 9           President of the United States perhaps more than any
10           other m<u>an</u> <u>or</u> woman in the country is t<u>e</u>rribly
11           terribly busy c<u>a</u>nnot p<u>o</u>s[sibly write <u>every</u> speech of=
12  PB:                              [Mhm
13  IR:      =his <u>o</u>wn, .hh <u>or</u> for that matter go over <u>every</u> speech
14           line by line as you sugg<u>e</u>st. [ .hhh ] Uh- an when that=
15  PB:                                   [Mhm]
16  IR:      =h<u>a</u>ppens, then people in positions such as your <u>own</u>,
17           .hh can sometimes get some of their <u>own</u> ideas across.
18  PB:      .h Well <u>sure</u>. you could get ideas in but l<u>oo</u>k every
19           speech in the White House Ted .hhhh g<u>o</u>:es through a pr<u>o</u>cess...
```

In response to this attack, the IR pursues two lines of defence
(lines 6–17). First, he characterises his previous question in a way
that detoxifies it, reducing much of its 'demeaning' character. That
is, he grants how 'terribly busy' the president is, suggesting that it is
perfectly understandable and indeed inevitable that Buchanan
would be wielding increased influence. More importantly for our
purposes, he presents the line of questioning (arrowed) as having
been motivated by 'what people <u>are</u> suggesting'. He thereby defends
his prior conduct, while also justifying his continued pursuit of the
matter.

Perhaps the most dramatic example of this sort occurred in Dan Rather's infamous interview with Vice President George Bush during the 1988 presidential campaign. The agenda for the interview was Bush's involvement in the Iran–Contra scandal. This agenda was set from the very beginning – it was the main focus of the hard-hitting taped segment that preceded the interview, as well as the IR's opening question. The agenda projected by this opening elicited a strong reaction from Bush – he registered a series of complaints against Dan Rather and the CBS *Evening News* team, accusing them, among other things, of having previously misrepresented the purpose of the interview. Specifically, he charged that he was led to believe that it would be a broad 'political profile' rather than a narrow investigation of his involvement in Iran–Contra. Following these accusations, he calls for 'fair play' (lines 1–3), and he bids to broaden the agenda of the interview as he claims he was promised.

(13) [CBS *Evening News* 25 Jan 1988: Bush–Rather]
```
 1  GB:    ...I'm_asking for: (0.3) fair play:, and I thought I was
 2         here to talk about my views on educa:tion, or on
 3         getting this deficit down=
 4  IR:    =Well Mr Vice Preside[nt we wanna talk about the re[cord    o]n=
 5  GB:                         [Yes.                         [Well let's]
 6  IR:    =this, .hh because it-
 7  GB:    Well let's talk
 8         abo[ut the (full) record, that's what I wanna talk about] Dan,
 9  IR: →     [th-the framework he::re:, is that one third of-    ]
10  IR: →  one third o'the Republicans in this poll[:, one third=
11  GB:                                            [Yeah
12  IR: →  =o'the the Republicans .hh and- and one fourth of the
13      →  people who say:: that- eh y'know they rather like you:,
14      →  .hh believe y[ou're hi]ding something.=Now if you=
15  GB:                 [(wha-) ]
16  IR:    =[are: here's a ch-]
17  GB:    [I              am] hid[ing something]
18  IR:                          [here's   a  ch]ance to get it out.
```

Rather simultaneously defends himself and justifies further questioning on Iran–Contra by reference to poll results (arrowed), indicating that a substantial segment of Bush's own supporters believe he's 'hiding something' (line 14). The concerns of the citizenry are thus offered as the rationale behind the adversarial line of questioning that Rather, despite the objections, continues to pursue.

9.5 Interactional consequences

To recap, journalist-interviewers sometimes present themselves explicitly as speaking for the public, but they do so in a highly selective manner, mainly during opening/resumptive questions, sensitive/aggressive questions and defensive/pursuing questions. In the latter two environments, a tribune of-the-people stance has the effect of neutralising and legitimating IRs' more aggressive conduct, thereby increasing the pressure on recalcitrant IEs.

Are such efforts actually successful? In other words, does the practice 'work'? The evidence indicates that for the most part it does, at least within the framework of the interview itself.

Consider first the problem of maintaining a formally neutral or 'neutralistic' posture. This is a generic problem that IRs face, but it becomes particularly acute when an IR does not come to a grammatically formatted question (as in excerpts (9) and (11) above). While interrogatives have a neutralistic quality, unvarnished declarative assertions threaten to undermine the IR's neutralism (Clayman, 1988; Heritage and Roth, 1995). By invoking the public at such moments, IRs present themselves as relaying the concerns of the populace rather than pursuing a personal agenda. One indication of the effectiveness of this claim to neutralism is that it is almost never challenged by IEs; indeed, IEs often respond in such a way as to validate the claim. This is perhaps most striking in excerpt (11), when the dog psychiatrist disputes the IR's 'poppy-cock' characterisation and – like the IR – attributes that viewpoint to the public: 'I say they are entitled to their opinion. .hh And I would also say to those people'. He thus presents himself as disagreeing, not with the IR per se, but with the public on whose behalf the IR was ostensibly speaking. (A similar pattern may be observed in excerpt (10), line 13.) In this way, IEs tacitly validate and reinforce the IR's neutralistic posture.

In a similar vein, IEs appear to accept the fundamental legitimacy of questions framed in this way, although once again this acceptance is registered tacitly rather than on an explicit level. In probing or adversarial environments, IRs are always in danger of being seen as exceeding their professional mandate, and in some cases they actually are criticised for overly aggressive questioning. However, when such questions are cast as responsive to the concerns and interests of the public, IEs generally proceed to answer them – or at least they present themselves as 'answering'. Acquiescent responses occur even when the line of questioning was previously the object of complaint. Consider excerpt (12) above – although Pat Buchanan vociferously attacked the question (lines 1–5) when it was initially raised, he subsequently gives in and answers it without complaint (lines 18–19) when it is reissued as something that 'people are suggesting'. There is only one exception to this general pattern of cooperation – George Bush continued to resist Dan Rather's Iran–Contra questions (following excerpt (13) above) even after Rather mobilised opinion poll statistics to justify his line of inquiry. That may well be the exception that proves the rule, since the resulting interaction was so argumentative that it became a major news story in its own right (Clayman and Whalen, 1988/89).

Of course, what impact all of this may or may not have on the viewing audience remains an open question which cannot be resolved with the present data. But at least within the confines of the interview itself, a tribune-of-the-people stance is remarkably effective in rendering a question defensible, thereby encouraging IEs to acquiesce – or at least feign acquiescence – even to highly aggressive interrogations.

9.6 A single case

The import of a tribune-of-the-people stance, and the effort IRs expend to achieve it, are richly illustrated in an episode from David Frost's famous 1977 interview with former President Richard Nixon. That widely anticipated interview focused on the Watergate affair and its aftermath, which culminated in Nixon's resignation of the presidency. At the time, there was much speculation concerning what Nixon would say about the events of Watergate. Would he accept responsibility for what transpired? Would he admit to wrongdoing? Or would he remain unrepentant?

As the interview unfolded, Frost succeeded in getting Nixon to admit to having made 'mistakes.' At one critical juncture, however,

Frost tries to induce Nixon to go further than this, pointing out that the word 'mistakes' seems 'n<u>o</u>t enough for <u>pe</u>ople to under-sta:nd' (lines 1–2). Thus, this initial push for a stronger admission of guilt is presented as being done on behalf of '<u>pe</u>ople' in general.

(14a) [Nixon–Frost]
```
 1   DF:  ...Would you go further than mistakes:: (.) the wor::d (0.9)
 2           that seems n- n- (.) not enough for people to understa:nd.
 3           (1.5)
 4   RN:  What wor::d would you:: (.) express,
 5           (3.8)
 6   DF:  My goodness that's a:: hhh (0.2) I:: think (.) that
 7             there're (.) three things. (.) since you ask me, (0.2)
 8             I:: would like to hear you sa:y >I think the
 9             American people would like to hear you say
10           ((question continues))
```

However, when Nixon invites Frost to indicate what word he would prefer (line 4), Frost momentarily strays from the safety of a tribune-of-the-people stance. Frost begins an extended question by indicating that there are three things that '<u>I</u>:: would like to hear you sa:y' (lines 6–8), emphasising the first person pronoun 'I' and thus framing the question-in-progress as an expression of his own personal preferences. Notice, however, that he carefully modulates this stance just as he launches into it, pointing out parenthetically that he is expressing his preferences at Nixon's request ('since you <u>ask</u> me') rather than on his own initiative.

Even this modulated stance is not maintained for long. Although Frost does not perform a complete about-face, he adds that this is also what 'the American <u>pe</u>ople would like to hear you say' (lines 8–9). Frost seems to treat the addition of this reference to the public as something of a priority – he speeds up (denoted in the transcript by the '>' symbol) just as he launches into the clause containing this attribution.

All of this manoeuvring to achieve a tribune-of-the-people stance is explicable given the gravity of the question that is eventually delivered. Frost pointedly asks Nixon to make three extraordinary admissions of guilt – the beginning of each is arrowed below.

(14b) [Nixon–Frost]

```
 8  DF:   I:: would like to hear you sa:y >I think the
 9             American people would like to hear you say. .hh (.)
10  1→    O:ne is::, (0.7) the:re was probably mo::re (0.2) tha::n, (0.4)
11             mista::kes there was:: (0.7) wro:ngdoing (0.2) whether it
12             was a cri::me >or not=yes it may have been a crime< too:. (0.6)
13  2→    Secondly:: (0.8) I did h (0.6) and I'm saying this without
14             (.) questioning the motives alright. I di:d h (0.2)
15             abu:se the power I had as President. (0.2) or:: ha::ve
16             (.) not fulfilled it (.) totality, .h (0.2) (eh)the
17             oath of office that- that's the second thing, (0.2)
18  3→    And thir::dly, (0.7) I: put the American peo-people
19             through two years of needless agony >an' I apologize for
20             that. (0.9) And I: say that- (.) you've explai:ned your
21             motives, (.) I think tho:se >are the categories.<
22             (0.7) And I kno:w how >difficult it is for anyone,< and
23             most of all you: but I: think h (0.8) that (.) people
24             need to hear it, (0.4) and I think unless you say it,
25             (0.6) you're gonna be hau:nted >for the rest of your life.<
26             (0.8)
27  RN:    I well remember: uh h (0.2) that (.) when I::...
```

Frost asks Nixon to admit: (1) that some of his actions were wrong and possibly criminal, (2) that he abused the power of the presidency, and (3) that he put the American people through two years of needless agony. Frost also asks Nixon to apologise for the latter offence. Frost himself acknowledges the magnitude of what he is requesting when he subsequently notes 'how >difficult it is for anyone,< and most of all you:' (lines 22–23). But as he completes this question, he reiterates that this is something that 'people need to hear' (lines 23–24). In so doing, he strives to neutralise and legitimate what is an extremely face-threatening and incriminating set of requests, while increasing the pressure on Nixon to comply with them.

Nixon's response is far too long and complex to analyse in detail here. It will suffice to observe that, while he doesn't actually do what Frost is requesting, he does at least gesture in the direction of an admission of guilt. Thus, he begins his response by recounting the story of the resignations of staff members Haldeman and Erlichman, noting that he told his speechwriter that perhaps he (Nixon) should resign too 'because I feel respo̱nsible' (arrowed).

(14c) [Nixon–Frost]
```
1   RN:   I we̱ll remember: uh h (0.2) that (.) when I:: (.) let
2         Ha̱ldeman and Erlichman (0.4) kno:w that the:y were t'
3         resi:gn (0.6) that I:: (0.4) had Ray Price bring in the::
4         fi̱nal dra̱:ft of the speech that I was t' make th' next
5         night. (0.6) and I said to him Ra::y, hh I said if you
6         think I oughtta resi:gn I said pu̱t that in too:
7   →     because I feel respo̱nsible
```

This certainly implies a modicum of responsibility, in a general way, for the events of Watergate.

On the other hand, Nixon's response falls short of a full-throated admission in a variety of ways. First, the assertion of responsibility at line 7 is markedly qualified – it is designed not as a straight factual assertion, but a statement about his subjective 'feelings' on the matter. Second, Since this comment is embedded within a story, it is supposed to reflect his feelings as they were expressed years ago, at an interpersonally difficult moment in his administration, when talking to a staff member. Thus contextualised, the remark is available to be interpreted as a gesture of solidarity with his beleaguered staff, rather than a literal admission of guilt for what transpired. Finally, by launching into this story as a way of responding to Frost's question, Nixon does not address any of the specific issues (criminality, abuse of power, causing needless public agony) that were raised in the original question. Although the story culminates in a highly general and unspecified admission, this is deferred until line 7, and the delay tends to obscure its lack of fit with the original question (cf. Clayman and Heritage, 2002: Chapter 7). Accordingly, while public-framed questions exert demonstrable pressure on IEs to answer in a particular way, they do not ensure a compliant outcome.

9.7 Conclusion

When interviewers present themselves as speaking on behalf of the public, they invoke a powerful symbolic resource. This practice both neutralises and legitimates lines of questioning, and exerts

pressure on interviewees to be genuinely forthcoming. It thus facilitates sensitive and aggressive modes of questioning, as well as
providing interviewers with resources for responding to criticisms
when they arise. For all of these reasons, the practice has a strategic
importance in the kind of adversarial questioning that has become a
hallmark of contemporary broadcast journalism (Clayman and
Heritage, 2002: Chapter 2).

While the import of the practice in dramatically conflictual
episodes can be readily appreciated, it is equally important to
recognise its more mundane uses. Sometimes interviewers invoke
the public simply to navigate from one phase of an interview to
another, or more specifically to manage the transition across, and
reconfiguration of, distinct participation frameworks.

Whatever its institutionally specific functions in the context of
news interviews, this practice is best understood as a specialised
variant of a much more general family of practices (e.g. direct
reported speech, indirect speech, footing shifts) that have the effect
of diffusing responsibility for what a speaker is saying. 'Speaking
on behalf of the public' exploits the basic properties and affor-
dances of these general practices of interaction, but it does so in a
highly distinctive way. By invoking a singular responsible party –
'the public' – with broad professional and cultural resonance, this
practice furthers certain specialised tasks associated with broadcast
journalism.

The dead in the service of the living

Robin Wooffitt

10.1 Introduction

In recent years there have been a number of studies of the use of reported speech in a variety of settings and discursive contexts: in everyday interaction (Tannen, 1986; Mayes, 1990; Holt, 1996); in courtroom interaction (Philips, 1986); in group discussions (Buttny, 1998; Myers, 1999; Buttny and Williams, 2000); in political discussion (Leudar, 1998) and in accounts of anomalous or paranormal experiences (Wooffitt, 1992). Many of these studies depart from the more linguistic and grammatical concerns with reported speech (for example, Coulmas, 1986; Li, 1986) and the exploration of its more psychological or cognitive aspects (Lehrer, 1989), and have instead begun to investigate more sociological questions which are raised when people incorporate another's utterances into ongoing encounters.

For example, Holt (1996) examined conversational instances of direct reported speech – in which the current speaker reproduces the words of another person in such a way as to suggest that this is what was actually said at the time. She reports a number of interactional functions of direct reported speech – for example, reported speech permits the speaker to demonstrate an assessment of the person whose talk is being reported in the way their words are reproduced. It allows

This chapter was prepared while I was a visiting researcher at the Koestler Parapsychology Unit (KPU) at the University of Edinburgh. I would like to thank the staff and students in the Unit for making me so welcome, and the Perrott-Warwick fund for providing generous financial support. I would also like to thank the editors of this volume for their insightful and helpful comments on an earlier version of this chapter.

the speaker to display what he or she considers to be, for example, the relevant attitudes, opinions, personality traits or general state of mind of the person whose talk they are reporting at the time it was originally produced. But, more relevant to the concerns of this chapter, it provides a key resource by which speakers can provide evidence for a position, or attest to the factuality of a claim or version of events (Potter, 1996). Reported speech can thus be examined as a resource through which the authenticity of a claim or the authority of a speaker can be established and defended.

In this chapter I examine some features of the way that direct reported speech can be used to warrant claims to have special parapsychological powers in interaction between members of the public and mediums: people who say that they are able to communicate with the dead on behalf of the living.

10.2 Mediumship and direct reported speech

The very notion of mediumship embodies a series of fantastically controversial claims: that some aspect of the human personality survives death; that spirits can monitor the ongoing lives of those they left behind; and that it is possible for some people to establish a parapsychological link with the spirit world so that they can pass on messages to the living. It is no surprise, therefore, to find that mediums (and psychic practitioners, more generally) are fully aware of the need to provide evidence of their claims. The importance of establishing proof of postmortem survival is a constant theme in their promotional flyers, in the *Psychic News* (the weekly newspaper for spiritualists and mediums) and in their autobiographies (for example, see O'Brien, 1992; Byrne and Sutton, 1993; Shine, 1996). Moreover, mediums are expected to demonstrate their claimed powers on every occasion they are consulted by members of the public, or address an audience or congregation. Their status as authentic mediums rests upon some form of display of knowledge gleaned from the spirit world and its acceptance by the sitter as evidence of the ability to communicate with the spirit world.

All psychic practitioners claim to be providing information for their sitters from a paranormal source: the tarot cards, the lines of the hand, or parapsychological cognitive abilities such as clairvoyance. But mediums are unique, in that ultimately their

source is a spirit *being*: an independent entity with agency which
can interact with the medium. And, while some mediums claim
merely to sense the intentions of the spirit, which are then conveyed
to the sitter, it is not uncommon for others to imply that they are in
some kind of direct verbal contact with the spirits, in much the
same way that the sitter and the medium are communicating.
Consider the following extract. This comes approximately twenty
minutes into a sitting. At this stage the medium claims to be in
contact with the spirit of the sitter's deceased husband.

(1) [JREF/VP: 35][1]
(Except where indicated, 'M' is the medium, 'S' is the sitter.)

```
 1   M:   mm hm because um, he's also a person (.) it's
 2         very hard to get to know him.(.) h he has
 3         very t- tough skins. he's very tough-skinned. h
 4         and it feels like (.) he doesn't let many
 5         people through, (0.2) but he let you through,
 6   S:   mm hm
 7   M:   you understand?
 8   S:   yes.
 9   M:   and this is what he is talking abou [t.
10   S:                                      ['kay=
11   M:   he said he let liz through. h
12         >did he ever call you< Lizzie?
13         (0.4)
14   S:   Ye:s:,
15         (0.4)
16   M:   because he says I let lizzie through.
17   S:   mm hm
18         (0.5)
```

---

[1] The data in this chapter come from a wider study of the discourse of psychic
practitioners. All data extracts come from recordings of private sittings
between mediums and one (or two) clients, except those identified by the
'DS/AUD' prefix, which come from public demonstrations of mediumship in theatres. (For an account of the various data sources, see Wooffitt,
2000.)

```
19   M:    °gotcha°
20         (0.4)
21   M:    .hhhhh hhhh
22         (0.7)
23   M:    right. .hh did you kinda wear a ri:ng? (th- hi(b)-
24         his, or some (kinda) his ri:ng?
           ((Continues))
```

This extract illustrates several ways in which the medium invokes his contact with a spirit. He talks directly to the spirit: the
quietly spoken 'gotcha' (line 19) displays his recipiency of information from the spirit source. He paraphrases the spirit: he reports
that the spirit is talking about aspects of the relationship he had
with his wife (the sitter) when alive. The medium also reports that
the spirit 'said he let liz through' (line 11). And, finally, the medium
directly reports the spirit's words: 'because he says I let lizzie
through' (line 16).

The use of reported speech in medium–sitter interaction is not
uncommon. Extract (2) provides another, lengthier, example.

(2) [JREF/Manchester: 7]

```
 1   M:    and your aunt was was such a sick. lady before
 2         she pa:ssed,
 3         (1.2)
 4   M:    I Feel that when she we:nt,
 5         (1.5)
 6   M:    she was just tired.
 7   S:    ye[s
 8   M:      [that's what she tells me, she sa[id I was s:o:
 9   S:                                       [yes
10   M:    tired.
11         (0.6)
12   M:    I didn't wan(t)o eat=I didn't want to do anything.
13         (0.3)
14   M:    I just was tired.
15   S:    mm hm
16   M:    I'd had enough. .hhh so I think I(d)- whatever they
17         put on her death certificate it would've
```

```
18        (0.3)
19   M:   REally the answer was she gave up sh[e didn't want
20   S:                                        [yes
21   M:   to (.) live an[y more. She'[d had enou]gh
22   S:                 [(           ) [had enough]
23        (.)
24   M:   .hhh ((clears throat)) I think she might have
25        had a little stroke, because .hhh I can feel
26        as if: (.) something went
27   S:   yes: she did
28        (0.3)
29   M:   .h:but (.) again (.) it was just (.) something (.)
30        to to (.) herald the en:d (.) .h and ellen,
31        ((continues))
```

Here reported speech is used to convey the spirit's account of their psychological state just prior to their death. If we remove the sitter's utterances, the stretch of reported speech is extensive: 'she said I was s:o: tired. (0.6) I didn't wan(t)o eat=I didn't want to do anything. (0.3) I just was tired. I'd had enough' (lines 8–16).

So, a medium can depict himself or herself as a recipient of spirit messages, or paraphrase their words, or even report the spirits' words directly. These are all activities which convey the sense that the medium is interacting with a co-present spirit (usually) with emotional ties with the sitter. They add drama to the moment, and at least provide for the possibility that the sitter may come to believe that it has been possible to communicate with loved ones who had passed over to the spirit world. And of these, direct reported speech is perhaps the most powerful resource: short of the actual materialisation of the spirit, it is the most compelling way to suggest the co-presence of a sentient, interactive entity.

But reported speech of the spirit's words is powerful not only because it vividly portrays the proximity, character and attention of the spirits. I want to argue that its inferential power derives as much from its sequential organisation in medium–sitter interaction as it does from the dramatic way it brings the dead to the attention of the living.

10.3 The sequential organisation of reported speech in successful demonstrations of the medium's powers

Instances of reported speech are not randomly distributed through-out medium–sitter interactions – they tend to cluster in particular sequential locations.

Mediums, along with other sorts of psychic practitioners, claim that they are able to gain knowledge about an individual through paranormal powers. The successful demonstration of these special powers exhibits some robust properties. In sittings, psychic practitioners will issue a series of utterances, usually (but not invariably) in the form of questions which hint at or imply that they have access to knowledge about the sitter or his or her circumstances. If the sitter finds the psychic's utterance to be accurate, or in some way relevant, it is receipted and accepted with a minimal turn, usually a simple 'Yes' or 'Yeah'. After the sitter's minimal acceptance or confirmation, the psychic practitioner moves swiftly to a turn in which the now-accepted knowledge is attributed to a paranormal source (Wooffitt, 2000). For example, the following extract comes from a sitting between a young woman and a psychic who uses tarot cards.

```
(3) [K/CC]
(Here 'P' designates the psychic)
((Discussing S's plans to travel after graduating.))
 1  S:  I graduate in June I'm probably going to work until
 2      about february [so: jus' (.) any old j[ob   ]y'know.
 3                     [RIght okay          [right]
 4  P:  and are you going to the states,
 5      (.)
 6  S:  yeah.
 7  P:  yea:h, c'z e I can see the old ehm:
 8      (.)
 9  S:  Hh[huh Hah .h]
10  P:    [ statue of ] liberty around you,
11  S:  heh heh h[e .hhh
12  P:           [there you are, there's contentment for
13      the future.
14  S:  oh go [od
15  P:        [who's pregnant around you?
```

The question 'and are you going to the states' may be heard as displaying the psychic's special knowledge that the sitter is indeed planning to visit the US. Once this has been accepted it is retrospectively cast as having been derived from the tarot cards: the psychic's utterance 'c'z e I can see the old ehm: statue of liberty around you' (lines 7–10) portrays her prior turn as a consequence of her ability to discern from the arrangement of cards a classic iconic representation of the US, and interpret its relevance to the sitter. Moreover, the turn is initiated with a derivation of 'because', thus explicitly establishing that the topic of her prior utterance was generated from the special powers claimed in her subsequent turn.

Once the attributive turn is complete, and the psychic has made a general remark about the sitter's future contentment, she initiates another topic with the question 'who's pregnant around you?' (line 15), which, should it be accepted by the sitter, would project the relevance of another attributive turn and further demonstration of special powers.

There is, then, a three-turn sequence which is a vehicle for demonstrations of ostensibly paranormal cognition:

T1 question (or statement) implying or hinting at knowledge of the sitter;
T2 minimal acceptance by the sitter;
T3 attribution of now-accepted knowledge to a paranormal source.

In this sequence the third turn is crucial, as it provides a slot in which psychic practitioners may establish their paranormal abilities.

This organisation informs success sequences in practitioners claiming a range of paranormal powers: tarot readers, palmists, astrologers, clairvoyants, psychics and mediums. And in medium–sitter interaction, it is noticeable that reports of spirit utterances cluster strongly in attributive third turns of success sequences. Consider extract (1) again:

(1) [JREF/VP: 35]

1 M: mm hm because um, he's also a person (.) it's
2   very hard to get to know him.(.) h he has

```
3              very t- tough skins. he's very tough-skinned. h
4              and it feels like (.) he doesn't let many
5              people through, (0.2) but he let you through,
6       S:     mm hm
7       M:     you understand?
8       S:     yes.
9       M:     and this is what he is talking abou[t.
10      S:                                        ['kay=
11      M:     he said he let liz through. h
12             >did he ever call you< Lizzie?         T1
13             (0.4)
14      S:     Ye:s:,                                 T2
15             (0.4)
16      M:     because he says I let lizzie through.  T3
17      S:     mm hm
18             (0.5)
19      M:     °gotcha°
20             (0.4)
21      M:     .hhhhh hhhh
22             (0.7)
23      M:     right. .hh did you kinda wear a ri:ng? (th- hi(b)-
24             his, or some (kinda) his ri:ng?
```

Here, the medium's utterance '>did he ever call you< Lizzie?' (line 12) hints or suggests that the medium has some intimate knowledge about a particular term of address used by the sitter's husband; there then follows a minimal acceptance from the sitter; and then the medium reveals that the source of the now-accepted information was the spirit of the sitter's deceased husband. Moreover, this attribution is accomplished by a report of the spirit's words: 'because he says I let lizzie through' (line 16). The inference available from this organisation is that it is because the spirit had said these words that the medium was able to inquire about – and to hint that he knew something of – this issue.

It is a common feature of ostensibly successful displays of the medium's powers that the spirit's own words occur in the third position and establish that the source of the medium's prior claim about the sitter was the spirit itself. Extract (4) provides another example:

(4) [JREF/VP: 4]

```
1   M:   hh number one thing is your >mother in spirit
2        please?<                                      T1
3        (0.2)
4   S:   Yes                                           T2
5   M:   >'cause I have (n-m) y'r mother standing
6        right over here, hh and she said I WANna      T3
7        TAlk to HEr and I want to speak to her
8        because hh your mother has very lou::d
9        when she comes through.
```

The medium's turn 'number one thing is your >mother in spirit please?<' (lines 1–2) is designed so that it could be heard as a genuine question about the sitter's mother (that is, it may be equivalent to 'has your mother passed on or is she still living?'), or it could be heard as a question which seeks confirmation of information already known to the medium. The sitter's minimal response does not disambiguate the prior turn, in that a simple 'yes' could be 'a telling' or 'a confirmation'. The medium's next turn, however, reveals that he is in contact with the spirit of the sitter's mother. His report that she said 'I WANna TAlk to HEr and I want to speak to her' (lines 6–7) implies that the knowledge that the sitter's mother has passed is now revealed to have come from the mother herself.

In the following extract the medium latches three of these three-turn sequences to establish a string of successful claims about the sitter:

(5) [EV]

```
1    M:   >'ave you 'ad< (.) bit >(o')< trouble with       T1
2         your back as well.
3         (0.2)
4    S1:  yes a little bi [t                                T2
5    M:                   [he says ah'd best send her       T3
6         a bit of sympathy down so you understand it,
7         .hh[h
8    S1:     [ye [s
9    M:         [coz y'know .h y'try to bottle things       T1
10        up and you don't always let people get close
```

```
11              to you in that sense do you
12   S1:        no.                                              T2
13   M:         he says she can be quite stubborn at times        T3
14              y'know
15              (.)
16   M:         is that true
17   S1:        °yes°
18   M:         an' he knows cz .h you are fussy about the        T1
19              bungalow aren't you [girl
20   S1:                            [yes I am                     T2
21   M:         bless her he says                                 T3
```

Here, there are three questions, each of which can be heard as
proposing that the medium has access to intimate knowledge about
the sitter: that she has a back trouble, that she can be withdrawn,
and that she is house-proud ('fussy about the bungalow' lines
18–19). To each of these questions the sitter provides minimal
positive responses. In each third position turn, reported speech is
used to imply that the spirit was the source of the accepted knowledge claim.

It is noticeable that in all kinds of psychic–sitter interaction, the
knowledge claim tentatively presented in first position turns is
invariably unattributed: psychic practitioners tend to declare the
paranormal source of their information only when it has been
accepted by the recipient. Similarly, mediums do not use reported
speech in first position turns. Indeed, there is often a marked footing
shift as the medium begins to build a clear first position knowledge
claim from an ongoing series of observations and comments.

In the following case, for example, the first position question is
'did you use to cook for him a lot?'

(6) [JREF/VP: 23]
```
1    M:         'e keeps > (keeps on with the) < was kitchen<
2               with you, .h and for (th-) some reason this
3               book, and I don't know why,.h good good good.
4               keep on going=He's talking about (0.2) you,
5               with=uhm cooking. (.) cooking, cooking,
6               cooking. .h andehm (.) missing some cooking.
7               (0.2) okay, you used tu- (.) did you use        T1
8               to cook for him a lot?
```

This first position turn arrives after the medium has been reporting the spirit's comments on the topic of cooking (with his then-wife, the sitter). During this, the medium paraphrases the spirit: he is said to be talking about cooking. He also displays his recipiency of the spirit's utterances: 'good good good. keep on going' (lines 3–4). There is clear evidence, then, that the medium positions himself as a verbal co-interactant with the spirit. But the design of the subsequent first position question does not suggest the spirit is in some way the origin of the hinted-at information: although there is a sense that the medium presents himself merely as the conduit for the spirit's information, this is left implicit.

Extract (7) provides a more stark illustration of the kind of footing shift which can accompany the introduction of a first position turn.

(7) [JREF/Manchester: 2]

```
1    M:    and she's pleased about that and she's (.) says
2          sh(e)- who's derek.                              T1
3          (0.5)
4    M:    who's derek.=
5    S:    =derek is a nephew                               T2
6          (0.2)
7    M:    .hh >she's<- sh:e's saying she's pleased about so T3
8          obviously
9          (0.3)
10   M:    there's something she's pleased about
11         where derek is concerned
```

Here the medium is providing closing comment on a prior topic by reporting the spirit's attitude: 'and she's pleased about that' (line 1). The utterance 'and she's (.) says sh(e)-' (lines 1–2) at the very least provides strong evidence of the onset of direct or indirect reported speech. We can infer, then, that the spirit is depicted as talking to the medium. And, when the sitter accepts that the name has some significance for him, the medium – albeit convolutedly – attributes her knowledge of the relevance of the name to the spirit's expression of a positive regard for this person. Yet the production of the first position turn gives no hint that the spirit may be the source of the query about Derek. Indeed, there seems to be a clear cut-off mid-production of those components of the turn which preface reported speech in favour of a non-attributive question.

There is a logic to the absence of reported speech in first position turns. If a medium makes a substantive claim which does not accord with the sitter's knowledge or experience, there is at least the basis to question the genuineness of his or her powers. But the inferential damage of such negative sitter responses can be minimised if that claim has not been attributed to a paranormal source. It can simply be ignored, and the medium can simply move on to another topic. In the following case, for example, the question 'an' are y' changing a ca:r' (line 1) receives an unequivocally negative response. The sequence projected by this candidate first turn is immediately abandoned and another initiated.

(8) [K/CC]
```
1   M:   an' are y' changing a ca:r,                    T1
2        (0.4)
3   S:   No [: .
4   M:        [and is your da : d, (0.2) 's your dad  T1
5        ehm, (0.8) generous?
```

However, if a first substantive claim is attributed to a spirit source, its subsequent rejection would constitute strong grounds for scepticism about the authenticity of the medium's powers. And if the spirits' own words were cited as the source of a subsequently rejected claim, the sitter would be left with one of two conclusions – either the medium had made it up, or the spirits had erred – and as people consult mediums to receive messages which offer evidence of the afterlife, both inferences would be damaging to mediums' credibility.

So far we have only considered the use of the spirits' words in cases where the sitter has been able to confirm or accept the first position substantive claims, thereby facilitating a sequential position in which this now-accepted information can be attributed to a spirit source. But reported speech may also be used to manage episodes which could, at the very least, be interpreted as evidence which disconfirms the medium's paranormal powers. In the rest of this chapter we examine the use of reported speech in three circumstances in which the medium's authenticity is in question: when the absence of an unequivocal acceptance leads to a revision of the first position claim; when the sitter's second position turn offers only a weak or hesitant acceptance, or even a hedged rejection; and in cases where the sitter's response exposes an error in a first position knowledge claim.

10.4 Revising first position claims

Jefferson (1989) has observed that participants in ordinary interaction may treat absences of talk which extend to approximately one second as indicating some form of difficulty or trouble in the exchange. This 'metric' may also be observed during medium–sitter interaction. A silence after the medium's tentative claim about the sitter which nears or exceeds the one-second mark invariably pre-monitors a negative or equivocal response from the sitter.

(9) [DS/AUD]
1   M: and you've got another Simon have you?
2   (0.8)
3   S: N-, No.

(10) [JREF/Manchester: 26]
1   M: who's been sw<u>i</u>mming,
2   (1.5)
3   S: nobody to <u>my</u> knowledge,

When mediums terminate a post-knowledge claim silence, they try to assist the sitter to see the relevance of the earlier claim.

(11) [DS/AUD]
1   M: Who's Bill?
2   (1.0)
3   M: Spirit side?

If the knowledge claim concerns the name of a person supposed to be relevant to the sitter, the medium's post-silence turn may suggest similar-sounding names.

(12) [JREF/Manchester: 5]
```
1   M:   colin, who's colin,
2        (0.8)
3   M:   or kevin.
4        (2.8)
5   S:   no (.) can't accept either of those
```

The absence of immediate sitter responses after first position turns is a valuable resource to mediums (and other psychic practitioners) because it invariably indicates that the sitter is unwilling or unable to accept the medium's claim, and thereby provide the possibility of a revised or amended claim prior to an explicit rejection by the sitter. This in turn allows the medium to sustain his or her claim to possess paranormal powers of communication when the sitter's behaviour would indicate that, at least for this occasion, it has deserted them.

However, if mediums propose a revised knowledge claim, they may be open to the charge that they are simply changing their claim in light of what can be plainly inferred from the sitter's silence. The offer and acceptance of any subsequent knowledge claim is therefore an inferentially sensitive moment. In these contexts, the design of reported speech displays some particularly delicate features.

Consider extract (2) again. Here, the medium's proposal about the spirit of the sitter's aunt does not receive either an acceptance or a rejection, but silence. After 1.2 seconds (the upper limit of Jefferson's (1989) tolerance interval) the medium produces a revised proposal: 'I Feel that when she we:nt, (1.5) she was just tired' (lines 4–6).

(2) [JREF/Manchester: 7]
```
1   M:   and your aunt was was such a sick. lady before
2        she pa:ssed,
3        (1.2)
4   M:   I Feel that when she we:nt,
5        (1.5)
6   M:   she was just tired.
7   S:   ye[s
8   M:     [that's what she tells me, she sa[id I was s:o:
9   S:                                      [yes
```

```
10   M:    tired.
11         (0.6)
12   M:    I didn't wan(t)o eat=I didn't want to do anything.
13         (0.3)
14   M:    I just was tired.
15   S:    mm hm
16   M:    I'd had enough. .hhh so I think I(d)- whatever they
17         put on her death certificate it would've
18         (0.3)
19   M:    REally the answer was she gave up sh[e didn't want
20   S:                                          [yes
21   M:    to (.) live an[y more. She'[d had  enou]gh
22   S:                   [(            )[had enough]
23         (.)
24   M:    .hhh ((clears throat))I think she might have
25         had a little stroke, because hhh I can feel
26         as if: (.) something went
27   S:    yes: she did
28         (0.3)
29   M:    .h:but (.) again (.) it was just (.) something (.)
30         to to (.) herald the en:d (.) h and ellen,
31         ((continues))
```

Both proposals deal with ostensibly the same topic: the condition of the sitter's aunt prior to her death. However, there is a significant amendment: the first implies that ill health was the cause of death. This is (potentially) a specific kind of claim, in that it suggests that a particular disease or set of medical problems was responsible for the aunt's death. The second proposes only that the aunt's demise was associated with tiredness, which invites the hearing that the death was more likely due to natural ageing. It is also prefaced by 'I Feel' (line 4), which modifies the epistemological status of the proposal, and is again in contrast to the more declarative design of the first proposal.

This revised claim is accepted by the sitter. Subsequently, in the third position turn the medium states that the spirit is saying that she was tired, and then introduces the spirit's voice as confirmation: 'I was s:o: tired. (0.6) I didn't wan(t)o eat=I didn't want to do anything. (0.3) I just was tired. I'd had enough' (lines 8–16). The spirit's words are thus presented as the source of the revised claim about the sitter's aunt, and also provide an endorsement of it.

There are more subtle features to the aunt's statement. Being tired is not a medical condition; it is not a sickness. There is, then, a clear difference between the medium's first claim and her subsequent version. Such a discrepancy is inferentially damaging: if the spirit's words are so clear and unequivocal, such that they can be reported directly, how did the medium fail to hear the spirit correctly in the first place? The reported speech addresses this problem in that it emphasises the extreme nature of the aunt's pre-mortem tiredness: she did not want to eat, she did not want to do anything, and so on. The aunt's tiredness prior to her death is thus hearably pathological or, at least, more severe than normal. This minimises the degree of error between the first and second first position knowledge claims.

The introduction of reported speech displays a similar organisation in the next extract. Here the initial claim about the sitter – that her husband wanted to return home from hospital before his death – is met initially by a 0.6-second gap. The medium reissues the proposal, this time as an explicit question, and this again receives no immediate reply.

(13) [JREF/VP: 32]

```
 1   M:    because he talks about being in the hospital
 2         before he passed over.
 3   S:    ye:s[:
 4   M:        [and wasn't there=he wanted to come home,
 5         (0.6)
 6   M:    did he wanna come ho:me?
 7         (0.4)
 8   M:    °hold on hol o(n)- no don't tell me, don't
 9         tell me.°(.)
10   M:    (°wha'dy'(ink))
11         (.)
12   M:    DId he die in a hospital?
13   S:    Yes
14   M:    (°goo:d°)                    ((whispered))
15         (0.3)
16   M:    he's like (.) I'm waiting for him to come
```

17		through with (iticals)=.h YEAH I <u>DIED</u> THEre.
18		(0.3)
19	M:	he <u>di</u>ed there..hh I also want to ask you, (.) ahm
20		I'm being shown initial <u>ai</u>tch

The medium's turn '°hold on hol o(n)- no don't tell me, don't tell
me.°' (lines 8–9) seems to be directed to two recipients. The sotto
voce 'hold on' thus displays that the medium is attending to spirits
who are communicating with him. However, the utterance '[N]o
don't tell me, don't tell me' seems to be directed at the sitter,
because it would be perverse for a medium to be seen to resist
information from the spirit world. Moreover, the medium exhibits
his understanding that the silences after his prior turns indicated a
problem, in that this part of the utterance is designed to forestall the
possibility that the sitter might reveal why she did not accept then
initial proposal. Eventually the medium offers a second proposal –
'DId he <u>di</u>e in a h<u>o</u>spital?' (line 12) – which displays a new characterisation of the husband's relationship with the hospital. This is
accepted. After a quietly spoken 'good' (line 14), the medium first
reports communication problems with the spirit (I think the sound
transcribed as 'iticals' on line 17 is an attempt at the word 'details'),
which provides an account as to why the initial proposal may have
been unacceptable (communication from the spirit world was
incomplete in some respect), and then reproduces the spirit's
emphatic words 'YEAH I <u>DIED</u> THEre' (line 17).

The spirit's words, then, may be incorporated to manage interactional episodes which could be interpreted as disconfirming the
medium's paranormal powers. Furthermore, the production and
then acceptance of a revised proposal displays both participants'
ongoing orientation to the three-part structure identified in cases in
which the proposal was accepted unequivocally and without delay.

10.5 Reported speech and hesitant or hedged sitter responses

On occasions a sitter may offer a distinctly lukewarm endorsement
of a medium's claim, or may offer a rejection which is designed to
minimise its force and, thereby, the degree to which it constitutes a
challenge to the authenticity of the medium's powers. In the
following extract the medium claims to be in contact with the spirit

of the sitter's husband and is describing, first, the sitter's sense of humour, and then, contrastively, the seriousness of the sitter's husband, now in spirit form, when he was still alive.

(14) [JREF/VP: 12]

```
 1   M:   you have the great sense of humour, you are the one
 2        who laughs at things, and you try to keep people up
 3        on a high level of laughter, do you understand that,
 4   S:   yes=
 5   M:   =laughing, laughter, laughter and this is what this
 6        man is talking about. .hh ahm I feel at times that
 7        your husband could be very serious (.) he could be
 8        very serious sometimes  very-c'd be very serious .h
 9        like his mind worked in a way where .h he was very
10        serious and rigid about certain ways of believing,
11        (.) and you kinda like hadduh (.) crack him up a little bit
12        and make make laughter make light of some situations.
13   S:   MMmmm I do[n't think so=
14   M:              [(th-)
15   M:   =th[e opposite,]>the opposi[te.<
16   S:      [so much.  ]              [Yes=
17   M:   =okay
18        (2.2)
19   M:   ((sniffs)) mm he said the laugh is on me. (0.2) so
20        (.) >°he's talking about himself °<
21   S:   okay °good°
22   M:   .hh good=I ALso want to ask you if you know of
23        anyone with the name of Jo::hn,
```

The knowledge claim embodied in the medium's lengthy turn is that the sitter had to defuse her husband's seriousness. After an extended 'mm' the sitter produces a modified rejection 'I don't think so so much' (lines 13–16). However, even as the sitter is articulating 'don't' the medium begins to speak in overlap. The first attempt appears to be the start of the word 'the'. He then temporarily abandons that turn, restarting it latched to the first transition relevance place in the sitter's turn, at the end of 'I don't think so'. He then says 'e opposite' (line 15), which is repeated in the clear of the sitter's turn.

If we accept the lay logic of mediumship – that the medium is receiving messages about the sitter from the spirits – rejection of a claim about the sitter should be news to the medium. Note, however, that the medium's turn does not address the prior turn with news receipts, such as 'oh' or 'really', which would display an orientation to new information. Instead the medium's utterance proposes a revised claim about the relationship, which in its bluntness seems to highlight and thereby exacerbate the degree of error now exposed by the sitter. However, this revised characterisation of the relationship between the sitter and her husband at least invites an assessment from the sitter, which in turn provides for the subsequent possibility of some form of acceptance or confirmation. And indeed, the sitter does confirm the medium's revised description, thereby demonstrating that she is treating it as another first position claim.

After an acknowledgement token latched to the sitter's acceptance, the medium moves to produce a third turn (albeit delayed by a 2.2-second gap). His turn is 'mm he said the laugh is on me. (0.2) so (.) >°he's talking about himself°<' (lines 19–20), which portrays the spirit confirming the now-accepted revised proposal.

It also offers an account for the medium's prior error. The spirit's utterance is ambiguous: it could mean that the spirit was the butt of jokes; or that the spirit was the originator of jokes. The latter interpretation is affirmed by the medium's subsequent utterance: '>°he's talking about himself°<' (line 20). However, the ambiguity of the spirit's utterance suggests a reason behind the medium's error: the implication is that the spirit was portraying the relationship correctly, but that the medium misinterpreted what was being said. This is a significant achievement, in that it reinstates the authority of the spirit source; and even the most committed sitter might question the value of a sitting in which he or she was presented with information from the spirits about such personal matters, which was plainly incorrect.

The requirement to ensure the infallibility of spirits is exemplified in extract (15). The medium's question proposes that the sitter is familiar with someone who lived in a house numbered seventeen. When this is rejected, the medium produces a revised proposal: 'Or number seven could it be?' (line 5).

(15) [DS/AUD]

1	M:	And who lived at number seventeen?
2		(1.5)
3	S:	I don't know Doris.
4		(0.4)
5	M:	Or number seven could it be?
6		(0.5)
7	S:	I lived at number seven.=
8	M:	=Sa-, sorry, I thought you said seventeen. They
9		said, Why don't you listen?

'I don't know Doris' (line 3) is a hedged negative response in that it allows for the possibility that someone relevant to the sitter did indeed live at number seven. The medium offers a revised claim, which is then accepted. Immediately after this, the medium apologises to the spirits, at the same time offering an account as to why she had asked the sitter about number seventeen, and then reports their response: 'Why don't you listen?' (line 9). This reported utterance confirms her account for the confusion between 'seventeen' and 'seven', while at the same time establishing that the spirits were the source of the revised first position turn.

10.6 Reported speech and correction

Mediums often make incorrect claims about the sitters. But, as we have seen, sitters have a range of strategies by which explicit correction can be avoided. This is not surprising: we might anticipate that people who go to mediums (which can involve payment, especially for the kind of large-scale demonstrations offered by Doris Stokes) have a belief that there is an afterlife and that some aspect of us survives physical death. Therefore, there will be a predisposition to receive evidence of a spirit existence, as opposed to evidence of the inauthenticity of the medium's powers, which will manifest itself in attempts to foreclose or avoid moments which seem to disconfirm the medium's powers.

But on occasions, correction can not be avoided. In this section we consider two instances. In the first, correction is managed artfully, and does not threaten the authenticity of the medium's powers. But in the second, it cuts right to the heart of the credibility of the on-going performance of mediumship. In each case, the spirits' words are used to account for the error. The next extract comes from a Doris Stokes performance to a large theatre audience. She is describing to a member of the audience the spirits of his colleagues from his wartime days in the Royal Air Force. At the start of the extract, Stokes is talking to a spirit identified here by his wartime nickname of 'Chalky'.

(16) [DS/AUD]

```
 1  M:    He's doing very well.  He's in, oh, I can't say that
 2         can I Chalky.
 3  AUD:  ((audience laughing))
 4  M:    I er, well I must say, are you in insurance now?
 5  S:    I have been.
 6  M:    You, I said what's he been doing since he came out
 7         of the mob like?  And he said, Oh, insurance. So,
 8         I'm very pleased to see you love, and, and er, that
 9         you've come through yes. 'Cos I'm in, I was in the
10         Air Force, so we're all one crowd together. God
11         bless you-
```

Initially, Stokes seems to demur from passing on information from the spirit about the sitter. But eventually she asks a question which proposes that she knows that the sitter *currently* works in insurance. It transpires, however, that Stokes is wrong: the member of the audience says 'I have been' (line 5), thereby revealing that he has *no* current involvement with that line of work. Stokes then recites an exchange with her spirit source: This exchange is introduced so that it is apparent that it occurred prior to the sitter's disclosure that he no longer works in insurance.

This reported exchange, and the spirit's own words, address the error revealed by the audience member's response. Stokes depicts herself as having asked the spirit what the sitter had been doing *after* leaving the RAF, referred to here as 'the mob' (line 7): the spirit's utterance 'Oh, insurance' (line 7) does not impose a time frame during which the sitter worked in insurance, nor does it preclude other occupations. So, whereas in the initial question she imposed a specific time frame for the sitter's occupation (that he was in insurance now), the subsequent reproduction of the spirit's words establish that she knew only that the sitter's employment in insurance was at some point after he left the Royal Air Force. And this information is consistent with the sitter's disclosure. The source of the error, then, is hearable as arising from the medium's incorrect interpretation of the spirit's response.

So, although the recipient of the medium's claim identifies an error, as in cases of embedded correction, neither party topicalises the error. Indeed, the sitter's turn 'I have been' (line 5) works to preserve the 'in general' accuracy of the medium's claim. And Stokes's subsequent turn subtly incorporates and accounts for the error, while at the same time attending to activities usually found in third position turns – establishing that the spirits were the source of the (corrected) information about the sitter.

Finally, consider the following extract. This is a rare sequence in that the sitters, a mother and daughter, unhesitatingly reject the medium's claim about their deceased husband/father, with whom the medium claims to be in contact. As the sequence unfolds, it is apparent that the sitters' rejection has potentially calamitous consequences for the medium's claim to be in contact with the spirit. What is significant is that even here – in the face of the most explicit and persistent resistance to his claims – the medium still invokes the words of the spirit to try to find an amended version which the sitters can accept.

(17) [EV]

```
 1   M:    'e did swear sometimes as ↑well didn't he.
 2   S1:       [no.
 3   S2:       [no.
 4   M:    sometimes he says>not [t (u) ] they WOn't (l)ow
 5   S1:                         [°no° ]
 6   M:    Me to do it [>d'y'understand it<]
 7   S1:               [we    never    hea].rd him.
 8   M:    no but that's why he's saying to me .hh °ah'm not°
 9         allowed to say those words c'n you understand it,
10         (.) it's just his character coming through (0.2) c's
11         he wouldn't allow me to do it but it was just a bit
12         of fu:n h cz had this lo:vely sense of humour didn't
13         he
14   S2:   [yes he did
```

15   S1:   [°yes°
16   M: °have you- (.) did you talk of mo̲ving as well
17   S2:   yes
18   S1:   yes

Prior to this sequence, the medium has made a number of claims about the sitters and their lives, which have been accepted and then attributed to the spirit (for example, extract (5) comes from the same sitting). In this extract the medium claims that, when he was alive, "e did swe̲a̲r sometimes as ↑well didn't he' (line 1). This points to a regular behaviour; moreover, the tag question 'didn't he' seeks confirmation, implying knowledge shared by medium and the sitters. However, both wife and daughter receipt this claim with a categorical rejection. The medium perseveres: 'sometimes he says' (line 4). This is ambiguous: it could be reported speech, as in "sometimes" he says', or it could be a repeat of 'sometimes' and then the projection of forthcoming reported speech. However, the rush through on the word 'not' implies that the end of 'he says' was a transition relevance place, and not a point within a turn construction unit. This suggests 'sometimes' was offered as reported speech. Consequently, there are two observations. First, the strength of the claim is amended and downgraded: the 'sometimes' here points not to the regularity of an event, but its infrequency. Second, the spirit is reported as the source of this downgraded version.

The medium continues, and it would seem that '(>no̲t t(u)' (line 4) was an attempt at 'not to', but it is abandoned as the first sitter (the wife) repeats the unequivocal rejection of the medium's downgraded version. This is admittedly speculative, but the medium could have been aiming for something like 'not to you', which would reconcile what can now be inferred to be the sitters' experience of their husband/father and the contradictory claims he has offered on behalf of the spirit. Clearly, though, the first sitter is adamant, issuing another categorical rejection of the medium's downgraded claim. The spate of reported speech which follows offers another amendment of the initial claim: 'they WOn't (l)ow Me to do it' (lines 4–6) suggests that the spirit, when alive, did have an inclination to swear but was prevented from doing so by his wife and daughter. This again is rebutted by the first sitter: 'we ne̲ver hea.rd him' (line 7) establishes that there was no evidence of propensity to swearing which required preventative measures. The medium's next utterance is also ambiguous: 'that's why he's saying to me .hh °ah'm not° allowed to s<u>a</u>y those words' (lines 8–9) could be a report of the spirit's utterance or a claim that the spirit is preventing the medium from swearing. The use of the present tense 'I'm not allowed' suggests that the medium is reporting constraints on him (and this is certainly consistent with his subsequent claim that *he* is not allowed to say 'those words'). At this point, then, it appears that even the spirit's own words cannot rescue this particular claim. The medium abandons any further attempts to amend the initial statement, and embarks on a series of positive observations about the spirit which are likely to elicit favourable responses from the sitters, before offering a new first position question.

10.7 Discussion

There are two points I'd like to make. The first concerns the importance of studying the sequential context of direct reported speech.

In conversational interaction, direct reported speech is an extremely effective method by which a speaker can produce an account or narrative which is engaging for the recipient. Reported speech adds immediacy to the narrative, provides for the vividness of the tale and facilitates the recipient's involvement in the account (Holt, 1996). This is certainly the case in reported speech in medium–sitter interaction. Given that most spirits seem to have some clear significance for the sitter, reports of their utterances present the sitter with evidence not only of their postmortem survival, but indicate the way the spirit's co-presence becomes manifest throughout the course of the sitting. And, as the spirits can be depicted as responding in real time to the topical trajectory of the exchanges between the sitter and the medium, they too become interactionally relevant. This in turn further enhances the sense that the spirit is an objective entity possessing everyday perceptual and cognitive abilities.

But the inferential impact of direct reported speech in this context does not stem solely from the way it offers to the sitter ostensibly dramatic evidence that their loved ones continue to exist in spirit form. Its power derives just as much from the kinds of discursive activities it is used to accomplish. It is surely significant that reports of the spirits' utterances tend to occur in third position turns in which accepted claims are attributed to a paranormal source; and it is perhaps no less significant that there is a conspicuous absence of reported speech in first position turns. And these two observations in turn underline why it is necessary to understand the sequential organisation of direct reported speech.

The spirit's words, though, may also be incorporated to manage interactional episodes which could be interpreted as disconfirming the medium's paranormal powers; and in studying these moments we increase our understanding of the ways in which reported speech works as a device to maintain the authority of knowledge claims and the authenticity of identities.

In the event of a sitter withholding talk after a medium's first position turn, a medium may issue an amended or revised version of that claim. But even if this subsequent version transpires to be more acceptable to the sitter (and subsequently leads to a third position slot in which the now-accepted information is attributed to a paranormal source), it is still possible that the medium may be open to the charge that they are guessing, or merely amending their utterances in light of what can be plainly inferred from the sitter's silence. That is, one inference is that the revised claim is generated from everyday human interpretative practices; this assessment is countered – or at least addressed – if the spirits themselves are presented as the source of any subsequent amendment.

On occasions, mediums make claims which seem to have little relevance for the sitter. If these troublesome moments are repaired, there remains this question: If the medium is correct now, why was he or she incorrect just seconds before? This in turn at least invites a sceptical assessment of the medium's ability, because it offers an alternative hypothesis: if the medium had no special powers, and was just guessing or using ordinary powers of deduction, we might expect errors would be a routine feature of the encounter. However, the spirits' own words can be marshalled here to reveal that there was a distinct problem that interfered with the smooth development of the sitting: the medium has misheard the spirits, for example. This in turn reinforces the sense that errors are an accountable deviation in the sitting, rather than a routine feature.

Finally, and relatedly, when the spirits reveal the nature of the problem that led to an error, it transpires that the medium is to blame. So, from extract (15), after an error concerning a house number, the medium says to the spirits (and for the benefit of the overhearing audience), 'sorry, I thought you said seventeen' and the spirits' reply is 'Why don't you listen?' This has two inferential benefits: the medium is able to portray her own normality and fallibility – she is just like members of her audience, or her clients. But, more important, it ensures that errors are attributed to earthly causes – the spirits remain infallible.

In so far as reported speech is directed to resolving what can be inferred to be problems or difficulties in the sitting, they can be regarded as a resource by which the medium's credibility and authenticity can be managed. As such, it offers resources for the maintenance of the sitting and expectations attendant upon it.

References

Aaron, U. E. (1992). Reported speech in Obolo narrative discourse. In S. J. J. Hwang and W. R. Merrifield (eds.) *Language in Context: Essays for Robert E. Longacre (Publications in Linguistics 107)*, pp. 227–240. Dallas/Arlington: Summer Institute of Linguistics and University of Texas.

Adelaar, W. F. H. (1990). The role of quotations in Andean discourse. In H. Pinkster and I. Genee (eds.) *Unity in Diversity: Papers Presented to Simon C. Dik on his 50th Birthday*, pp. 1–12. Dordrecht: Foris.

Adelsward, V., K. Aronsson, L. Jonsson and P. Linell (1987). The unequal distribution of interactional space: dominance and control in courtroom interaction. *Text* 7(4): 313–346.

Aikhenvald, A. Y. and R. M. W. Dixon (eds.) (2003). *Studies in Evidentiality*. Amsterdam: John Benjamins.

Antaki, C. (1994). *Explaining and Arguing: the Social Organization of Accounts*. London: Sage.

Atkinson, J. M. and P. Drew (1979). *Order in Court*. London: The Macmillan Press.

Atkinson, J. M. and J. Heritage (eds.) (1984). *Structures of Social Action: Studies in Conversation Analysis*. Cambridge: Cambridge University Press.

Bakhtin, M. M. (1981). *The Dialogic Imagination*, ed. M. Holquist, trans. C. Emerson and M. Holquist. Austin: University of Texas Press.

Bally, C. (1914). Figures de pensée et formes linguistiques. *Germanisch–Romanische Monatsschrift* 6: 456–470.

Banfield, A. (1973). Narrative style and the grammar of direct and indirect speech. *Foundations of Language*, 10: 1–39.

(1982). *Unspeakable Sentences: Narration and Representation in the Language of Fiction*. Boston, MA: Routledge and Kegan Paul.

Basso, E. (1986). Quoted dialogues in Kalapalo narrative discourse. In J. Sherzer and G. Urban (eds.) *Native South American Discourse*, pp. 119–168. Berlin: Mouton de Gruyter.

Beach, W. A. (2000). Inviting collaborations in stories about a woman. *Language and Society*, 29: 379–407.

Bergmann, J. (1992). Veiled morality: notes on discretion in psychiatry. In P. Drew and J. Heritage (eds.) *Talk at Work: Interaction in Institutional Settings*, pp. 137–162. Cambridge: Cambridge University Press.

Bergmann, J. R. (1993). *Discreet Indiscretions: The Social Organization of Gossip*. Walter de Gruyter: New York.

Besnier, N. (1993). Reported speech and affect on Nukulaelae Atoll. In J. H. Hill and J. T. Irvine (eds.) *Responsibility and Evidence in Oral Discourse*, pp. 161–181. Cambridge: Cambridge University Press.

Blyth, C. Jr, S. Recktenvald and J. Wang (1990). I'm like, 'say what?!': a new quotative in American oral narrative. *American Speech*, 65(3): 215–227.

Bolden, G. (2004). The quote and beyond: defining boundaries of reported speech in conversational Russian. *Journal of Pragmatics*, 36: 1071–1118.

Buttny, R. (1997). Reported speech in talking race on campus. *Human Communication Research*, 23: 477–506.

 (1998). Putting prior talk into context: reported speech and reporting context. *Research on Language and Social Interaction*, 31(1): 45–58.

Buttny, R. and P. L. Williams (2000). Demanding respect: the use of reported speech in discursive constructions of interracial contact. *Discourse and Society*, 11: 109–133.

Byrne, J. and J. Sutton (1993). *The Psychic World of James Byrne*. London: The Aquarian Press.

Clark, H. H. and R. J. Gerrig (1990). Quotations as demonstrations. *Language*, 66: 764–805.

Clayman, S. E. (1988). Displaying neutrality in television news interviews. *Social Problems*, 35(4): 474–492.

 (1992). Footing in the achievement of neutrality: the case of news interview discourse. In P. Drew and J. Heritage (eds.) *Talk at Work: Interaction in Institutional Settings*, pp. 163–198. Cambridge: Cambridge University Press.

Clayman, S. E. and J. Heritage (2002). *The News Interview: Journalists and Public Figures on the Air*. Cambridge: Cambridge University Press.

Clayman, S. E. and J. Whalen (1988/1989). When the medium becomes the message: the case of the Rather–Bush encounter. *Research on Language and Social Interaction*, 22: 241–272.

Clements, G. N. (1975). The logorophic pronoun in Ewe: its role in discourse. *Journal of West African Languages*, 10(2): 141–177.

Clift, R. (1999). Irony in conversation. *Language in Society*, 28(4): 523–553.

 (2003). Synonyms in action: a case study. *International Journal of English Studies*, 3(1): 167–187.

 (2005) Discovering order. *Lingua*, 115: 1641–1665.

Cohen, D., M.-C. Simeone-Senelle and M. Vanhove (2002). The grammaticalisation of 'say' and 'do': an areal phenomenon in East Africa. In T. Güldemann and M. von Roncador (eds.) *Reported Discourse: A Meeting Ground for Different Linguistic Domains*, pp. 227–251. Amsterdam: John Benjamins.

Collins, J. (1987). Reported speech in Navajo myth-narratives. In J. Vershueren (ed.) *Linguistic Action: Some Empirical-Conceptual Studies (Advances in Discourse Processes 23)*, pp. 69–84. Norwood, NJ: Ablex.

Conley, J. M. and W. M. O'Barr (1990). *Rules versus Relationships: The Ethnography of Legal Discourse*. University of Chicago Press: Chicago.

Coulmas, F. (ed.) (1986). *Direct and Indirect Speech*. Berlin: Mouton de Gruyter.

Couper-Kuhlen, E. (1999). Coherent voicing: on prosody in conversational reported speech. In W. Bublitz and U. Lenk (eds.) *Coherence in Spoken and Written Discourse: How to Create it and How to Describe it*, pp. 11–32. Amsterdam: Benjamins.

(2003). Prosodische Stilisierungen im Gespräch. To appear in A. Assmann, U. Gaier and G. Trommsdorf (eds.) *Zwischen Literatur und Anthropologie: Performanzen, Diskurse, Medien*. Tübingen: Narr.

Cukor-Avila, P. (2002). She say, she go, she be like: verbs of quotation over time in African American Vernacular English. *American Speech*, 77(1): 3–31.

Danet, B. (1980). Language in the legal process. *Law & Society Review*, 14(3): 445–564.

Davidson, D. (1968–9). On saying that. *Synthèse*, 19: 130–146.

(1980). *Essays on Actions and Events*. Oxford: Clarendon Press.

(1984). Quotation. In D. Davidson (ed.), *Inquiries into Truth and Interpretation*, pp. 79–92. Oxford: Pergamon.

Davidson, J. (1984) Subsequent versions of invitations, offers, requests, and proposals dealing with potential or actual rejection. In J. M. Atkinson and J. Heritage (eds.) *Structures of Social Actions: Studies in Conversation Analysis*, pp. 102–128. Cambridge: Cambridge University Press.

Dersley, I. and A. Wootton (2000). Complaint sequences within antagonistic argument. *Research on Language and Social Interaction*, 33(4): 375–406.

Drew, P. (1979). The production of justifications and excuses by witnesses in cross-examination. In J. M. Atkinson and P. Drew (eds.) *Order in Court*, pp. 136–187. London: The Macmillan Press.

(1984). Speakers' reportings invitation sequences. In J. M. Atkinson and J. Heritage (eds.) *Structures of Social Actions: Studies in Conversation Analysis*, pp. 129–151. Cambridge: Cambridge University Press.

(1987). Po-faced receipts of teases. *Linguistics*, 25: 219–253.

(1992). Contested evidence in courtroom cross-examination: the case of a trial for rape. In P. Drew and J. Heritage (eds.) *Talk at Work: Interaction in Institutional Settings*, pp. 470–520. Cambridge: Cambridge University Press.

(1998a). Complaints about transgressions and misconduct. *Research on Language and Social Interaction*, 31: 295–325.

(1998b). Mis-alignments between doctor and callers in 'after-hours' telephone calls to a British GP's practice: a study in telephone medicine. Forthcoming in J. Heritage and D. Maynard (eds.) *Doing Medicine*. Cambridge: Cambridge University Press.

Drew, P. and J. Heritage (1992). Analyzing talk at work: an introduction. In P. Drew. and J. Heritage (eds.) *Talk at Work: Interaction in Institutional Settings*, pp. 3–65. Cambridge: Cambridge University Press.

Drew, P. and E. Holt (1998). Figures of speech: idiomatic expressions and the management of topic transition in conversation. *Language in Society*, 27: 495–522.

Dubois, B. L. (1989). Pseudoquotation in current English communication: 'Hey, she didn't really say it'. *Language in Society*, 18: 343–359.

Edwards, D. and J. Potter (1993) Language and causation: a discursive action model of description and attribution. *Psychological Review*, 100: 23–41.

Ferrara, K. and B. Bell (1995). Sociolinguistic variation and discourse function of constructed dialogue introducers: the case of be+like. *American Speech*, 70: 265–289.

Fludernik, M. (1993). *The Fictions of Language and the Languages of Fiction: the Linguistic Representation of Speech and Consciousness*. London: Routledge.

Ford, C. E. (2001). At the intersection of turn and sequence: negation and what comes next. In M. Selting and E. Couper-Kuhlen (eds.) *Studies in Interactional Linguistics*, pp. 51–79. Amsterdam: John Benjamins.

Galatolo, R. (2003). Les stratégies de changement de *footing* dans le témoignage commun au tribunal: une resource pour la construction de crédibilité. In M. Bondi and S. Stati (eds.) *Dialogue Analysis 2000*, pp. 209–218. Niemeyer: Tubingen.

Galatolo, R. and M. Mizzau (2003). Quoting dialogues and the construction of the narrative point of view in legal testimonies. Unpublished manuscript submitted for publication.

Goffman, E. (1972). The neglected situation. In P. P. Giglioli (ed.) *Language and Social Context*, pp. 61–66. Baltimore: Penguin. Reprinted from *American Anthropologist*, 66: 133–136 (1964).

Goffman, E. (1974/1986). *Frame Analysis: An Essay on the Organization of Experience*. York, Pennsylvania: Northeastern University Press.

(1981). *Forms of Talk*. Oxford, England: Blackwell.

Golato, A. (2000) An innovative German quotative for reporting on embodied actions: und ich so/und er so 'And I'm like/and he's like'. *Journal of Pragmatics* 32(1): 29–54.

(2002). Self-quotation in German: reporting on past decisions. In T. Güldemann and M. von Roncador (eds.) *Reported Discourse: A Meeting Ground for Different Linguistic Domains*, pp. 49–70. Amsterdam: John Benjamins.

Goodwin, C. (1979). The interactive construction of a sentence in natural conversation. In. G. Psathas (ed.) *Everyday Language: Studies in Ethnomethodology*, pp. 97–121. New York: Irvington Publishers.

(1980). Restarts, pauses, and the achievement of mutual gaze at turn-beginning. *Sociological Inquiry*, 50: 272–302.

(1981).*Conversational Organization: Interaction Between Speakers and Hearers*. New York: Academic Press.

(1984). Notes on story structure and the organization of participation. In M. Atkinson and J. Heritage (eds.) *Structures of Social Action: Studies in Conversation Analysis*, pp. 225–246. Cambridge: Cambridge University Press.

(1986a). Audience diversity, participation and interpretation. *Text*, 6(3): 283–316.

(1986b). Between and within: alternative treatments of continuers and assessments. *Human Studies*, 9: 205–217.

(1987). Forgetfulness as an interactive resource. *Social Psychology Quarterly*, 50: 115–130.

(1996). Transparent vision. In E. Ochs, E. Schegloff and S. A. Thompson (eds.) *Interaction and Grammar*, pp. 370–404. Cambridge: Cambridge University Press.

(2000a). Action and embodiment within situated human interaction. *Journal of Pragmatics*, 32: 1489–1522.

(2000b). Pointing and the collaborative construction of meaning in aphasia. *Texas Linguistic Forum* (Proceedings of the seventh annual Symposium About Language and Society Austin SALSA), 43: 67–76.

(2002). Time in action. *Current Anthropology*, 43 (Supplement August–October 2002): S19–S35.

(2003a). The body in action. In J. Coupland and R. Gwyn (eds.) *Discourse: The Body and Identity*, pp. 19–42. Houndsmill, Hampshire and New York: Palgrave/Macmillan.

(2003b). Pointing as situated practice. In S. Kita (ed.) *Pointing: Where Language, Culture and Cognition Meet*, pp. 217–241. Hillsdale, NJ: Lawrence Erlbaum.

Goodwin, C. and M. H. Goodwin (1987). Concurrent operations on talk: notes on the interactive organization of assessments. *IPrA Papers in Pragmatics*, 1(1): 1–52.

(in press). Participation. In A. Duranti (ed.) *A Companion to Linguistic Anthropology*. Oxford: Basil Blackwell.

Goodwin, M. H. (1980). Processes of mutual monitoring implicated in the production of description sequences. *Sociological Inquiry*, 50: 303–317.

(1990). *He-Said-She-Said: Talk as Social Organization among Black Children*. Bloomington: Indiana University Press.

(1997). By-Play: negotiating evaluation in story-telling. In G. R. Guy, C. Feagin, D. Schriffin and J. Baugh (eds.) *Towards a Social Science of Language: Papers in Honor of William Labov*, vol. II, *Social Interaction and Discourse Structures*, pp. 77–102. Amsterdam/Philadelphia: John Benjamins.

Güldemann, T. and M. von Roncador (eds.) (2002). *Reported Discourse: A Meeting Ground for Different Linguistic Domains*, pp. 227–251. Amsterdam: John Benjamins.

Güldemann, T., M. von Roncador and W. van der Wurff (2002). A comprehensive bibliography of reported discourse. In T. Güldemann and M. von Roncador (eds.) *Reported Discourse: A Meeting Ground for Different Linguistic Domains*, pp. 363–415. Amsterdam: John Benjamins.

Günthner, S. (1997a). Complaint stories: constructing emotional reciprocity among women. In H. Kotthoff and R. Wodak (eds.) *Communicating Gender in Context*, pp. 179–218. Amsterdam: John Benjamins.

(1997b). The contextualization of affect in reported dialogues. In S. Niemeier and R. Dirven (eds.) *The Language of Emotions: Conceptualization, Expression and Theoretical Foundation*, pp. 247–275. Amsterdam: John Benjamins.

(1998). *Polyphony and the 'layering of voices' in reported dialogues. (InList 3)*. Konstanz, Germany: University of Konstanz.

(1999). Polyphony and the 'layering of voices' in reported dialogues: an analysis of the use of prosodic devices in everyday reported speech. *Journal of Pragmatics*, 31: 685–708.

Haakana, M. (1999). Laughing matters: a conversation analytical study of laughter in doctor–patient interaction. Unpublished doctoral thesis. University of Helsinki, Department of Finnish.

(2005). Sanottua, ajateltua ja melkein sanottua. Puheen ja ajatusten referointi valituskertomuksissa [Said, thought and almost said. Reported speech and thought in complaint stories]. In M. Haakana and J. Kalliokoski (eds.) *Referointi ja Moniäänisyys* [Reported speech and polyphony]. Suomalaisen Kirjallisuuden Seura: Helsinki.

(unpublished). From misconduct to misunderstanding: responding to patients' complaints about a third party in Finnish medical interactions. Manuscript.

Haiman. J. (1985). *Natural syntax*. Cambridge: Cambridge University Press.

Halliday, M. A. K. (1985). *An Introduction to Functional Grammar*. London: Arnold.

Hanks, W. F. (1990). *Referential Practice: Language and Lived Space Among the Maya*. Chicago: University of Chicago Press.

Hayashi, M. (1997). An exploration of sentence-final uses of the quotative particle in Japanese spoken discourse. In H.-m. Sohn and J. Haig (eds.) *Japanese/Korean Linguistics*, vol. VI, pp. 565–581. Stanford: CSLI Publicatons.

Heath, C. (1986). *Body Movement and Speech in Medical Interaction.* Cambridge: Cambridge University Press.

Heider, F. (1958). *The Psychology of Interpersonal Relations.* New York: Wiley.

Heritage, J. (1984a). *Garfinkel and Ethnomethodology.* Cambridge: Polity Press.

(1984b). A change-of-state token and aspects of its sequential placement. In J. M. Atkinson and J. Heritage (eds.) *Structures of Social Action: Studies in Conversation Analysis*, pp. 299–345. Cambridge: Cambridge University Press.

(1985). Analyzing news interviews: aspects of the production of talk for an overhearing audience. In T. A van Djik (ed.) *Handbook of Discourse Analysis*, vol. III, pp. 95–117. London: Academic Press.

(1988). Explanations as accounts: a conversation analytic perspective. In C. Antaki (ed.) *Analysing Everyday Explanation: A Casebook of Methods*, pp. 127–144. London: Sage.

Heritage, J. and G. Raymond (2005). The terms of agreement: indexing epistemic authority and subordination in talk-in-interaction. *Social Psychology Quarterly*, 68(1): 15–38.

Heritage, J. and A. Roth (1995). Grammar and institution: Questions and questioning in the broadcast news interview. *Research on Language and Social Interaction*, 28(1): 1–60.

Heritage, J. C. and D. R. Watson (1979). Formulations as conversational objects. In G. Psathas (ed.) *Everyday Language. Studies in Ethnomethodology*, pp. 123–162. New York: Irvington.

(1980). Aspects of the properties of formulations in natural conversations: Some instances analysed. *Semiotica*, 30: 245–262.

Holt, E. (1996). Reporting on talk: the use of direct reported speech in conversation. *Research on Language and Social Interaction*, 29(3): 219–245.

(1999). Just gassing: an analysis of direct reported speech in a conversation between employees of a gas supply company. *Text*, 19: 505–538.

(2000). Reporting and reacting: Concurrent responses to reported speech. *Research on Language and Social Interaction*, 33: 425–454.

Hyvättinen, E. (1999). Ajatteleminen ja referointi: nuortenpalstojen ajatella-verbin sisältävien referaattirakenteiden analyysia [Thinking and reporting]. Unpublished MA thesis, Department of Finnish, University of Helsinki.

Irvine, J. T. (1996). Shadow conversations: The indeterminacy of participant roles. In M. Silverstein and G. Urban (eds.) *Natural Histories of Discourse*, pp. 131–159. Chicago: The University of Chicago Press.

Iso suomen Kieloppi [The Descriptive Grammar of Finnish] (2004). Auli Hakulinen (ed. in-chief), Maria Vilkuna, Riitta Korhonen, Vesa Koivisto, Tarja Riitta Heinonen and Irja Alho. Suomalaisen Kirjallisuuden Seura: Helsinki.

Jakobson, R. (1971). Shifters, verbal categories and the Russian verb. In Roman Jakobson *Selected Writings*, vol. II, *Word and Language*, pp. 130–147. The Hague: Mouton.

Jefferson, G. (1973). A case of precision timing in ordinary conversation: overlapped tag-positioned address terms in closing sequences. *Semiotica*, 9: 47–96.

(1979). A technique for inviting laughter and its subsequent acceptance/ declination. In G. Psathas (ed.) *Everyday Language: Studies in Ethnomethodology*, pp. 79–96. New York: Irvington.

(1983). Caveat speaker: preliminary notes on recipient topic-shift implicature. *Tilburg Papers in Language and Literature*, 30.

(1984a). Notes on a systematic deployment of the acknowledgement tokens 'yeah' and 'mm hm'. *Papers in Linguistics*, 17: 197–216.

(1984b). On stepwise transition from talk about a trouble to inappropriately next-positioned matters. In J. M. Atkinson and J. Heritage (eds) *Structures of Social Action: Studies in Conversation Analysis*, pp. 191–222. Cambridge: Cambridge University Press.

(1986). On the sequential organisation of troubles talk in ordinary conversation. *Social Problems* 35(4): 418–441.

(1989). Notes on a possible metric for a 'standard maximum silence of approximately one second in conversation'. In D. Roger and P. Bull (eds.) *Conversation: An Interdisciplinary Perspective*, pp. 166–196. Clevedon and Philadelphia: Multilingual Matters.

Jefferson, G. (1990). List construction as a task and resource. In G. Psathas (ed.) *Interaction Competence*, pp. 63–92. Washington, DC: University Press of America: 63–92.

Jefferson, G., H. Sacks and E. Schegloff (1987). Notes on laughter in the pursuit of intimacy. In G. Button and J. R. E. Lee (eds.) *Talk and Social Organisation*, pp. 152–205. Clevedon and Philadelphia: Multilingual Matters.

Jespersen, O. (1924). *The Philosophy of Grammar*. London: Allen and Unwin.

Kendon, A. (1990). Behavioral foundations for the process of frame-attunement in face-to-face interaction. In A. Kendon (ed.) *Conducting Interaction: Patterns of Behavior in Focused Encounters*, pp. 239–262. Cambridge: Cambridge University Press.

Kerby, J. and Rae, J. (1998). Moral identity in action: young offenders' reports of encounters with the police. *British Journal of Social Psychology*, 37: 439–456.

Klewitz, G. and E. Couper-Kuhlen (1999). Quote-unquote: the role of prosody in the contextualization of reported speech sequences. *Pragmatics*, 9: 459–485.

Komter, M. L. (1998). *Dilemmas in the Courtroom: A Study of Violent Crime in The Netherlands*. Mahwah, NJ: Lawrence Erlbaum.

Koppel, T. and K. Gibson (1995). *Nightline: History in the Making and the Making of Television*. Norwalk, CT: Crown Publishing.

Kuiri, K. (1984). *Referoiniti Kainuun ja pohjois – karjalan murteissa* [Reported speech in the dialects of Kainuu and North Carelia]. Suomalaisen Kirjallisuuden Seura: Helsinki.

Labov, W. (1972). *Language in the Inner City*. Philadelphia: University of Pennsylvania Press.

Labov, W. and J. Waletzky (1967). Narrative analysis: oral versions of personal experience. In J. Helm (ed.) *Essays on the Verbal and Visual Arts*, pp. 12–44. Washington: University of Washington Press.

Larson, M. L. (1987). *The Functions of Reported Speech in Discourse*. Arlington: Summer Institute of Linguistics.

Leech, G. N. and M. H. Short (1981). *Style in Fiction: A Linguistic Introduction to English Fictional Prose*. New York: Longman.

Lehrer, A. (1989) Remembering and presenting prose: quoted speech as a data source. *Discourse Processes*, 12: 105–125.

Lerner, G. H. (1991). On the syntax of sentence-in-progress. *Language in Society*, 20: 441–458.

    (1993). Collectivities in action: establishing the relevance of conjoined participation in conversation. *Text*, 13(2): 213–45.

Leudar, I. (1998). Who is Martin McGuinness 1: on contextualizing reported. political talk. In S. Cmejrkova et al. (eds.) *Dialogue Analysis*, 6(2): 217–224. Tubingen: Niemeyer.

Levinson, S. C. (1988). Putting linguistics on a proper footing: explorations in Goffman's concepts of participation. In P. Drew and A. Wootton (eds.) *Erving Goffman: Exploring the Interaction Order*, pp. 161–227. Berlin: Mouton de Gruyter.

Li, C. (1986). Direct and indirect speech: a functional study. In C. Coulmas (ed.) *Direct and Indirect Speech*, pp. 29–45. Berlin: Mouton de Gruyter.

Longacre, R. (1985). Sentences as combinations of clauses. In T. Shopen (ed.) *Language Typology and Syntactic Description*, pp. 235–286. Cambridge: Cambridge University Press.

Luchjenbroers, J. (1997). 'In your own words...' Questions and answers in a Supreme Court trial. *Journal of Pragmatics* 27(4): 477–503.

Lucy, J. A. (ed.) (1993). *Reflexive Language: Reported Speech and Metapragmatics*. Cambridge: Cambridge University Press.

Macaulay, R. (2001). You're like 'why not': the quotative expressions of Glasgow adolescents. *Journal of Sociolinguistics*, 5(1): 3–21.

McCawley, J. (1999) Participant roles, frames, and speech acts. *Linguistics and Philosophy*, 22: 595–619.

McGregor, W. (1994). The grammar of reported speech and thought in Gooniyandi. *Journal of Linguistics*, 14: 63–92.

McHale, B. (1978). Free indirect discourse: a survey of recent accounts. *PTL: A Journal for Descriptive Poetics and Theory of Literature* 3: 249–287.

McNeill, D. (1992). *Hand & Mind: What Gestures Reveal about Thought.* Chicago: University of Chicago Press.

Mandelbaum, J. (1991/1992). Conversational non-cooperation: an exploration of disattended complaints: *Research on Language and Social Interaction* 25: 97–138.

Mathis, T. and G. Yule (1994). Zero quotatives. *Discourse Processes*, 18: 63–76.

Mayes, P. (1990). Quotation in spoken English, *Studies in Language* 14: 325–363.

Maynard, D. W. (1996). Introduction to Harold Garfinkel for the Mead Cooley award. *Social Psychology Quarterly*, 59: 1–4.

Maynard, D. W. and C. L. Marlaire (1999). Good reasons for bad testing performance: the interactional substrate of educational testing. In D. Kovarksky, J. Duchan and M. Maxwell (eds.) *Constructing (In)Competence: Disabling Evaluations in Clinical and Social Interaction*, pp. 171–196. Mahwah, NJ: Lawrence Erlbaum Associates.

Maynard, S. K. (1996). Multivoicedness in speech and thought representation: the case of self-quotation in Japanese. *Journal of Pragmatics*, 25: 207–226.

Mills, C. Wright (1940). Situated actions and vocabularies of motive. *American Sociological Review*, 5: 904–913.

Mizzau, M. (1999). Parola a più voci: il discorso riportato. In R. Galatolo and G. Pallotti (eds.) *La Conversazione*, pp. 187–204. Milano: Raffaello Cortina Editore.

Moore, R. E. (1993). Performance form and the voices of characters in five versions of the Wasco Coyote Cycle. In J. A. Lucy (ed.) *Reflexive Language: Reported Speech and Metapragmatics*, pp. 213–240. Cambridge: Cambridge University Press.

Myers, G. (1999). Functions of reported speech in group discussions. *Applied Linguistics*, 20(3): 376–401.

O'Barr, W. (1982). *Linguistic Evidence.* San Diego, New York and Boston: Academic Press.

O'Brien, S. (1992). *In Touch With Eternity: Contact With Another World.* London: Bantam Books.

Parmentier, R. J. (1993). The political function of reported speech: a Belauan example. In J. A. Lucy (ed.) *Reflexive Language: Reported Speech and Metapragmatics*, pp. 261–286. Cambridge: Cambridge University Press.

Partee, B. H. (1973). The syntax and semantics of quotation. In S. R. Anderson and P. Kiparsky (eds.) *A Festschrift for Morris Halle*, pp. 410–418. New York: Holt, Rinehart and Wilson.

Penman, R. (1987). Discourse in courts: cooperation, coercion and coherence. *Discourse Processes*, 10(3): 201–218.

Philips, S. U. (1986). Reported speech as evidence in an American trial. In D. Tannen and J. E. Alatis (eds.) *Languages and Linguistics: The Interdependence of Theory, Data and Application*, pp. 154–179. Washington DC: Georgetown University Press.

(1992). Evidentiary standards for American trials: just the facts. In J. H. Hill and J. T. Irvine (eds.) *Responsibility and Evidence in Oral Discourse*, pp. 248–259. Cambridge: Cambridge University Press.

Polanyi, L. (1982). Literary complexity in everyday storytelling. In D. Tannen (ed.) *Spoken and Written Language: Exploring Orality and Literacy*, pp. 155–170. Norwood, NJ: Ablex.

Pomerantz, A. (1978). Compliment responses: notes on the co-operation of multiple constraints. In J. Schenkein (ed.) *Studies in the Organization of Conversational Interaction*, pp. 79–112. New York: Academic Press.

(1980). Telling my side: 'limited access' as a 'fishing' device. *Sociological Inquiry*, 50: 186–198.

(1984a). Agreeing and disagreeing with assessments: some features of preferred/dispreferred turn shapes. In J. M. Atkinson and J. Heritage (eds.) *Structures of Social Action: Studies in Conversational Analysis*, pp. 57–101. Cambridge: Cambridge University Press.

Pomerantz, A. M. (1984b). Giving a source or basis: the practice in conversation of telling 'how I know'. *Journal of Pragmatics* 8: 607–625.

Pomerantz, A. (1986). Extreme case formulations: a way of legitimizing claims. *Human Studies*, 9: 219–230.

Potter, J. (1996). *Representing Reality: Discourse, Rhetoric and Social Construction*. London: Sage.

Psathas, G. (1995). *Conversation Analysis: The Study of Talk in Interaction*. London: Sage.

Quine, W. V. O. (1960). *Word and Object*. Cambridge, MA: MIT Press.

Rae, J. (2001). Organizing participation in interaction: doing participation framework. *Research on Language and Social Interaction*, 34(2): 253–278.

Raymond, G. (2000). The structure of responding: type-conforming and nonconforming responses to yes/no type interrogatives. Unpublished Ph.D dissertation, UCLA.

Romaine, S. and D. Lange (1991). The use of *like* as a marker of reported speech and thought: a case of grammaticalization in progress. *American Speech*, 66(3): 227–279.

Routarinne, S. (2003). Tytöt äänessä. *Parenteesit ja nouseva sävelkulku kertojan vuorovaikutuskeinovia* [Girls talking. Parenthesis and rising intonation as narrators' interactional devices]. Suomalaisen Kirjallisuuden Seura: Helsinki.

Sacks, H. (1970). Hypothetical second stories and explanations for first stories: sound-related terms (Poetics); 'what I didn't do'. In G. Jefferson (ed.) (1992) *Lectures on Conversation*. Oxford: Blackwell.

(1971). Produced similarities in first and second stories; poetics; 'fragile stories'; etc. In G. Jefferson (ed.) (1992) *Lectures on Conversation*. Oxford: Blackwell.

(1987). On the preference for agreement and contiguity in sequences in conversation. In G. Button and J. R. E. Lee (eds.) *Talk and Social Organization*, pp. 54–69. Clevedon: Multilingual Matters.

(1992a). *Lectures on conversation*, vol. I, ed. G. Jefferson. Oxford: Blackwell.

(1992b). *Lectures on conversation*, vol II, ed. G. Jefferson. Oxford: Blackwell.

Sacks, H., E. Schegloff and G. Jefferson (1974). A simplest systematics for the organization of turn-taking for conversation. *Language* 50(4): 696–735.

Sapir, E. (1968). Language defined. In P. Gleeson and N. Wakefield (eds.) *Language and Culture: A Reader*, pp. 3–19. Columbus, OH: Charles E. Merrill.

Schegloff, E. A. (1982). Discourse as an interactional achievement: some uses of 'uh uh' and other things that come between sentences. In D. Tannen (ed.) *Georgetown University Roundtable on Languages and Linguistics*, pp. 71–93. Washington DC: Georgetown University Press.

(1984). On some questions and ambiguities in conversation. In J. M. Atkinson and J. Heritage (eds.) *Structures of Social Actions: Studies in Conversation Analysis*, pp. 28–52. Cambridge: Cambridge University Press.

(1988). Goffman and the analysis of conversation. In P. Drew and A. Wootton (eds.) *Erving Goffman: Exploring the Interaction Order*, pp. 89–135. Cambridge: Polity Press.

(1993). Reflections on quantification in the study of conversation. *Research on Language and Social Interaction*, 26(1): 99–128.

(1995). Sequence organization. Unpublished manuscript.

(1996a). Confirming allusions: toward an empirical account of action. *American Journal of Sociology*, 102(1): 161–216.

(1996b). Some practices for referring to persons in talk-in-interaction: a partial sketch of a systematics. In B. Fox (ed.) *Studies in Anaphora*, pp. 437–485. Amsterdam: John Benjamins.

(1996c). Turn organization: one intersection of grammar and interaction. In E. Ochs, E. A. Schegloff and S. A. Thompson (eds.) *Interaction and Grammar*, pp. 52–133. Cambridge: Cambridge University Press.

(1997). Whose text? Whose context? *Discourse and Society*, 8(2): 165–187.

(2000a). On granularity. *Annual Review of Sociology*, 26: 715–720.

(2000b). Overlapping talk and the organization of turntaking for conversation. *Language in Society*, 29(1): 1–63.

Schegloff, E. A. and H. Sacks (1973). Opening up closings. *Semiotica*, 7: 289–327.

Schegloff, E. A., G. Jefferson and H. Sacks (1977). The preference for self-correction in the organization of repair in conversation. *Language*, 53: 361–382.

Schenkein, J. (ed.) (1978). *Studies in the Organization of Conversational Interaction*. New York: Academic Press.

Schudson, M. (1978). *Discovering the News*. New York: Basic Books.

Scott, M. B. and S. M. Lyman (1968). Accounts. *American Sociological Review*, 33: 46–62.

Selting, M. (2003). Lists as embedded structures and prosody of list construction as an interactional resource. *InList 35*, Konstanz, Germany: University of Konstanz.

Shine, B. (1996). *My Life as a Medium*. London: Thorsons.

Shoaps, R. (2004) 'Moral irony': modal particles, moral persons and indirect evaluative stance-taking in Sakapultek discourse. Unpublished manuscript.

Sorjonen, M.-L. (2001). *Responding in Conversation: A Study of Response Particles in Finnish*. Amsterdam: John Benjamins.

Sternberg, M. (1982). Proteus in quotation-land: mimesis and the forms of reported discourse. *Poetics Today*, 3: 107–156.

Stivers, T. and J. Heritage (2001). Breaking the sequential mold: answering 'more than the question' during comprehensive history taking. *Text*, 21: 151–185.

Stygall, G. (1994). *Trial Language*. Amsterdam: John Benjamins.

Tagliamonte, S. and R. Hudson (1999). *Be like* et al. Beyond America: the quotative system in British and Canadian youth. *Journal of Sociolinguistics* 3: 147–172.

Tannen, D. (1986). Introducing constructed dialogue in Greek and American conversational and literary narrative. In F. Coulmas (ed.) *Direct and Indirect Speech*, pp. 311–332. Berlin: Mouton de Gruyer.

Tannen, D. (1989). *Talking Voices: Repetition, Dialogue and Imagery in Conversational Discourse*. Cambridge: Cambridge University Press.

ten Have, P. and Psathas, G. (1995). *Situated Order: Studies in the Social Organization of Talk and Embodied Activities*. Washington, DC: University Press of America.

Thompson, G. (1984). Voices in the text: discourse perspectives on language reports. *Applied Linguistics*, 17: 501–530.

Tuchman, G. (1972). Objectivity as strategic ritual: an examination of newsmen's notions of objectivity. *American Journal of Sociology*, 77: 660–679.

Urban, G. (1993). The represented functions of speech in Shokleng myth In J. A. Lucy (ed.) *Reflexive Language: Reported Speech and Metapragmatics*, pp. 241–259. Cambridge: Cambridge University Press.

Vincent, D. and L. Perrin (1999). On the narrative vs non-narrative functions of reported speech: a socio-pragmatic study. *Journal of Sociolinguistics*, 3: 291–313.

Volosinov, V. N. (1971). Reported speech. In L. Matejka and K. Pomorska (eds.) *Readings in Russian Poetics: Formalist and Structuralist Views*, pp. 149–175. Cambridge, MA: MIT Press.

(1973). Exposition of the problem of reported speech. In *Marxism and the Philosophy of Language*, pp. 115–174. New York and London: Seminar Press.

Wierzbicka, A. (1974). The semantics of direct and indirect discourse. *Papers in Linguistics*, 7(3/4): 267–307.

Wilkinson, R., S. Beeke and J. Maxim (2003). Adapting to conversation: on the use of linguistic resources by speakers with fluent aphasia in the construction of turns at talk. In C. Goodwin (ed.) *Conversation and Brain Damage*, pp. 59–89. Oxford: Oxford University Press.

Wooffitt, R. (1992). *Telling Tales of the Unexpected: the Organisation of Factual Discourse*. Hemel Hempstead: Harvester Wheatsheaf.

(2000). Some properties of the interactional organisation of displays of paranormal cognition in psychic–sitter interaction. *Sociology*, 43: 457–479.

(2001). Raising the dead: reported speech in medium–sitter interaction. *Discourse Studies*, 3: 351–374.

Yule, G. (1995). The paralinguistics of reference: representation in reported discourse. In G. Cook and B. Seidlhofer (eds.) *Principle & Practice in Applied Linguistics*, pp. 185–196. Oxford: Oxford University Press.

Yule, G., T. Mathis, et al. (1992). On reporting what was said. *ELT Journal* 46: 245–251.

Index